Reference Architectures for Critical Domains

Elisa Yumi Nakagawa • Pablo Oliveira Antonino
Editors

Reference Architectures for Critical Domains

Industrial Uses and Impacts

 Springer

Editors
Elisa Yumi Nakagawa
Department of Computer Systems
University of São Paulo
São Carlos, Brazil

Pablo Oliveira Antonino
Virtual Engineering
Fraunhofer IESE
Kaiserslautern, Germany

ISBN 978-3-031-16959-5   ISBN 978-3-031-16957-1   (eBook)
https://doi.org/10.1007/978-3-031-16957-1

This Springer imprint is published by the registered company Springer Nature Switzerland AG
The registered company address is: Gewerbestrasse 11, 6330 Cham, Switzerland

Foreword

It is our great pleasure to write a foreword on this very important subject, one that is relevant for every software architect everywhere. It is our belief that this book is very timely. Reference architectures are important today, and we see no signs of this changing: they will be at least as important tomorrow.

For the past four decades, as today, reference architectures have influenced how we think about the process of software and system architecture, and they can be an important starting point for designing an architecture in a well-established domain. Beyond the obvious conceptual advantages of reference architectures, they can also help to foster a component marketplace, giving architects a practical "toolkit" to work with once they have chosen a specific reference architecture. For example, Microsoft realized this years ago when they created the "Microsoft Application Architecture Guide," an e-publication that provided, among other things, many examples of reference architectures for popular domains—web applications, service applications, mobile applications, etc.—and these various reference architectures were all supported by Microsoft's .NET framework and many of the components that they sold. Today, Microsoft is doing exactly the same thing with Azure Stack; AWS is doing the same with their Well-Architected Framework.

Reference architectures give us a structured way of thinking about a complex problem in a well-established domain. They give us definitions—a vocabulary of design—along with clear examples guiding us to make architectural choices. This is because a reference architecture is typically a comprehensive treatment of the domain it is addressing. Of course, reference architectures will evolve over time, as technology changes, but they should evolve much more slowly than any given technology stack and, in this way, act as a fixed point of calm in what might be a very volatile, tumultuous technology landscape.

In addition to the obvious benefits of reference architectures in design and development, they can also be a useful starting point for requirements gathering and analysis, acting as a kind of checklist for architects. And, in this way, they can be a great aid to stakeholder communications.

Nowadays, many reference architectures rely on a variety of industrial standards and provide the necessary blueprint for building complex systems (e.g., AUTOSAR in the automotive domain, IIRA for engineering IoT and Industry 4.0 solutions). As companies inevitably face technology changes, this motivates the continuous evolution of these architectures, to guard against obsolescence and architecture erosion.

In this regard, the editors of this volume are uniquely qualified by their academic and industrial experience to provide a modern and comprehensive treatment of key industrial reference architectures in a wide variety of application domains. They nicely guide the reader throughout a set of chapters offering a coherent perspective, one that positions today's reference architectures as key design artifacts for building modern systems. This book helps software architects and practitioners to understand how reference architectures are used today and how they perceive the needs for future architectures in the marketplace.

University of Hawaii, HI, USA and Software   Rick Kazman
Engineering Institute, Baltimore, MD, USA
Rey Juan Carlos University (Spain)   Rafael Capilla

Preface

Reference architectures have now been in existence for several years, and the community around them is growing more and more. It is time for us to paint a picture of both the state of the practice and the state of the art regarding these architectures. This is the first book that explicitly addresses reference architectures, particularly those for software-intensive systems.

Attracted by the many possibilities of reference architectures as a value-adding reusable artifact for systems engineering, we have worked for more than a decade conducting research and designing and using reference architectures in different application domains and contexts. We have coordinated industry and academic research projects addressing reference architectures, supervised Ph.D. and post-doctoral projects, and collaborated with researchers from areas as diverse as healthcare, manufacturing, automotive, and other core areas, such as software architecture, on the topic of reference architectures. With this book, we intend to share what we have learned about these architectures along our journey.

Aiming to include exciting contributions in this book, we chose a group of hand-picked experts and invited them to share their knowledge about reference architectures and enrich the book with practical and industry experiences. More than 2 years have passed since the first concrete idea of what this book would be. Now, after several iterations with the authors of all the chapters, we can proudly present our work.

Our main intention with this book is to contribute to consolidating the area of reference architecture. For that, we provide the theoretical foundation on reference architecture and a panorama of several reference architectures proposed over the years, emphasizing successful industrial cases and delving deeper into a set of critical application domains, including defense, healthcare, automotive, avionics, and Industry 4.0. In order to make this a helpful book for advances in this area, too, we discuss the most prominent and necessary directions for future expansion of the field of reference architecture.

This book is positioned at a point midway between an academic and an industry-focused book. Hence, it is not exactly a didactical book but provides references to the main scientific literature in the field, meaning it can serve as a guide for scientific and academic work.

We hope that the content of this book will prove helpful for researchers and practitioners from the areas of computing and engineering and from critical application domains. In the academic environment, this book can also enrich graduate courses with real-world cases using reference architectures, particularly in courses that address software architecture education.

Finally, we extend our most sincere thanks to all our friends, colleagues, students, and many collaborators who directly (and even indirectly) contributed to making it possible to organize and write this book.

São Carlos, Brazil   Elisa Yumi Nakagawa
Kaiserslautern, Germany   Pablo Oliveira Antonino

Acknowledgments

This book was supported by the São Paulo Research Foundation (FAPESP) (Grants: 2015/24144-7, 2019/19730-5, 2020/00835-9) and the Brazilian National Council for Scientific and Technological Development (CNPq) (Grants: 312634/2018-8, 313245/2021-5). Our special thanks go to Sonnhild Namingha for her excellent proofreading.

Contents

8   Domain-Independent Reference Architectures and Standards 181
Silverio Martínez-Fernández, Xavier Franch, and Claudia Ayala

Chapter 1
Introduction

Elisa Yumi Nakagawa and Pablo Oliveira Antonino

Abstract This first chapter of the book introduces reference architectures and offers a brief view of their context and surroundings. It also presents an overview of the book by summarizing each of the following nine chapters.

Reference architectures have been considered one of the key means for reusing consolidated knowledge and experience regarding the development, evolution, and standardization of dependable and secure software-intensive systems. Evidence of the value and potential of such architectures is seen in the increasing attention being paid to these architectures by large consortia composed of companies, research institutions, universities, and others. The notable industrial adoption of reference architectures has been accompanied by a growing interest from academia, regulatory bodies, and independent organizations in designing a diversity of reference architectures. Examples of these are the broad use of the Automotive Open System Architecture (AUTOSAR) in the automotive industry [2], the Reference Architectural Model Industrie 4.0 (RAMI 4.0) [3] and the Industrial Internet Reference Architecture (IIRA) [5] in the production industry, the Architecture Reference for Cooperative and Intelligent Transportation (ARC-IT) for transportation systems [9], the European Interoperability Reference Architecture (EIRA) for interoperable e-Government systems [7], and the Service-Oriented Architecture Reference Architecture (SOA RA) for service-oriented systems [8].

At the same time, the scientific literature is reporting an increasing number of reference architectures, currently more than 160, mostly published in the last 15 years [4]. We can also note several reference architectures in the industrial context where companies, research groups, and other interested entities have joined

E. Y. Nakagawa (✉)
University of São Paulo, São Carlos, Brazil
e-mail: elisa@icmc.usp.br

P. O. Antonino
Fraunhofer IESE, Kaiserslautern, Germany
e-mail: pablo.antonino@iese.fraunhofer.de

efforts to build and maintain reference architectures of different categories. These architectures have been successfully used in diverse domains like automotive, avionics, industrial production plants, medical, telecommunications, as well as traditional IT systems and emergent cross-domain smart ecosystems.

In this regard, this book provides an overview of the field of reference architecture in its diverse issues, from architectural design to industry-wide adoption. Over 20 leading experts from both industry and academia contribute chapters that together provide a detailed view of the role and contribution of reference architectures in different critical domains.

This book is positioned in a scenario where the development, interoperation, and evolution of heterogeneous, distributed systems have become challenging and can result in large-scale or even ultra-large-scale systems. To deal with the new challenges that such systems entail, reference architectures offer a suitable solution.

This book can be considered as the first to address reference architectures, including those associated with critical domains. Composed of ten standalone chapters that may be read in any order, the book starts by providing a general introduction of reference architectures in Chap. 2, followed by six chapters that cover reference architectures in different critical domains. Chapters 3, 4, 5, 6 and 7 each cover one domain, namely, telecommunications, healthcare, automotive, avionics, and Industry 4.0, while Chap. 8 focuses on non-specific domain reference architectures. Chapter 9 deepens the discussion about the future of reference architectures and presents open issues and research perspectives. Chapter 10 concludes this book.

In more details, Chap. 2 sets out to create an understanding of what a reference architecture is, contrasting it with other similar terms being used to refer to this architecture, and also provides a categorization of reference architectures to make it easier to understand their various purposes in the context of software and systems engineering. This chapter also addresses reference architecture engineering, which encompasses the main activities for designing architectures, namely, architectural analysis, synthesis, and evaluation.

The evolution of communication systems improved with the aggregation of mobility associated with high data rates made possible by advances in radiofrequency technology and new services enabled by enhanced computational power on end-user devices. In the last decades, wireless communication utilization has reached low latency systems, online gaming, entertainment, massive machine communication, and other applications requiring mobility and/or high performance. Nowadays, the telecommunications industry faces significant business and technology challenges due to growing competition, a multitude of services, and convergence. Based on this scenario, they have proposed reference architectures for developing such systems as a common approach to generalizing knowledge and standardizing integration, deployment, and operation between the leading players and their associated stakeholders. Chapter 3 presents examples of these architectures focusing on 5G, digital TV, and future scenarios.

Chapter 4 provides an up-to-date scenario of software systems and associated technologies for the area of healthcare. Based on new technologies, such as IoT, cloud computing, and microservices-based architectures, a considerable number of technological solutions for healthcare have emerged, and, as a result, they have contributed to leverage this area. This chapter also provides a rich experience report that details the instantiation of a reference architecture in this area.

The development of the architectures of modern passenger cars involves a multitude of systems ranging from multimedia features to safety-critical driving assistant systems. Manifold standards, design approaches, modeling notations, and tools have been developed to tackle these challenges, above all the AUTOSAR, which has become a reference architecture standard in the automotive domain. In this regard, Chap. 5 provides an overview and comparison of historical and current automotive architecture design approaches on the system and software level along with their advantages and drawbacks. This chapter also discusses standards, such as ISO 26262 [6] and Automotive SPICE [1], as well as the use of architecture modeling frameworks such as AADL in the automotive domain. Finally, this chapter presents a discussion of the impact of emerging trends such as automotive ecosystem infrastructures, e.g., Car2Car and Car2X, and the integration of machine learning components into the architecture design and corresponding design approaches.

Chapter 6 discusses reference architectures in the avionics domain. Avionics refers to the electronic systems used on aircraft, satellites, and spacecraft. It includes a broad range of systems, from displays, communication, and navigation to any other electronic equipment used by the aircraft to perform individual functions, including engine management, collision avoidance, and flight control. The design of avionics software onboard modern commercial aircraft follows the integrated modular avionics (IMA) architecture. IMA focuses on modularity and integration to aggregate multiple aircraft functions on the same execution platform. Due to the inherent consequences of resource sharing, IMA systems are extremely complex. As a result, the development, integration, and certification of commercial avionics software must follow a strict process aligned with the overall system design and with the aircraft certification plan—all of which must be communicated to, and overseen by, international Airworthiness Authorities (AAs). In this setting, Chap. 6 explores the fundamental concepts involved in the development and certification of commercial avionics software, emphasizing its role in the overall system design and aircraft safety assessment.

Chapter 7 addresses a prominent application domain: the Industry 4.0. Industry 4.0 mainly refers to the end-to-end communication among all production-relevant assets on the production floor and IT, leveraging big challenges regarding vertical and horizontal integration. Reference architectures for Industry 4.0 have been designed and adopted to support the concretization of Industry 4.0 processes and the building and integration of a range of heterogeneous technological solutions. This chapter discusses the most relevant reference architectures in the Industry 4.0 ecosystem.

Besides the reference architectures for specific application domains like those described in the previous chapters, another category of architectures with considerable importance are those for non-specific domains (or for a specific technology), such as for IoT, big data, cloud computing, and artificial intelligence. Hence, Chap. 8

provides an overview of domain-independent reference architectures, some of them published as standards by standardization organizations such as ISO/IEC.

This book is also about the state of the art of reference architectures; hence, Chap. 9 points out the most recent research directions addressing such architectures and also discusses the next steps and open issues that still require attention from the research community and industry to mature the field of reference architectures.

Finally, Chap. 10 concludes this book by highlighting the main takeaway messages and associating them with the contents of this book.

References

1. Automotive Special Interest Group and the Quality Management Center in the German Association of Automotive Industry (VDA QMC). Automotive SPICE (2021). http://www.automotivespice.com
2. AUTOSAR. AUTomotive Open System ARchitecture (AUTOSAR) (2022). https://www.autosar.org
3. DIN: German Institute for Standardization. DIN SPEC 91345: Reference Architecture Model Industrie 4.0 (RAMI 4.0) (2016)
4. L. Garcés, S. Martínez-Fernández, L. Oliveira, P. Valle, C. Ayala, X. Franch, E. Nakagawa, Three decades of software reference architectures: a systematic mapping study. J. Syst. Softw. **179**, 111004, 1–27 (2021)
5. Industrial Internet Consortium. Industrial Internet Reference Architecture (IIRA) (2021). https://www.iiconsortium.org/IIRA.htm
6. International Organization for Standardization. ISO 26262: Road Vehicles - Functional Safety (2018)
7. Joinup. European Interoperability Reference Architecture (EIRA) (2022). https://joinup.ec.europa.eu/solution/eira
8. Open Group. SOA Reference Architecture (2022). http://www.opengroup.org/soa/source-book/soa_refarch
9. U.S. Department of Transportation. Architecture Reference for Cooperative and Intelligent Transportation (ARC-IT) (2019). https://local.iteris.com/arc-it/html/architecture/architecture.html

Chapter 2
An Overview of Reference Architectures

Elisa Yumi Nakagawa and Pablo Oliveira Antonino

Abstract This chapter provides a characterization of what reference architectures are precisely and how they differ from similar architecture types, such as software product architectures, reference models, and product line architectures (PLA). This chapter also presents the main categories of reference architectures and their roles in developing and evolving software-intensive systems, including those critical ones. Reference architecture engineering is also addressed, as it can organize the tasks associated with the analysis, synthesis (i.e., description or documentation), and evaluation of these architectures.

2.1 Characterization of Reference Architectures

The notion of reference architectures emerged decades ago when the need for standardization, interoperability, maintainability, and other qualities in systems arose. Some examples are architectures for compilers [26], software engineering environments [10], and testing tools [11]. But at that time, the term reference architecture was not widespread. To refer to some standardization of systems, many terms were then proposed from that time on, such as architectural style, pattern, tactic, and standard, as well as architecture framework, enterprise architecture, and many others, including reference architecture.

A *reference architecture* (or software reference architecture) is a special type of software architecture that serves as a blueprint for building similar systems of a given domain or technology and that comprises reusable information to support the design of *product architectures* (also referred to as *concrete architectures* or *architectural instances*) through an instantiation process, as presented in Fig. 2.1.

E. Y. Nakagawa (✉)
University of São Paulo, São Carlos, Brazil
e-mail: elisa@icmc.usp.br

P. O. Antonino
Fraunhofer IESE, Kaiserslautern, Germany
e-mail: pablo.antonino@iese.fraunhofer.de

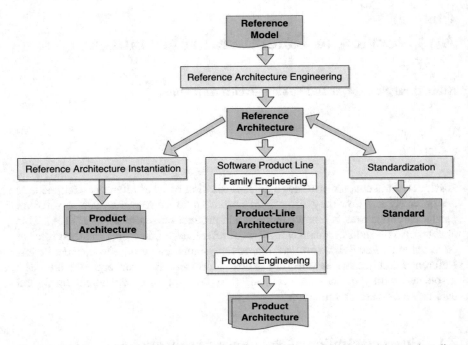

Fig. 2.1 Reference architecture and its positioning regarding reference models, product line architectures, product architectures, and standards

Hence, reference architectures are usually found at a higher level of abstraction compared with product architectures. The literature provides different definitions of reference architecture [1, 3, 5, 23, 29]. All of them somehow point out the reuse of knowledge and experience in developing software systems in a given context. Hence, reference architectures capture the essence (or commonalities) of the architectures of these systems and provide a significant body of knowledge regarding how to architect new systems. Besides serving as a guidance for new systems, they can also promote the standardization and evolution of these systems, impacting important aspects such as system quality and productivity in the software development process.

The knowledge and experience contained in reference architectures are specified through different elements, such as business drivers, key functional and quality requirements, architectural decisions, architectural styles and patterns, software and hardware elements (electronics and even mechanical parts), constraints (e.g., those associated with the domain as well as legal, organizational, and technical constraints), and engineering best practices, that have successfully supported or could support the development and evolution of a set of similar systems. Besides, the description of these elements uses a common vocabulary of the target application domain or technology, aiming to spread a unique understanding of the architecture.

In general, we can categorize elements present in reference architectures into four sets: (i) application domain (such as domain-relevant quality attributes, regulation compliance, domain legislation, standards, and constraints), (ii) infrastructure (which makes it possible to realize product architectures, e.g., software elements, hardware elements, and architectural styles and patterns), (iii) crosscutting elements (those spread along with the whole documentation of the reference architectures, e.g., architectural decisions and domain terminology), and (iv) the reference architecture itself (e.g., the reference architecture's goal, its risks, usage contexts, scope, constraints, and limitations) [31]. All these elements depend directly on the purpose of the reference architecture.

A *reference model* (cf. Fig. 2.1) refers to an abstract framework that presents a set of unifying concepts, axioms, and relationships within a particular problem domain, independent of specific standards, technologies, implementations, or other concrete details [3]. Conceptual models (containing concepts and their relationships) and ontologies of a given domain can be considered as reference models. According to Bass et al. [3], a reference model mapped onto software elements (which cooperatively implement the functionality defined in the reference model) and the data flows between them can be considered a reference architecture. Hence, reference models can be used together with other elements, such as architectural styles and software elements, to create reference architectures. Therefore, although similar, reference models and reference architectures are quite different things.

In *software product lines* (SPL), an approach for developing a family of similar software products (or members of an SPL) in which variability is a central element [39, 40], the term reference architecture is sometimes used as a synonym for PLA [6, 39]. PLA (also referred to as software PLA, domain-specific architecture, and domain architecture) is a software architecture that captures the high-level design for all software products of a given SPL and is therefore shared by all these products. It includes their commonalities and variabilities with their variation points and variants captured through variability models [39]. Other similar definitions of PLA can also be found [14, 33]. PLA is thus the core architecture used to support an SPL and is the basis for the architecture of all product line members. Hence, while a PLA is more specialized, focusing sometimes on a subset of software systems of a domain and providing standardized solutions for a family of systems, reference architectures deal with the range of knowledge of an application domain or technology, providing standardized solutions for that broader context. Besides, while PLA are concerned with the variabilities among products, reference architectures usually are not. In this regard, reference architectures can be used as a basis for PLA [28], as shown in Fig. 2.1. A reference architecture can be specialized to different PLA, each for a specific SPL. Reference architectures can also be used as the basis of other elements of the SPL core assets, for example, product feature lists, product descriptions, variability models, and product line components.

Reference architectures, product architectures, reference models, and PLA each have their specific purposes, although some of them have been used as synonyms due to the subtle differences among them. As illustrated in Fig. 2.1, there exist possible relationships among them. While the existence of a given architecture or model is not necessarily a requirement to the design of others, one may benefit from another to support its design. For instance, a reference model in a given domain can support the construction of a reference architecture. Similarly, a reference architecture can be the foundation of the design of a PLA, which serves as a basis for the product architectures resulting from that SPL. Reference architectures can also support the design of product architectures through an instantiation process. Hence, while reference models are usually at the highest level of abstraction, the others are more specific, all the way to product architectures, which are found at the lowest level of abstraction.

Reference architectures have also been referenced in documents produced by certification authorities, as in the case of Reference Architectural Model Industrie 4.0 (RAMI 4.0) [38], which is described in DIN SPEC 91345 [8]. At the same time, reference architectures can be built to better describe standards. For example, ISO 23247 [20], a standard that provides a digital twin framework for manufacturing, contains a reference architecture represented in functional views and describes the ways that entities within the architecture exchange information.

2.2   Categories of Reference Architectures

Reference architectures can be classified into different categories ranging from *industry-oriented* to *research-oriented*; *preliminary* to *classic*; *facilitation* to *standardization*; *domain-specific* to *non-domain-specific*; *high-level* to *low-level* abstraction; *single-organization* to *multiple-organization*; and *large-*, *medium-*, or *small-*scale (or scope). Figure 2.2 illustrates a categorization of reference architectures that aggregates the abovementioned categories. Also, existing architectures are sometimes positioned at the intersection of these different categories, like most architectures discussed throughout this book. Architectures

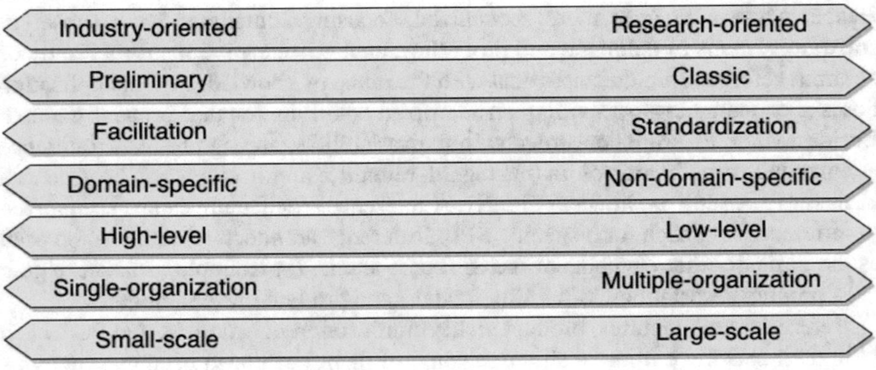

Industry-oriented	Research-oriented
Preliminary	Classic
Facilitation	Standardization
Domain-specific	Non-domain-specific
High-level	Low-level
Single-organization	Multiple-organization
Small-scale	Large-scale

Fig. 2.2 Categorization of reference architectures

can also be positioned between both extremes, for instance, at some point between high-level and low-level abstraction.

In more detail, *industry-oriented* reference architectures are led by consortia of organizations (e.g., companies, research centers, universities, standardization organizations, non-profit organizations, governmental and non-governmental organizations), which design and update large-scale architectures like Industrial Internet Reference Architecture (IIRA) [19] for Industry 4.0 and AUTOSAR for the automotive sector, intending to serve the interests of industry. On the other hand, *research-oriented* architectures sometimes result from an interest in making progress in a research topic through an architecture that supports the development of systems for that topic. Research projects and PhD projects have proposed several research-oriented architectures, like those reported in [13].

Reference architectures can also be either preliminary or classical [1]. *Preliminary* reference architectures are defined when there is no large set of software systems in the domain yet, but only research experiments. These architectures can also provide an innovative architectural design considering the existing state-of-the-art research. New application domains or fields whose systems are not still well-established are candidates for having preliminary architectures; an example is the reference architecture for digital twins whose field is maturing [20]. *Classic* reference architectures (or practice-oriented architectures) aggregate the knowledge gathered from (preferably diverse) existing software systems of a given context. There is a prevalence of classic architectures (making up around two thirds), while one third are preliminary architectures.

The purpose of reference architectures can be used to classify them into *facilitation* or *standardization* [1]. While the former intends to facilitate the design of new product architectures, the latter refers to those architectures designed to mainly state a standardization in new systems, such as architectures for CoT systems that aim at mainly promoting system/component interoperability, since this is a major requirement in these systems [7]. A review of reference architectures found in the literature revealed that around three-quarters of them are classified as facilitation, while the others aim at standardization.

Reference architectures that encompass the experience and knowledge of a specific application domain, such as automotive, transportation, or healthcare, are classified as *domain-specific* architectures. Chapters 3, 4, 5, 6 and 7 of this book address architectures in this category. On the other hand, *non-domain-specific* architectures address a specific technology or class of systems, or specific quality attributes, like the architectures discussed in Chap. 8. Architectures for SOA [37] and IoT [21] are examples in this category that are also suitable as a basis for the development of systems in different application domains.

Most existing reference architectures present *high-level* abstraction in the sense that details are left aside and the focus is on providing an overall organization for systems, for instance, the current version of RAMI 4.0 destined for Industry 4.0. Still, architectures with *low-level* abstraction present considerable detailing through extensive documentation, like IIRA for Industry 4.0 and Architecture Reference for Cooperative and Intelligent Transportation (ARC-IT) [41] for transportation.

They are intended to support the planning, definition, design, and interoperation of systems in those domains.

Another possible categorization concerns the context for which reference architectures are destined, i.e., single or multiple organizations [1]. *Single-organization* architectures usually benefit only the development of systems in the scope of that organization or a given research group, while *multiple-organization* ones target several organizations that share common properties (e.g., a market or a geographical property, such as a region or country) and benefit multiple organizations. The latter is the case for most of the architectures addressed in the next chapters of this book.

Considering the categories that reference architectures can pertain to, they can also be categorized as *small-scale* to *large-scale*. It is worth highlighting that successful reference architectures continually evolve over the years and can change their category, starting, for instance, from small-scale, high-level abstraction, and a research-oriented focus and becoming large-scale, low-level abstraction, and industry-oriented architectures. Moreover, some categories indicate the occurrence of others, e.g., an architecture categorized as standardization is also likely to be industry-oriented. A non-domain-specific architecture is possibly a multi-organization architecture intending to benefit several organizations. Otherwise, most categories are mutually independent.

Finally, understanding of the categorization of reference architectures can help to understand *why* an architecture is being designed, *what* information should be included in the architecture, *which* elements should be aggregated and detailed, *who* the possible stakeholders are, and *how* to better design, describe, and document it, all of which is aimed at reaching and adequately addressing the stakeholders.

2.3   Engineering Reference Architectures

The construction of reference architectures becomes interesting when knowledge and experience regarding how to architect a set of similar systems, sometimes gained through industry and research projects, are available and a means for communicating, disseminating, and reusing such knowledge and experience is needed.

These architectures have sometimes been designed and evolved in an ad hoc way, i.e., without exactly following a systematic or formal architectural process even in critical application domains. Considering the set of reference architectures found in the literature, most of them (around 80%) were created without following a systematic process or method. At the same time, a systematized process is certainly relevant as it could result in more effective architectures in terms of better covering their requirements. Considering the necessity of such systematization, initiatives have emerged over the years [2, 5, 9, 12, 27, 32].

Reference architecture engineering is defined as the process of analyzing the requirements of a reference architecture, synthesizing this architecture (i.e., representing it through a suitable description), and then evaluating it against its

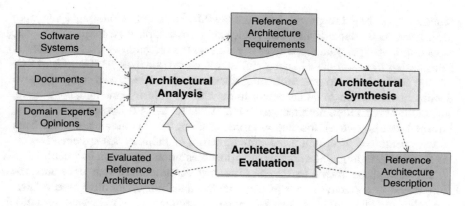

Fig. 2.3 ProSA-RA: Process for engineering reference architectures

requirements. This process is iterative, considering that successful reference architectures are continually updated and evolved following the inherent evolution of the application domains, research topics, classes of systems, and technologies for which the architectures are intended. In this scenario, ProSA-RA is an architectural process for reference architecture engineering [32] and has supported the design of architectures of different application domains, for example, those published in [24, 25, 30, 34]. Based on the general architectural process [15], this three-phase process encompasses architectural analysis, synthesis, and evaluation, as illustrated in Fig. 2.3.

To obtain success in the design of a reference architecture, its intention must be defined first (i.e., its categories). This intention can be found by mainly considering the set of systems that should be produced or integrated using that architecture.

The first phase of ProSA-RA comprises the *architectural analysis*, which selects and examines relevant, comprehensive sources of information to gather the architecture's requirements. Existing software systems can provide the overall structure of systems as well as their capabilities and features. Another source is the set of stakeholders, such as customers, users, researchers, systems developers, and others, who provide what should be included in the architecture. Documents, such as books, articles, theses, and technical reports, can also be used to collect relevant information. In this phase, international standards can also be examined, mainly those associated with the domain. For instance, RAMI 4.0 aggregates the standards IEC 62264 [17], IEC 61512 [16], and IEC 62890 [18]. After identifying the information sources and analyzing the requirements, a set of functional and nonfunctional requirements is specified.

In the *architectural synthesis* phase, the architectural description is developed. Considering the effective use of traditional architectural viewpoints and views to represent software architectures [4], they can also be used to describe reference architectures. Besides, different modeling languages and techniques, including formal ADL (Architecture Description Languages) and semi-formal ones like UML

(Unified Modeling Language) [35] and SysML (Systems Modeling Language) [36], have been adopted [42]. The choice of architectural viewpoints and views, modeling languages, and techniques depends on the intention of that architecture. Considering the example of successful architectures, such as AUTOSAR, ARC-IT, and IIRA, they also present textual documentation. Therefore, comprehensive documentation seems to be necessary in the case of industry-oriented, large-scale, and multi-organization architectures. Otherwise, RAMI 4.0 is represented by an informal and high-level abstraction representation, but this architecture has been widely mentioned to design the overall structure of Industry 4.0 systems. Hence, the size and detailing of the architectural documentation depend on its intention.

The last phase refers to the *architectural evaluation*, which considers the completeness, correctness, consistency, understandability, viability, ease of use, and other qualities relevant for that reference architecture. Traditional scenario-based methods like ATAM (Architecture Tradeoff Analysis Method) [22] and its derivations such as DCAR [43] may be suitable with adaptations for evaluating reference architectures. Besides, a checklist-based inspection can complement the evaluation by focusing on the architecture's documentation and examining the various elements that describe it.

To be effective and useful over time, reference architectures should be continually updated according to advances and changes, for instance, in the application domains, such as new standards, technologies, and needs in systems of these domains. Hence, the phases of ProSA-RA should be continuously revisited and performed iteratively.

Depending on the categories of the reference architecture, ProSA-RA involves different numbers of different stakeholders, e.g., a small number of researchers in the case of research-oriented architectures and many stakeholders as part of a large consortium in the case of large-scale architectures.

2.4 Final Remarks

While reference architecture as a research area is relatively new with advances concentrated in the last decade, many reference architectures of diverse categories have been designed and disseminated and have gained considerable value, drawing attention from both industry and academia. Examples are architectures in critical domains, such as those addressed throughout this book.

The term reference architecture is still used interchangeably with other close terms such as reference model, but the establishment of a definition can contribute to consolidating it as a field to be researched. Such a definition can facilitate the understanding and communication among researchers, practitioners, and other interested stakeholders. Similarly, a better understanding of the diverse existing categories of these architectures can serve as guidance for building and evolving them.

In general, most reference architectures have been designed in an ad hoc way, but systematizing the entire process of engineering reference architectures is a way to assure quality in the architectures and, as a consequence, their longevity and sustainability. At the same time, a considerable number of reference architectures do not survive after their first release or publication in scientific journals or events.

It is also worth highlighting that the effective reuse of knowledge and experience held in these architectures depends directly on the quality and adequacy of their description, also in terms of reaching a wide variety of stakeholders (e.g., customers, product managers, project managers, and engineers). However, most architectures are still represented in an informal way (using box and lines, for instance).

The next chapters will present reference architectures in different critical application domains. They were written by industry experts and researchers who have worked with such architectures and have collected experience about the role of these architectures for the system engineering process.

References

1. S. Angelov, P. Grefen, D. Greefhorst, A classification of software reference architectures: Analyzing their success and effectiveness, in *8th Working IEEE/IFIP Conference on Software Architecture (WICSA)* (2009), pp. 141–150
2. S. Angelov, P. Grefen, D. Greefhorst, A framework for analysis and design of software reference architectures. Inf. Softw. Technol. **54**(4), 417–431 (2012)
3. L. Bass, P. Clements, R. Kazman, *Software Architecture in Practice*, 3rd edn. (Addison-Wesley, Boston, 2012)
4. P. Clements, F. Bachmann, L. Bass, D. Garlan, J. Ivers, R. Little, P. Merson, R. Nord, J. Stafford, *Documenting Software Architecture: Views and Beyond*, 2nd edn. (Addison-Wesley, Boston, 2011)
5. R. Cloutier, G. Muller, D. Verma, R. Nilchiani, E. Hole, M. Bone, The concept of reference architectures. Syst. Eng. **13**(1), 14–27 (2010)
6. J.-M. DeBaud, O. Flege, P. Knauber, PuLSE-DSSA - A method for the development of software reference architectures, in *3rd International Workshop on Software architecture (ISA)* (1998), pp. 25–28
7. D. Dias, F. Delicato, P. Pires, A. Rocha, E. Nakagawa, An overview of reference architectures for cloud of things, in *35th Annual ACM Symposium on Applied Computing (SAC)* (2020), pp. 1498–1505
8. DIN: German Institute for Standardization. DIN SPEC 91345: Reference Architecture Model Industrie 4.0 (RAMI 4.0) (2016)
9. L. Dobrica, E. Niemela, An approach to reference architecture design for different domains of embedded systems, in *International Conference on Software Engineering Research and Practice (SERP)* (2008), pp. 287–293
10. ECMA and NIST. Reference model for frameworks of software engineering environments, Dec. 1991. Special Publication Report No. ECMA TR/55, 2nd edn. (1991)
11. N. Eickelmann, D. Richardson, An evaluation of software test environment architectures, in *18th International Conference on Software Engineering (ICSE)* (1996), pp. 353–364
12. M. Galster, P. Avgeriou, D. Weyns, T. Mannisto, Empirically-grounded reference architectures: A proposal, in *7th ACM Sigsoft International Conference on the Quality of Software Architectures (QoSA)* (2011), pp. 153–157

13. L. Garcís, S. Martínez-Fernández, L. Oliveira, P. Valle, C. Ayala, X. Franch, E. Nakagawa, Three decades of software reference architectures: a systematic mapping study. J. Syst. Softw. **179**, 111004, 1–27 (2021)
14. H. Gomaa, *Designing Software Product Lines with UML: : From Use Cases to Pattern-Based Software Architectures*. Object Technology Series (Addison-Wesley Professional, Boston, 2004)
15. C. Hofmeister, P. Kruchtenb, R.L. Nordc, H. Obbinkd, A. Rane, P. Americad, A general model of software architecture design derived from five industrial approaches. J. Syst. Softw. **80**(1), 106–126 (2007)
16. IEC - International Electrotechnical Commission. IEC 61512-1 Batch Control - Part 1: Models and Terminology (1997)
17. IEC - International Electrotechnical Commission. IEC 62264-1:2013 Enterprise-control system integration — Part 1: Models and terminology (2013)
18. IEC - International Electrotechnical Commission. IEC 62890:2020 Industrial-process measurement, control and automation - Life-cycle-management for systems and components (2020)
19. Industrial Internet Consortium. Industrial Internet Reference Architecture (IIRA) (2021). https://www.iiconsortium.org/IIRA.htm
20. ISO: International Organization for Standardization. ISO 23247-1:2021 Automation systems and integration — Digital twin framework for manufacturing — Part 1: Overview and general principles (2021)
21. ISO/IEC - International Electrotechnical Commission/International Electrotechnical Commission. ISO/IEC 30141:2018: Internet of Things (IoT) - Reference Architecture (2018)
22. R. Kazman, M. Klein, M. Barbacci, T. Longstaff, H. Lipson, J. Carriere, The architecture tradeoff analysis method, in *4th IEEE International Conference on Engineering Complex Computer Systems (ICECCS)* (1998), pp. 68–78
23. P. Kruchten, *The Rational Unified Process: An Introduction* The Addison-Wesley Object Technology Series, 2nd edn. (Addison-Wesley, Boston, 2000)
24. B. Kumar, B. Sharma, E. Nakagawa, Architectural support for context-aware mobile learning applications. Educ. Inf. Technol. **27**, 3723–3741 (2022). https://link.springer.com/article/10.1007/s10639-021-10771-1
25. W. Mizutani, F. Kon, Unlimited rulebook: A reference architecture for economy mechanics in digital games, in *IEEE International Conference on Software Architecture (ICSA)* (2020), pp. 58–68
26. S. Muchnick, *Advanced Compiler Design & Implementation*, 1st edn. (Morgan Kaufmann, Burlington, 1997)
27. G. Muller, P. Laar, Right sizing reference architectures - how to provide specific guidance with limited information, in *18th Annual International Symposium of the International Council on Systems Engineering (INCOSE)* (2008), pp. 1–8
28. E. Nakagawa, P. Antonino, M. Becker, Exploring the use of reference architectures in the development of product line artifacts, in *2nd International Workshop on Knowledge-Oriented Product Line Engineering (KOPLE), 15th International Software Product Line Conference (SPLC)* (2011), pp. 28:1–28:8
29. E. Nakagawa, P.O. Antonino, M. Becker, Reference architecture and product line architecture: A subtle but critical difference, in *5th European Conference on Software Architecture (ECSA), LNCS 6903* (2011), pp. 207–211
30. E. Nakagawa, F. Ferrari, M. Sasaki, J. Maldonado, An aspect-oriented reference architecture for software engineering environments. J. Syst. Softw. **84**(10), 1670–1684 (2011)
31. E. Nakagawa, F. Oquendo, M. Becker, RAModel: A reference model of reference architectures, in *10th Working IEEE/IFIP Conference on Software Architecture & 6th European Conference on Software Architecture (WICSA/ECSA)* (2012), pp. 297–301
32. E. Nakagawa, M. Guessi, F. Feitosa, F. Oquendo, J.C. Maldonado, Consolidating a process for the design, representation, and evaluation of reference architectures, in *11th Working IEEE/IFIP Conference on Software Architecture (WICSA)* (2014), pp. 143–152

33. L. Northrop, P. Clements, R. Little, J. McGregor, L. O'Brien, F. Bachmann, J. Bergey, G. Chastek, S. Cohen, P. Donohoe, L. Jones, R. Krut Jr, A framework for software product line practice, version 5.0 (2012). https://resources.sei.cmu.edu/library/asset-view.cfm?assetID= 495357

34. L. Oliveira, E. Nakagawa, A service-oriented reference architecture for the software testing tools, in *5th European Conference on Software Architecture (ECSA)* (2011), pp. 405–421

35. OMG - Object Management Group. UML - Unified Modeling Language (2017). https://www.omg.org/spec/UML/

36. OMG - Object Management Group. SYSML - OMG System Modeling Language (2019). https://www.omg.org/spec/SysML

37. Open Group. SOA Reference Architecture (2021). http://www.opengroup.org/soa/sourcebook/soa_refarch

38. Plattform Industrie 4.0. RAMI 4.0 - A Reference Framework for Digitalisation (2016). https://www.plattform-i40.de/IP/Redaktion/EN/Downloads/Publikation/rami40-an-introduction.pdf

39. K. Pohl, G. Böckle, F. van der Linden, *Software Product Line Engineering: Foundations, Principles, and Techniques* (Springer, Berlin, 2011)

40. M. Raatikainen, J. Tiihonen, T. Männistö, Software product lines and variability modeling: a tertiary study. J. Syst. Softw. **149**, 485–510 (2019)

41. U.S. Department of Transportation. Architecture Reference for Cooperative and Intelligent Transportation (ARC-IT) (2019). https://local.iteris.com/arc-it/html/architecture/architecture.html

42. P. Valle, L. Garcés, T. Volpato, S. Martínez-Fernández, E. Nakagawa, Towards suitable description of reference architectures. Peer J. Comput. Sci. **7**, e392, 1–36 (2021)

43. U. van Heesch, V.-P. Eloranta, P. Avgeriou, K. Koskimies, N. Harrison, Decision-centric architecture reviews. IEEE Softw. **31**(1), 69–76 (2014)

Chapter 3
Reference Architectures for Telecommunications Systems

Edmar Candeia Gurjão, Jean Felipe Fonseca de Oliveira, and Pablo Oliveira Antonino

Abstract The evolution of communications systems has improved with the aggregation of mobility concepts, high data rates enabled by advances in radiofrequency technology, and new services enabled by enhanced computational power on end-user devices. In recent decades, wireless communication utilization has reached low-latency systems such as self-driving cars, remote surgery, online gaming, entertainment, massive machine communication such as sensor networks and the Internet of Things (IoT), and other applications requiring mobility and high performance. Moreover, the telecommunications industry faces significant business and technology challenges due to increased demands for new services, incorporation of new paradigms, and the technical challenges associated with implementing market demands and complying with regulatory standards. In this regard, reference architectures have been proposed for the development of such systems as a common approach for generalizing knowledge and standardizing integration, deployment, and operation between the leading players and associated stakeholders. This chapter presents examples of these architectures focusing on 5G, digital TV, and future scenarios.

3.1 Introduction

Telecommunications is a continuously evolving engineering area that rapidly takes advantage of technological advances to improve system capabilities. These

E. C. Gurjão (✉)
Federal University of Campina Grande, Campina Grande, Brazil
e-mail: ecg@dee.ufcg.edu.br

J. F. F. de Oliveira
NOS Innovation, Lisbon, Portugal
e-mail: jean.f.oliveira@parceiros.nos.pt

P. O. Antonino
Fraunhofer IESE, Kaiserslautern, Germany
e-mail: pablo.antonino@iese.fraunhofer.de

© The Author(s), under exclusive license to Springer Nature Switzerland AG 2023
E. Y. Nakagawa, P. Oliveira Antonino (eds.), *Reference Architectures for Critical Domains*, https://doi.org/10.1007/978-3-031-16957-1_3

17

improvements directly affect users who adopt telecommunications systems in their routine and who continuously demand new services, resulting in the need to improve technologies in order to improve the development of telecommunications systems. In this regard, reference architectures are fundamental as a means to provide guidance.

Out of the variety of communications systems, in this chapter, we focus on reference architectures for fifth-generation (5G) communications systems and digital TV systems.

3.2 Fifth Generation of Mobile Telephony (5G)

Due to increasing user demands, competition, and strategic business, telecommunications systems demand the utilization of the state-of-the-art technologies. As a result, mobile communications systems, particularly cellular systems, have evolved and have been a disruptive technology ever since their first generation appeared in the 1970s [1].

The evolution from analog to digital systems, voice to data, low to high data rates, and other features has marked improvements from the first to the fifth generation of cellular communications.

Some features of 5G systems are:

- High coverage: reaching challenging locations
- Ultra-low energy: more than 10 years of battery life
- Ultra-low complexity: tens of bits per second
- Ultra-high density: one million nodes per km^2
- Enhanced mobile broadband (eMBB):

  - Extreme capacity: 10 Tbps per km^2
  - Extreme data rates: multiple peak rates of Gbps and 100+ Mpbs of average rates in the user equipment
  - Rapid and efficient user location and resources optimization

- Strong security
- Ultra-high reliability: $< 10^{-5}$ per 1 ms
- Ultra-low latency: as low as 1 ms
- Extreme mobility: up to 500 km/h

To better understand 5G architectures, it is necessary to understand the concepts of network slicing and network functions. Network slicing is a novel concept for setting up logical networks on a shared common physical infrastructure. As depicted in Fig. 3.1, each logical network can serve different use case requirements considering all network resources [2]. This technology utilizes service isolation, customization of network functions, virtualization, independent management, and dynamic orchestration to enable efficient network resource utilization.

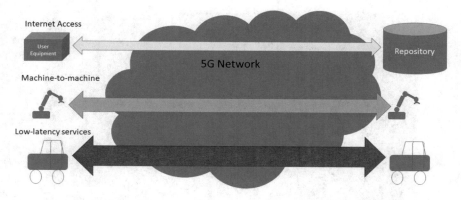

Fig. 3.1 Network slicing

Another critical concept in 3GPP 5G architecture is *network functions (NF)*, which consist of a module (hardware, software, or a virtualized function on a platform) built using microservice methodologies and service orchestration. Each network function exposes its functionality through a service-based interface (SBI) employing a well-defined interface. Thus, a 5G network can provide different functionalities of distinct quality of service by combining network functions.

3.2.1 5G Architecture Network

As depicted in Fig. 3.2, the basic architecture of a 5G system (5GS) comprises the following components: user equipment (UE), access network (including "new radio" or NR), and core network (5GC or 5GCN) [3].

The user equipment (UE) is the system's entry point from the mobile network user point of view. Access to the other UE in the same or another region happens via the radio access network (RAN), which is responsible for over-the-air communication. The radio access network (RAN) connects to the core network, which, in turn, connects to the other components of the system (Internet, other cellular networks, backbones, etc.).

In the remainder of this chapter, the essential components presented in Fig. 3.2 will be used to describe the 5G system reference architecture.

3.2.1.1 User Equipment

The entrance point of the 5G system can be considered the user equipment (UE), which consists of the mobile terminal and a tamper-resistant security element like a SIM (subscriber identity module) card or another unique identification module. The

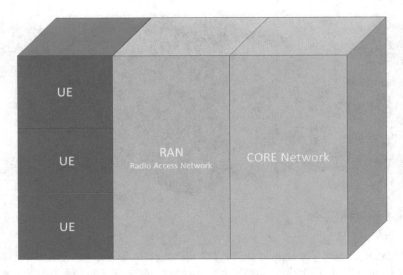

Fig. 3.2 Basic components of a 5G network

UE can be a sensor, a machine, or even a mobile vehicle, i.e., any object connected to a 5G modem that establishes a wireless connection with the radio access network.

Compared to fourth-generation (4G) mobile access terminals, a new aspect of the UE in 5G is the possibility of using more than one form of connection to transmit data, known as multiple transmission points (multi-TRP). For example, a UE can simultaneously transmit data over the 5G network and over a reachable wireless network in the location, which implies throughput increase. Also, a UE uses full-power transmission from multiple UE antennas in the uplink (UL).

The UE architecture is vendor-dependent, and the standards are mode-centered in the access network and the core network, which are interconnected, as shown in Fig. 3.3. The following sections will provide more details about these elements.

3.2.2 Radio Access Network

The 3GPP 38.300 technical specification describes the radio interface, i.e., the connection with UE and functionalities [4]. It is an evolving document that continuously presents new definitions and details about the architecture.

As depicted in Fig. 3.3, the gNB (next-generation NodeB) is the base station connecting the UE and the core network. In the 5G architecture, there is a logical separation between data networks and signaling; this separation is represented in Fig. 3.3 by the user plane and the control plane, respectively. The control plane connects to the AMF (Access and Mobility Management Function) and the user

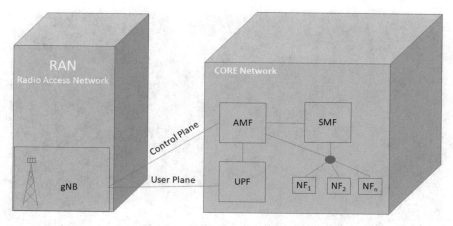

Fig. 3.3 Internal elements and connections between RAN and core network

plane to the UPF (User Plane Function). The roles of these functions will be explained in the next section.

The gNB performs functions such as radio resource management (RRM) (modulation, frame size, etc.), routing, connection setup, release, and others, as specified in the 3GPP 38.300 technical specification [4]. In addition, TS 38.210 details the physical layer, and TS 30.202 defines the radio protocol architecture.

The architecture depicted in Fig. 3.3 presents a standalone 5G architecture where the system's deployment uses only 5G components. However, considering the already installed 4G systems and a smooth transition to 5G, non-standalone architectures are also proposed. As depicted in Fig. 3.4, setting up a 5G network can benefit the 4G system already implemented. Two options (3 and 7×) with connections (solid, dashed, and green lines) exist that are configured to provide 5G connections. The choice of the specific architecture depends on the needs of the telecommunications operator.

3.2.3 The Core Network (5GC or 5GCN)

The core network (cf. Figure 3.3) is the crucial point that enables advances in the data rate and flexibility of 5G. Such advances are based on the cloud concept, which enables increasing intelligence of the network. A combination of network functions configures a service, permitting adjustment of the system to the UE and the network resources' capabilities and necessities. One of these adjustments is the provision of different network slices for different users. These network slices are software-configurated and allow, for example, variations according to the user profile, such as the reduction of the slice for and industry in the night shift.

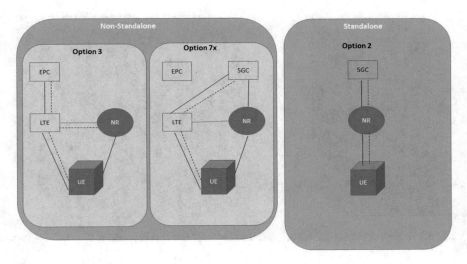

Fig. 3.4 Architecture for 5G implementation

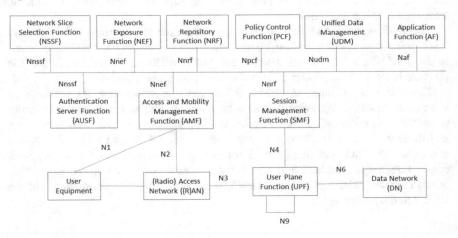

Fig. 3.5 Non-roaming reference architecture

Considering the interconnection of network functions, there are two basic reference architectures for 5G: non-roaming, where the UE user connects with a base station, and roaming, where the UE has to communicate with several base stations simultaneously.

Figure 3.5 presents a non-roaming reference architecture, where each block represents a network function and links represent connection interfaces. Figure 3.6 depicts a roaming architecture.

In the core network, the Access and Mobility Management Function (AMF) acts as a single-entry point for the UE connection according to the service requested

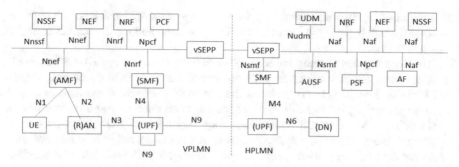

Fig. 3.6 Roaming reference architecture

by the UE. The AMF selects the respective Session Management Function (SMF) to manage the user session. The User Plane Function (UPF) transports the IP data traffic (user plane) between the user equipment (UE) and the external networks. The Authentication Server Function (AUSF) allows the AMF to authenticate the UE and access the 5G core services. Other functions like the Session Management Function (SMF), the Policy Control Function (PCF), the Application Function (AF), and the Unified Data Management (UDM) function provide the policy control framework, applying policy decisions and accessing subscription information governing the network behavior [5].

Another fundamental advance in 5G systems is the massive utilization of Multi-Access Edge Computing (MEC) to perform computation in the location closest to the UE to provide low-latency services. This new capability implies the capacity to migrate computing processes according to the movement of the UE. Some architectures are under development that aim to implement this multi-access edge computing [6, 7].

5G network capabilities will both enable new services and the improvement of essential services. In the next section, we will discuss the architecture for one of these services, digital TV.

3.3   Digital TV

Nothing has shown the central role of video streaming more than the crisis caused by the Covid-19 pandemic, during which billions of people around the world remained at home, which greatly increased the demand for television services. With segment revenue forecast close to $223.98 billion globally by 2028 [8], and companies like Disney, HBO, and Amazon investing heavily in the industry, over-the-top (OTT) media is becoming an essential asset for the telecommunications market.

Mobile is an essential part of the OTT sector, whether in the living room or on the street. In addition, emerging technological advancements such as the implementation of blockchain technology in video streaming and artificial intelligence to improve video quality are expected to boost the demand for the market over the forecast period.

The fast adoption of cloud-based video-streaming solutions based on 5G network enhancements directly influences growth. Potential technologies for reconfigurable networks such as 5G network architectures and SDN (software-defined networking) have been investigated to achieve better transmission efficiency and build efficient network infrastructures for video-streaming applications. SDN is regarded as a revolutionary technology for virtualizing networks in order to configure and maintain servers and routers easily. It will likely play a critical role in designing 5G wireless communication networks [9].

The reasons attributed to the market's growth are rapid digitalization, increasing use of mobile devices, and the growing popularity of online video and game streaming. In mobile video streaming, the bandwidth demand of users is expected to increase dramatically in the next generation of mobile networks [10, 11], driven by the capabilities of the upcoming 5G systems. In on-demand video streaming, caching the most popular large-size video content at the network edge can help to significantly reduce the high contention on the origin server [12]. In contrast to static HTTP-based video streaming, edge caching is more challenging in dynamic adaptive video streaming since, for each request from a mobile client, the requested chunk and its specific bitrate need to be efficiently cached [9].

3.3.1 Multiple-System Operator

Multiple-system operator (MSO) is a designation often used for cable companies that offer services beyond television broadcast. Their traditional business models are becoming outdated, while dominant players are under attack by new entrants. Realizing the need to evolve, MSOs have begun to focus on other areas to drive revenue growth and explore new business models in order to remain competitive.

Recent improvements and changes in the associated technologies and consumer behavior as well as new and innovative services, such as over-the-top (OTT) content, peer-to-peer networking, and content provision by new players, are eroding the revenue streams. These changes have altered the MSOs' competitive landscape and present numerous challenges to the position of MSOs as leading providers and aggregators of video content.

3.3.2 Video Services

One of the biggest trends in the TV industry at present is disaggregation and fragmentation. This industry is moving from a world in which most people consume, almost exclusively, pay TV content through a traditional infrastructure and a set-top box to one in which people consume a variety of video content through many different channels. 2014 was the first year in media history where US consumers spent more time using mobile screens than watching TV, according to Flurry, a Yahoo-owned mobile analytics service [13].

This fact was named the cord-cutting phenomenon. Regarding television viewing, cord-cutting is defined as the dropping of a cable or satellite television subscription service in favor of one or more alternatives. The decision to cut the cord frequently results from a consumer performing a cost-benefit analysis and concluding that a cable or satellite package costs more than it is worth.

The scope of video services includes many different services, applications, and technologies and can be split into two different types: linear and nonlinear. Linear, or broadcast, networks are one-way networks where the end-user receives content live or records it using a set-top box (STB). Nonlinear networks are IP-based, two-way networks, meaning they are duplex and more endowed. They support many devices, including smartphones, tablets, TVs, laptop/desktop computers, and gaming consoles, streaming content using IPTV or hybrid fiber-coaxial (HFC) networks.

3.3.3 Adaptive Bitrate Systems

An adaptation mechanism is needed to allow applications to adapt to the changing environment gracefully and to improve and tailor the video quality to the device and network context. HTTP adaptive streaming (HAS) systems, or adaptive bitrate (ABR) streaming, are the most recent attempts regarding video quality optimization in transmission environments of varying or unstable bandwidth. They enable cheap and easy-to-implement streaming technology without the need for a dedicated infrastructure. Moreover, combining TCP and HTTP offers the advantage of reusing all the existing technologies designed for the ordinary web [14]. Figure 3.7 shows a general architecture organization of one of the two most frequently adopted ABR algorithms, the HLS.

3.3.4 MPEG-DASH

The MPEG-DASH, an open-source international standard developed by the ISO/IEC MPEG Committee [15], is one of the most popular video-streaming protocols and is currently widely used to deliver media via either video on demand (VOD) or live streaming to various end-user devices, including smartphones, tablets, smart TVs, gaming consoles, etc. MPEG-DASH is primarily designed in client pull-based environments with HTTP as the protocol of choice for media streaming. An MPEG-DASH client first retrieves a manifest file, known as Media Presentation Description (MPD). Then it selects, retrieves, and renders content segments based

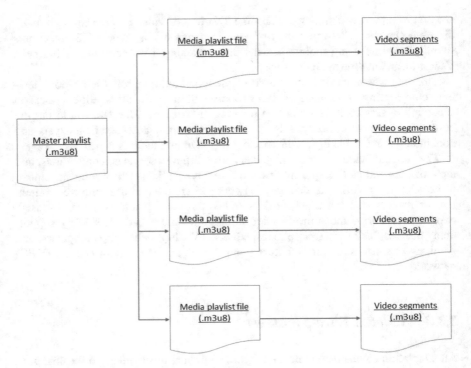

Fig. 3.7 General organization of HLS and DASH systems

on that metadata, as seen in Fig. 3.8. The real benefits of the MPEG-DASH standard over other traditional streaming technologies, such as RTP, are [16]:

- MPEG-DASH request and response messages can pass firewalls like any other HTTP message. As the content is typically hosted on plain HTTP servers and no specific media servers are necessary, DASH is highly scalable.
- MPEG-DASH segments can be cached in HTTP caches and delivered via content delivery networks (CDN).
- Most importantly, a DASH client constantly measures the available bandwidth, monitors various resources, and dynamically selects the next segment based on that information.

The MPEG-DASH-related files in the HTTP server consist of two parts: the Media Presentation Description (MPD), which defines a manifest of the available content, its various representations, their URL addresses, and other characteristics, and data segments, which contain the actual multimedia bitstreams in the form of chunks [16]. The MPD defines the timeline of a media presentation, which serves as the baseline for all scheduling decisions made during DASH presentation playback. It also enables the client to obtain media samples and dynamically switches between different bit rates of the same content to adapt to the network bandwidth conditions.

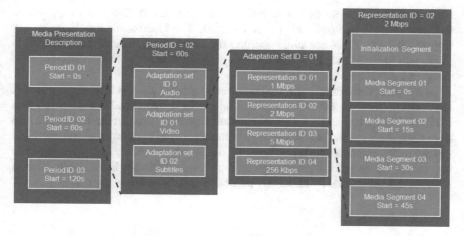

Fig. 3.8 General organization of HLS and DASH systems

The following data structures, depicted in Fig. 3.8, are most relevant to locating and scheduling the samples:

- The MPD consists of consecutive periods that map data onto the MPD timeline.
- Each period contains one or more representations, providing media samples inside a sequence of media segments.
- Representations within a period are grouped into adaptation sets, which associate related representations and metadata.

If there is a reduction in bandwidth, the DASH clients select lower quality and size segments. As a result, a buffer underrun is prevented, and the end-user retains a continuous media consumption experience. Many studies show that startup delays and buffer underruns are among the most severe quality issues in an Internet video and DASH constitutes a solution for overcoming and minimizing such problems.

3.3.5 HLS

In 2009, Apple released an HTTP-based streaming media communication protocol called HLS to transmit bounded and unbounded multimedia data streams. At first, HLS was exclusive to iPhones, but today almost every device supports this protocol, becoming a proprietary format.

According to this specification, the overall stream is broken into a sequence of small HTTP-based file downloads, where users can select alternate streams encoded at different data rates. Initially, users download an extended M3U playlist that contains several Uniform Resource Identifiers (URIs) corresponding to media files, where each file must be a continuation of the encoded stream. Each media file must be formatted as an ISO-BMFF fMP4 container, an MPEG-2 transport stream (TS), or an MPEG-2 audio elementary stream. The video-streaming industry has converged to the fMP4 container solution for all HTTP-based streaming protocols (including MPEG-DASH). These video files typically contain AVC/H.264-encoded video and AAC-encoded audio.

In a typical configuration, a hardware encoder takes audio-video input, encodes it as HEVC video and AC-3 audio, and outputs a fragmented MPEG-4 file or an MPEG-2 transport stream. A software stream segmenter then breaks the stream into a series of short media files placed on a web server. The segmenter also creates and maintains the extended M3U playlist. The URL of the index file is published on the webserver. Client software reads the index, then requests the listed media files in order, and displays them without any pauses or gaps between segments.

3.3.6   Low-Latency Streaming

Adaptive bitrate protocols are designed to ensure an optimal visual experience, but at the cost of an important aspect: the latency of delivery, also known as camera-to-display delay or glass-to-glass delay, which in current deployments can reach the order of tens of seconds. Many different steps in the creation and distribution process contribute to this build-up in the delay. Still, ultimately, the very nature of adaptive bitrate protocols requires a valuable amount of time, mainly due to the segmentation and distribution phases [17].

Latency is intrinsically introduced at different stages in the OTT video-streaming pipeline:

- Video encoding
- Ingest and packaging
- Network propagation delays
- Transport protocol
- Content delivery network (CDN)
- Segment length (MPEG-DASH, HLS, HDS, Microsoft Smooth Streaming)
- Video player policies (buffering, played positioning, resilience)

One possible solution for reducing end-to-end latency is to use a shorter segment duration (1 second or less). Although this solution can control the latency to within target limits, it has the disadvantages of reducing encoding efficiency, suffering from frequent quality changes, and increasing the number of HTTP requests and responses.

To avoid these problems while keeping latency low, chunked transfer encoding (CTE) with MPEG Common Media Application Format (CMAF; ISO/IEC 23000-19) [18] has recently emerged as the standard segmenter for low-latency delivery. CTE allows the delivery of a segment in small pieces called chunks, the smallest referenceable unit of a segment. A chunk can be as small as a single frame to be delivered to the client in real time.

Although the CTE and CMAF solution is a step forward in low-latency streaming, it alone is not enough to reduce latency. It requires efficient content delivery networks (CDNs), efficient encoders, and optimized adaptive rate algorithms.

3.3.7   The Over-the-Top Model

Over-the-top (OTT) is a generic term for a service used over a network that the operator does not offer. It is usually described as "over-the-top" because these services work over an existing service infrastructure and do not require any affiliation with technologies or business models associated with the telecommunications operator. It can also be defined as multimedia content (television and video content, e.g.) distributed over a high-speed Internet connection, not through cable or satellite service providers. The introduction of OTT service providers has enabled the creation of new business models for network-based services. OTT service providers collaborate with telecommunications operators to integrate their services with telecommunications network infrastructures.

The most common application of the OTT model is undoubtedly digital video-streaming services, where content providers depend on a telecommunications operator to make content (often interactive content) available for televisions, cable boxes, and personal computers. Examples of this type of service include Netflix, Amazon, iTunes, etc.

The most significant growth in the telecommunications market in recent times has been in the field of video streaming. There is considerable interest among users in consuming on-demand content and accessing it on any device (television, desktops, laptops, smartphones, etc.). The evolution of video streaming and digital content offerings facilitates access to video content from any place or device. In the entertainment area, it is estimated that video streaming represents 30% of total Internet traffic.

For telecommunications operators, the proliferation of video-streaming services implies greater network bandwidth requirements and, sometimes, a significant redesign of their infrastructure. Video streaming has expanded beyond the entertainment industry to areas such as education and health, among others. Trainers make documentaries, films, and instructional videos available as a vital part of the teaching process. The exponential growth of video content in different areas requires vast investments by telecommunications service providers (Internet connection providers). In addition, users need connections that are fast enough to also view and share other content.

Video-on-demand (VoD) applications are interactive multimedia systems that work like cable television, differentiating themselves from the possibility of selecting a video or program from an extensive content library. Instead, individual users can access different contents according to their preferences, making this system a video rental store accessible from anywhere. However, video on demand is a recent technology and not yet very standardized.

Services such as Spotify and Deezer were the first OTT platforms in the music industry, with Netflix as a corresponding OTT platform in the film industry. Their overall business model is based on OTT technology which aggregates contents delivered through an MSO communication infrastructure, such as pay TV or Internet service provision.

3.3.8 CDN (Content Delivery Network)

Video streaming makes up most of the network traffic on today's Internet. YouTube accounts for more than a billion hours of video streaming every day [11], including the largest single source of downstream traffic. Content delivery networks (CDNs) help deliver content globally. Providing caches close to the users relieves the content provider from traffic load, and low initial video buffering time can be achieved. CDNs are used, among others, for streaming both on-demand and live video [19].

3.3.9 The New Generation of TV Broadcasting Systems

Considering the scenario in which users are increasingly used to multi-screen environments, it is expected that the broadcasting industry should evolve substantially, at least to match the upcoming demands of this new era, offering high-quality content with full connectivity. The main difference to the previous DTV standards requirements is that users want to experience HDTV or even UHDTV services on the move or even on personal devices at home due to the new mass media.

Broadcasters are being pushed to include new broadcasting standards in their deployed networks to cope with those bit rates [20]. In the following subsection, a brief overview of the new generation of TV broadcasting systems will be provided. The ATSC 3.0 standard will be explained in more detail below as broadcast and broadband technologies converge in it.

3.3.9.1 DVB-T2

This standard for digital terrestrial television was the second of a series of new-generation digital television systems inside the DVB consortium. The first one was DVB-S2 (satellite systems) and the third DVB-C2 (cable systems). DVB-T2 was designed to fulfill the requirements of flexibly increasing the spectral efficiency and robustness. Different reception scenarios can be covered with the same system by choosing the best configuration options available. Like many modern terrestrial broadcasting and radio communication systems, DVB-T2 uses OFDM (orthogonal frequency-division multiplexing) modulation. DAB (Digital Audio Broadcasting) and DVB-T were the first digital terrestrial broadcasting standards to use this technique in the 1990s.

Since the introduction of the first DVB-based DTT standards, many other wireless communications systems, such as IEEE 802.11, IEEE 802.16, and LTE, have adopted OFDM as their transmission technique [20]. As stated above, the DVB-T2 standard originated from the need to increase the spectral efficiency of digital terrestrial systems in the UHF/VHF bands. The standard provides high flexibility in multiplex allocation, coding, modulation, and RF parameters.

Another important novelty introduced in DVB-T2 was the Physical Layer Pipes (PLP) concept, allowing service-specific robustness with different coding and modulation schemes within the same frame. This feature can be understood as the first attempt to simultaneously deliver mobile and stationary services based on the time-division multiplexing (TDM).

Moreover, the last update to the standard has been to incorporate a new profile known as LITE, designed to deliver mobile services to the final user. The silicon footprint required for this profile demodulation is about half that of DVB-T2 as the required configuration parameters are reduced to a minimum.

3.3.9.2 ATSC 3.0

The all-IP transmission of ATSC 3.0 offers distinct features over traditional broadcasting, as it enables convergence or cooperation with IP-based broadband networks. For example, leveraging uplink transmission as a return channel, a broadcaster can provide interactive or personalized services that will bring more attraction from audiences. Also, a broadcasting service could cooperate with available broadband networks such as mobile networks or Wi-Fi. Further enhanced features of broadcasting services will be possible, including quality improvement, service area extension, and rich media services [12].

In ATSC 3.0, the format of transmitted signals is IP-based to enhance the feasibility of convergence and cooperation with other IP-based networks such as mobile networks. The signaling, delivery, synchronization, and error protection standard of ATSC 3.0 allow two options for service delivery over a broadcast network, known as MMT and ROUTE. For service delivery over a broadband network, only DASH may be used.

3.3.9.3 MMT (MPEG Media Transport)

MPEG-2 TS (transport stream) has been adopted worldwide for multiplexing compressed audio and video data in digital broadcasting applications, such as DTV (digital television) systems, IPTV (Internet protocol television), and DMB (digital multimedia broadcasting). It was established in the early 1990s. However, after more than two decades since its first establishment, many parts of MPEG-2 TS have

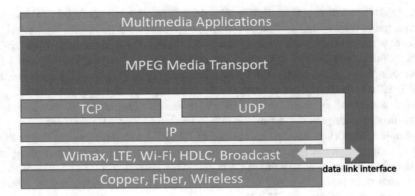

Fig. 3.9 MMT architecture [22]

turned out to be unsuitable for today's broadcast and communications environment due to the rise of broadband video-streaming technologies [21].

Given this scenario, in 2014, MPEG (ISO/IEC JTC 1 SC 29/WG 11) released ISO 23001-13 as the MMT standard for specifying the next-generation multimedia transport technologies that can replace MPEG-2 TS. Figure 3.9 illustrates how MMT interacts with the other layers.

The MPEG Media Transport Protocol (MMTP) is a transport layer protocol designed to download and stream multimedia content and applications simultaneously. MMTP optimizes the delivery of multimedia data encapsulated on ISO-BMFF (ISO/IEC base media file format) packets by specifying a new media streaming mode and provides a GFD (Generic File Delivery) mechanism. It is agnostic to media encoding standards so that any type of ISOBMFF media data format can be packetized into MMTP payloads. In addition, MMTP implements Application Layer Forward Error Correction (AL-FEC), which provides additional repair information to recover lost data at the receiver. AL-FEC is integrated into content delivery protocols, such as the MMT protocol, to support reliable delivery [23].

The MPEG Media Transport Protocol defines an appropriate protocol for exploiting hybrid streaming scenarios because it is a multimedia application layer protocol with the inherent ability to transmit video in heterogeneous network environments. Hybrid media delivery refers to the combination of media components delivered over different types of networks. This could be, for example, one broadcast channel and one broadband channel or two broadband channels. MMT was standardized in 2013 and has already been adopted by several other standards to replace the old MPEG-2 TS protocol [22].

MMTP inherently supports multiplexing media data from different sources and coming through different paths by allowing the simple combination of MMTP packets received from other sources into a single MMTP flow. The end-to-end delay is governed by a Hypothetical Receiver Buffer Model (HRBM), which operates on a fixed end-to-end delay. Therefore, the service provider can decide to cover different delays on different transmission paths. The HRBM also instructs the receiver about the required buffer size to receive and consume the service while preserving the fixed end-to-end delay.

3.3.9.4   Enhanced Multimedia Broadcast Multicast Service

This solution can be considered a point-to-multipoint interface specification for 3GPP cellular networks, designed to provide efficient broadcast and multicast services delivery. It was defined to overcome the potential limitation of 3G networks for unicast streaming of high-usage TV traffic. It is designed to allocate part of the spectrum (or some carrier resources) to the multicast transport channels in each cell, delivering both unicast and multicast channels.

Currently, eMBMS is supported for all defined bandwidths of LTE, including frequency-division duplexing (FDD) and time-division duplexing (TDD). In addition, it is defined for one effective transmitter antenna and two receiver antennas, as the MIMO gain obtained for broadcast services is not as large as expected.

3.3.9.5   Hybrid Television Systems

An Integrated Broadcast-Broadband (IBB) system uses a combination of the technologies of both broadband and broadcasting. In such systems, a hybrid terminal (HT) is either a TV device or an external set-top box (STB) that, in addition to receiving the video and audio signals through traditional media (air, cable, or satellite), is connected to the Internet via broadband. This additional connection enables access to complimentary audiovisual content and software applications. Furthermore, unlike a classic smart TV with an Internet connection, a hybrid terminal can receive and display online broadband information and synchronize with the broadcast content [24].

Different IBB standards are currently in use or under development, including HbbTV, Hybridcast, ATSC 3.0, and Ginga. They are not reciprocally compatible. Each is designed and developed with a specific broadcast standard (HbbTV with DVB, Hybridcast, and Ginga with ISDB-T). They all share the same concepts and use particular protocols to integrate the broadcasting signals available via broadband Internet connections. These protocols describe content synchronization methods, network access, and how to register and use companion screens along with the main screen. Although all IBB standards share the same fundamental concepts, interoperability between them is currently not supported.

3.3.10   QoE Monitoring

The advancements in video streaming have recently resulted in the emergence of both video-on-demand and live-streaming services. It is evident that video streaming is not a niche market anymore and there exist a wide range of options for consumers to choose from. Hence, as a service provider, it is no longer sufficient to just provide a service; rather, it is equally important to make sure that the needs and expectations of the end-user of the offered services are met [25]. In conventional video-streaming systems, the measurement of quality of experience (QoE) uses traditional subjective metrics such as mean opinion score (MOS) or objective metrics such as peak signal-to-noise ratio (PSNR).

However, video providers do not commonly use these metrics because they are difficult to measure in a large-scale operational system, especially MOS, which requires the direct participation of the users [26]. In this way, objective video evaluation techniques work as a reasonable trade-off because they are faster and cheaper and can efficiently indicate the existence of slight degradations [27]. The main factors that affect the QoE in dynamic adaptive video streaming are:

- Video stalling – A video stall event refers to when the client's buffer gets empty (playback freezes) due to streaming the video on a player with high bitrates under low achievable throughput.
- Video quality – Refers to the quality that clients perceive during the video-streaming session, which is directly related to the streaming bitrate.
- Bitrate switching – High bitrate switching also negatively impacts the satisfaction of mobile clients.
- Initial playback buffering time – Also known as initial/startup delay, refers to the time duration from the arrival time at the client until the time that the data in the playback buffer reaches the maximum capacity.

3.3.11   Convergence of Broadband and Broadcast Systems

The possible future cooperation of broadband and broadcast is not transparent so far. Traditionally, both groups of standards have followed independent development and deployment paths. However, there has been fierce competition between them to get various spectrum bands at the international regulatory bodies. Moreover, each system's business model and infrastructure has also been very different until now.

Despite the differences and the competition, there have been significant efforts to find possible convergence scenarios. However, so far, none of the convergence proposals has been available commercially. In some cases, the main reasons were technical difficulties, but mostly, the major drawback has been the absence of an actual commercial use case for converged systems, networks, or services. Figure 3.10 depicts an evolution of the convergence scenario where the 5G infrastructure increasingly encompasses more network features [10].

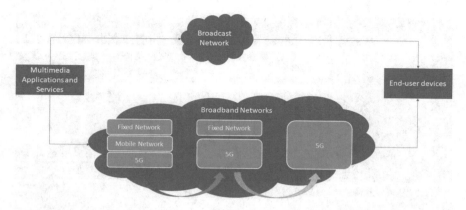

Fig. 3.10 5G infrastructure increasingly encompasses more network features

3.3.12   Software Architectures for DTV Receivers

3.3.12.1   RDK

The Reference Design Kit, commonly known as RDK, is a pre-integrated open-source software distribution that accelerates the deployment of next-gen video and broadband services. It provides a common framework for powering customer-premises equipment (CPE) such as set-top boxes, modem/routers, and other devices from communications service providers. In addition, it helps service providers to standardize some aspects of these devices, enabling them to quickly launch new services or customize applications and user experiences. As a result, the RDK accelerates time to market while allowing flexibility and competitive differentiation [28].

RDK provides common methods for video tuning, conditional access, DRM, stream management, and diagnostics. Companies can also benefit from the RDK App Framework to build and manage their apps, select an RDK pre-integrated app store solution, or choose an RDK Video Accelerator, a fully integrated IP set-top box, from leading suppliers. The RDK-V (Video) software stack gives communication providers a common framework for developing STB software. It incorporates tuning, IP video, and media streaming/DLNA, but allows for the telecommunications operator to be in charge of user interface control and development. Figure 3.11 depicts all the subsystems that make up the RDK-V architecture.

3.3.12.2   Android TV and Android AOSP

The Android TV platform consists of the Google environment and its applications, including some features such as location services for maps. However, the essential

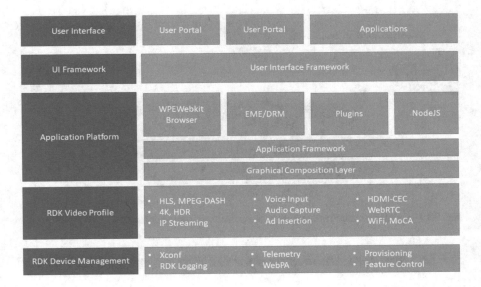

Fig. 3.11 RDK-V architecture

feature is the Google Play store with the Android TV platform. A multichannel video programming distributor (MVPD) is required to provide a fully open Google Play store, allowing users to download any app they want onto the STB, like on a smartphone [29]. The MVPD is a service that supports multiple television channels, for instance, cable or satellite television services like Comcast and DirecTV. These were often formerly known as operators or MSOs.

The main component of the Android TV platform is the Android TV Input Framework (TIF). It defines a standard API capable of creating input modules for controlling Android TV, live content search, recommendations engine, and handling of the delivery mechanism of live content. The framework does not seek to implement TV standards or regional requirements but does make it easier for device manufacturers to meet regional digital TV broadcast standards without re-implementation [30]. In addition, the Android Open Source Project (AOSP) is a subset of Android TV designed as an open-source platform to allow developers to create any type of application for an Android environment. The main benefits of adopting the AOSP over Android TV are:

- No requirement to meet Google's licensing requirements
- Complete control over user interface and user experience aspects
- Definition of a proprietary ecosystem of applications
- Regular updates of the core codebase by Google

On the other hand, some critical disadvantages also need to be considered in the product development process of an AOSP-enabled set-top box:

- No access to the Google Play app store and its ecosystem of thousands of apps
- No third-party OTT services without certification
- Porting of the Widevine DRM mechanism
- Additional complexity to implement Android updates

3.3.12.3 Challenges of the Video-Streaming Industry

There are several challenges that the video-streaming industry is facing. First, content is not an issue anymore; there is a lot of content, but making all this content available to the appropriate audiences with high quality of experience (QoE) is still a challenge [24].

Global service providers are attempting to propose new mobile architectures and solutions for high performance of video-streaming services, which means high quality of experience along with high resource efficiency. In addition, the video traffic associated with the increasing number of mobile users represents a significant portion of resource consumption in the upcoming 5G networks. This scenario defines a new landscape of challenges to service providers in terms of supporting high quality of experience that is characterized by the following aspects:

- Precise arrival of received video chunks to guarantee continuous playback on low-latency applications
- High peak signal-to-noise ratio (PSNR) of the received video packets to gain high playback quality
- Low-quality fluctuation among the received segments to ensure smooth playback

Consequently, service providers need an immediate solution for a disruptive video-streaming technique to address requirements, such as the increasing number of connected mobile users, perceived quality, and bandwidth consumption [31], and for providing users with adaptive streaming services between 5G wireless communication networks and software-defined networking.

Future work should go toward developing QoE-aware video adaptation systems that leverage the 5G-QoE frameworks to analyze and optimize user perception of quality for ultra-high-definition video streams.

3.4 Future Directions

Telecommunications systems are constantly evolving, and reference architectures have to evolve as well to reflect new features. Considering this fact, in this chapter, we presented the principles of 5G and digital TV architectures, leaving details to the specific release of the system.

The continuous evolution of mobile telecommunications systems brings us 5G systems with new capabilities that have the potential to be disruptive in some areas, like IoT and autonomous vehicles. However, despite continuous improvements in 5G architecture, the vicious cycle of more bandwidth allowing new services that require more bandwidth means that the 6G system, which will use new architectures, is already under discussion.

References

1. D.U. Campos Delgado, C.A. Gutierrez, O. Caicedo, 5G and beyond: Past, present and future of the Mobile communications. IEEE Lat. Am. Trans. **19**(10), 1702–1736 (2021)
2. S. Zhang, An overview of network slicing for 5G. IEEE Wirel. Commun. **26**(3), 111–117 (June 2019). https://doi.org/10.1109/MWC.2019.1800234
3. 3GPP TR 21.915 version 15.0.0 Release 15, Technical Report
4. NR; NR and NG-RAN Overall description; Stage-2. Technical Specification
5. Introduction to 5G Core Service-Based Architecture (SBA) Components. https://5g.security/5g-technology/5g-core-sba-components-architecture/ Accessed 10 December 2021
6. Edge Computing for 5G Networks. 5G PPP Technology Board. https://doi.org/10.5281/zenodo.3698117
7. MEC in 5G Networks. ETSI White Paper No. 28. First edition – June 2018
8. Video streaming market growth trends. https://www.grandviewresearch.com/press-release/global-video-streaming-market. Accessed 10 April 2021
9. C. Lai, R. Hwang, H. Chao, M.M. Hassan, A. Alamri, A buffer-aware HTTP live streaming approach for SDN-enabled 5G wireless networks. IEEE Network **29**(1), 49–55 (Jan.–Feb. 2015). https://doi.org/10.1109/MNET.2015.7018203
10. L. Fanari, E. Iradier, J. Montalban, P. Angueira, S.-I. Park, N. Hur, S.-Y. Kwon, Trends and challenges in broadcast and broadband convergence, in *2019 IEEE International Conference on Electrical Engineering and Photonics (EExPolytech)*, (IEEE, St. Petersburg, 2019), pp. 153–156
11. Youtube for press – Youtube in numbers. https://www.youtube.com/intl/en-GB/about/press/. Accessed 10 June 2021
12. J.-y. Lee, S.-I. Park, H.-J. Yim, B.-M. Lim, S. Kwon, S. Ahn, N. Hur, Ip-based cooperative services using atsc 3.0 broadcast and broadband. IEEE Trans Broadcast **66**(2), 440–448 (2020)
13. S. Khalaf. Consumers time-spent on mobile crosses 5 hours a day. flurrymobile.tumblr.com/post/157921590345/us-consumers-time-spent-on-mobilecrosses-5, 2017. Flurry Analytics Blog
14. G. Bichot, G. Deen, D. Lucas, B. Stevenson, A. C. Begen, Y. Gressel, The viability of multicast ABR in future streaming architectures. https://streamingvideoalliance.docsend.com/view/kzg6cekcrosses-5, 2019. Streaming Video Alliance, Fremont, CA, USA
15. 23001-6 Dynamic Adaptive Streaming over HTTP (DASH), MPEG-4 Systems, ISO International Organisation for Standardization
16. I. Sodagar, The mpeg-dash standard for multimedia streaming over the internet. IEEE MultiMedia **18**(4), 62–67 (October 2011)
17. P.K. Yadav, A. Bentaleb, M. Lim, J. Huang, W.T. Ooi, R. Zimmermann, Playing chunk-transferred DASH segments at low latency with QLive, in *Proceedings of the 12th ACM Multimedia Systems Conference (MMSys' 21). Association for Computing Machinery*, (ACM, New York, NY, 2021), pp. 51–64. https://doi.org/10.1145/3458305.3463376

18. Rdk-V   architecture.   https://wiki.rdkcentral.com/display/RDK/RDK-V+Architecture. Accessed 11 June 2021
19. C. Koch, S. Hacker, D. Hausheer, Vodcast: Efficient sdn-based multicast for video on demand, in *2017 IEEE 18th International Symposium on A World of Wireless, Mobile and Multimedia Networks (WoWMoM)*, (IEEE, Macau, 2017), pp. 1–6
20. I. Eizmendi, M. Velez, D. Gomez-Barquero, J. Morgade, V. Baena-Lecuyer, M. Slimani, J. Zoellner, Dvb-t2: The second generation of terrestrial digital video broadcasting system. IEEE Trans. Broadcast. **60**(2), 258–271 (2014)
21. M.K. Park, Y. Kim, An overhead comparison of MMT and MPEG-2 TS in broadcast services. J Broadcast Eng **21**, 436–449 (2016 May)
22. S. Afzal, V. Testoni, J.F.F. de Oliveira, C.E. Rothenberg, P. Kolan, I. Bouazizif, A novel scheduling strategy for MMT-based multipath video streaming, in *2018 IEEE Global Communications Conference (GLOBECOM)*, (IEEE, Abu Dhabi, 2018), pp. 206–212
23. B. Furht, S. Ahson, T. Stockhammer, A. Shokrollahi, M. Watson, M. Luby, T. Gasiba, Application layer forward error correction for mobile multimedia broadcasting, in *Handbook of Mobile Broadcasting: DVB-H, DMB, ISDB-T, and MEDIAFLO*, (CRC Press, Boca Raton, 2008, April)
24. R. Sotelo, J. Joskowicz, N. Rondan, An integrated broadcast-broadband system that merges isdb-t with hbbtv 2.0. IEEE Trans. Broadcast. **64**(3), 709–720 (2018)
25. N. Barman, M.G. Martini, Qoe modeling for http adaptive video streaming: A survey and open challenges. IEEE Access **7**, 30831–30859 (2019)
26. A. Mehrabi, M. Siekkinen, A. Yl-Jaaski, Qoe-traffic optimization through collaborative edge caching in adaptive mobile video streaming. IEEE Access **6**, 52261–52276 (2018)
27. J.V.M. Cardoso, A.C.S. Mariano, C.D.M. Regis, M.S. Alencar, Comparison of objective video quality metrics based on structural similarity and error sensitivity. Revista de Tecnologia da Informação e Comunicação **1**(2), 33–40 (2012, April)
28. Rdk   documentation.   https://wiki.rdkcentral.com/display/RDK/RDK+Documentation. Accessed 11 June 2021
29. Android Platforms in Television - Mapping Out a Strategy, Susan Crouse, 2016, Alticast, https://www.digitaltveurope.com/files/2016/01/AndroidWhitePaperDec2015final1.pdf
30. The android TV input framework. https://source.android.com/devices/tv. Accessed 19 June 2021
31. N. Vo, T.Q. Duong, H.D. Tuan, A. Kortun, Optimal video streaming in dense 5G networks with D2D communications. IEEE Access **6**, 209–223 (2018). https://doi.org/10.1109/ACCESS.2017.2761978

Chapter 4
Reference Architectures for Health

Sabrina Souto, Paulo Barbosa, Lucas Oliveira, Eugenio Gaeta, Adilson Batistel, and Leire Bastida

Abstract We provide an overview on reference architectures for health and address non-functional validation as an important issue for this domain. We applied the approaches through a case study of a microservices architecture. Through experiments, we demonstrate how performance and resilience can be addressed.

4.1 Introduction

Typically, the motivation to use modern information and communications technologies (ICT) in health systems is to offer promising solutions for efficiently delivering all kinds of medical healthcare services to patients, referred to as e-health, such as telemedicine systems, personalized devices for diagnosis, etc. E-health involves a broad group of activities that use electronic means to deliver health-related information, resources, and services. At the heart of e-health is a vision of improving the quality of health information, strengthening national health systems, and ensuring accessible, high-quality healthcare for all [51].

Health applications, specially the IoT-based ones, can be used in a diverse array of fields, including care for pediatric and elderly patients, the supervision

S. Souto · P. Barbosa (✉) · L. Barbosa
Center for Strategic Health Technologies—NUTES, Campina Grande, Brazil
e-mail: sabrina.souto@nutes.uepb.edu.br; paulo.barbosa@nutes.uepb.edu.br; lucas.barbosa@nutes.uepb.edu.br

E. Gaeta
Life Supporting Technologies—LifeSTech, Universidad Politécnica de Madrid, Madrid, Spain
e-mail: eugenio.gaeta@lst.tfo.upm.es

A. Batistel
Research and Development Center in Telecommunications—CPQD, Campinas, Brazil
e-mail: adilsonb@cpqd.com.br

L. Bastida
TECNALIA, Basque Research and Technology Alliance (BRTA), Derio, Spain
e-mail: leire.bastida@tecnalia.com

E. Y. Nakagawa, P. Oliveira Antonino (eds.), *Reference Architectures for Critical Domains*, https://doi.org/10.1007/978-3-031-16957-1_4

41

of chronic diseases, and the management of private health and fitness, among others. The Gartner Company [25] presents IoT applications in health as a key trend coming out in the year of 2021 due to the digital transformation driven by the pandemic. Among the current IoT-based applications for health, Ambient-Assisted Living (AAL) technologies have the potential to improve people's quality of life [12]. According to Blackman et al. [8], three generations of AAL systems can be distinguished. The first generation includes wearable devices, usually alarms for emergency situations. The second generation is home sensors that provide automatic response to the detection of hazards. Finally, the third generation is based on the integration of wearable devices and home sensors, applicable for the monitoring of patient situation and prevention of health risks.

Another e-health- and IoT-related component is mHealth. The World Health Organization (WHO) [52] defined mHealth or mobile health as a medical and public health practice supported by mobile devices, such as mobile phones, patient monitoring devices, personal digital assistants (PDAs), and other wireless devices. mHealth involves the use and capitalization on a mobile phone's core utility of voice and short message service (SMS) as well as more complex functionalities and applications including general packet radio service (GPRS), third- and fourth-generation mobile telecommunications (3G and 4G systems), global positioning system (GPS), and Bluetooth technology [52].

Finally, the main scenarios of usage of IoT-based health applications, supported by e-health and ICT, are monitoring physiological and pathological signals; self-management, wellness monitoring, and prevention; medication intake monitoring; personalized healthcare; cloud-based health information systems; disease monitoring and telepathology; assisted living; and rehabilitation. All mentioned applications require a high-quality level of the e-health systems.

About the features of IoT-based health applications, there are some important non-functional requirements (quality attributes) that represent a concern in this kind of applications. The non-functional requirements refer to scalability, reliability, ubiquity, portability, interoperability, robustness, performance, availability, privacy, integrity, authentication, and security.

At the same time, software architectures constitute the backbone for any successful software-intensive system and play a fundamental role in determining the system quality (e.g., performance, resilience, security). In this context, reference architectures refer to a special type of software architecture that captures the essence of the architectures of a collection of systems in a given domain. The purpose of a reference architecture is to provide guidance for the development, standardization, and evolution of system architectures of a specific domain [45].

In the health domain, several reference architectures have been proposed. According to Garcés et al. [23], and taking the domain of AAL and e-health systems, examples of reference architectures for health are UniversAAL [61], OASIS [37], Continua [63], and PERSONA [58]. At that time, these works were proposing solutions based on high levels of interoperability, requiring the implementation of protocols by manufacturers that could lead to more productive infrastructures. Unfortunately, most devices that were included in these initiatives were based on episodic measurements (a single measurement of a variable), such as weight scales, thermometers, glucometers, and blood pressure monitors, among others. The requirements of connections and synchronization such as Bluetooth could involve much more effort for the users than the normal measurement. This generated problems of adoption by manufacturers, which could not find commercial applicability to justify such investment. The adoption became restricted to the initial proposers, such as OMRON and A&D. In 2018, Garcés, in her thesis [22], proposed a reference architecture for healthcare supportive home systems. This work brought clarifications on issues of aging. It addressed the problem that, so far, none of the existing reference architectures were oriented to support the self-management of multiple chronic conditions and assist patients at home.

Nowadays, some works are still emerging adding value to reference architectures for health. More recently, [59] have proposed a reference architecture for health information systems, meeting the concerns of various stakeholders. Atos [1] delivered recently a white paper entitled IT Reference Architecture for Healthcare. However, the discussion is very open, based on the classification of solutions as healthcare, supporting, basic, and infrastructure. Dependency models are introduced, and discussions about quality attributes, such as performance, scalability, adaptability, and maintainability, are developed, but without more clear benefits for the software industry.

The qualities of a software architecture go beyond functionality, which is the primary statement of the system's capabilities, services, and behavior. For example, systems are often redesigned not because they are functionally deficient, but because they are difficult to maintain, port, or scale or they are too slow. Thus, when it refers to these characteristics, it is referring to quality attributes.

A quality attribute is a measurable or testable property of a system used to indicate how well the system satisfies the needs of its stakeholders. This way, it can understand that a quality attribute is a measure of "how good" a system is along with some dimension of how interesting it is to a stakeholder [6]. Quality attributes or non-functional requirements, these requirements are qualifications of the functional requirements or the overall product. A qualification of a functional requirement is an item such as how fast the function must be performed or how resilient it must be to erroneous input. A qualification of the overall product is an item such as the time to deploy the product or a limitation on operational costs.

In this context, the identification and definition of a software architecture consist of a complex process, once the architect must consider both functional and non-functional requirements, domain constraints, and so on, and reference architectures provide guidelines to standardize such process. In the context of Health IoT software, building a software architecture may be more challenging due to the requirements of this area, specially the non-functional ones, such as faulty tolerance, scalability, security, and so on.

Microservices [33, 41, 47] are a popular trend in software architecture in recent years for building large-scale distributed systems. Microservices employ architectural design principles leading to explicit domain-based bounded contexts and loose coupling [55], exploit modern cloud-based technologies including containerization and self-healing [19], and are suitable for modern software engineering paradigms such as DevOps [7] including agile development methods and continuous delivery.

Microservices have emerged as an architectural style for developing distributed applications. Microservice-based architectures (MSAs) consist of small services that focus on one particular functionality. Some benefits of microservices include increased flexibility, scalability, and a smaller granularity of the offered functionality by a service. The benefits of microservices for functional testing are often praised, as the focus on one functionality and their smaller granularity allow for more targeted and more convenient testing.

Due to the mentioned benefits, and the high flexibility and evolvability characterizing microservices architectures, many organizations, like Netflix, Amazon, eBay, and Twitter, have already evolved their business applications to MSA [21]. Based on that, Nichol [48] and some recent research [24, 31] suggest to implement healthcare applications using microservice-based architectures.

Microservices architecture transfers healthcare providers and payers from one large application into smaller applications. These little applications or "micro" applications provide specialization using service-oriented architectures (SOA) by building dependent and flexible components. Microservices combine lightweight mechanisms that offer scalability (Netflix supporting 800 different devices and 1 billion calls a day) and can support a range of platforms and interactions (the web, mobile, IoT, wearables) [48].

Considering the critical characteristics of e-health systems, building such kind of system consists in a challenging task, and reference architectures can help to address the quality attributes (non-functional requirements), which are very relevant for this type of system. In this context, the microservice-based architectures are likely to be a great option to implement e-health systems, due to many benefits related to the needs of these systems. However, there is still needing to check how the MSAs deal with the quality attributes.

In that regarding, we conduct an empirical study in order to observe how a microservice-based architecture deals with some relevant non-functional requirements for an Health IoT system developed during the H2020 OCARIoT project[1] The OCARIoT microservice-based architecture can be seen in this chapter as a candidate for a reference architecture in health, and previous results in publishing its main components already exist [3, 4]. Both performance and resilience are considered important non-functional requirements for this project. Ueda et al. [60] observed performance degradation of microservices architectures as compared to an equivalent monolithic deployment model. Moreover, Heorhiadi et al. [29] pointed that many popular highly available Internet services have experienced various failures and outages (e.g., cascading failures due to database overload), and according to the post-mortem reports, most of such outages were caused by missing or faulty recovery logic, with an acknowledgement that unit and integration tests are insufficient to catch bugs in the fault-handling logic.

---

[1] https://ocariot.eu/.

With respect to performance, we built a performance testing approach and applied it to the OCARIoT project to evaluate service degradation in terms of both memory and CPU usage, response time, and error rate. Concerning resilience, we built a resilience testing approach that intentionally causes the outage of a service (or a combination of them) during the execution of existing API tests (from the system under test (SUT)) to detect failures or service degradation. We applied that approach to the OCARIoT project, evaluated service unavailability, and observed failures related to timeout, server error, network, and unexpected behaviors.

The remainder of this chapter is organized as follows. Section 4.2 presents essential concepts and summarizes the reviewed literature related to the two main non-functional requirements evaluated. Section 4.3 presents the OCARIoT architecture description. Section 4.4 contains the proposed approach to validate performance and its implementation. Then, we detail the evaluation and discuss the results and limitations. Section 4.5 explains the proposed approach to validate resilience and its implementation. Then, we detail the evaluation and discuss the results and limitations. Section 4.6 contains the lessons learned during this process.

4.2   Background and Related Work

This section introduces essential concepts and terminology to support the discussion of the remaining sections and summarizes the reviewed literature related to the two main non-functional requirements that are relevant to be considered in both reference architectures for health and associated health systems.

4.2.1   Performance

Similar to other software systems, product quality plays an important role for microservices and microservice-oriented architectures. An important non-functional quality attribute is performance, which describes a system's properties with respect to timeliness and resource usage, including aspects, such as scalability and elasticity [30]. Timeliness may seem to be achievable more easily by cloud features such as auto-scaling. However, resource usage becomes extremely relevant because inefficient architectures and implementations lead to high costs as a part of pay-per-use charging models for cloud resources.

The performance of a system can be assessed through several performance engineering techniques such as performance testing [9, 35]. Performance testing is traditionally done by establishing the baseline performance of a software version, which is then used to compare the performance testing results of later software versions. Performance testing is already considered challenging in traditional systems [40]. Even worse, the architectural, technological, and organizational changes that are induced by microservices have an impact on performance engineering practices as well [28]. While some of these changes may facilitate performance testing, others may pose considerable challenges. For example, establishing such a baseline performance is challenging in microservice applications.

4.2.1.1 Related Work

Despite the performance being one of the major aspects considered when adopting microservices, there exists a body of research on the testing of microservices, but focusing on functional tests [47]. There are few approaches for testing performance of microservice-based architectures documented in literature.

There is some research that highlights the challenges related to performance testing in microservice-based architectures. Knoche [39] presented a simulation-based approach for transforming monolithic applications into microservice-oriented applications while preserving their performance. Heinrich et al. [28] argued that traditional performance modeling and monitoring approaches in most cases cannot be reused for microservices. Dragoni et al. [16] argued that network overhead will be the major performance challenge for microservice-oriented applications.

Recently, Simon et al. [18] pointed the benefits and challenges of microservices from a performance tester's point of view. Through a series of experiments, they demonstrate how microservices affect the performance testing process and that it is not straightforward to achieve reliable performance testing results for a microservice application.

Assessing the performance of architecture deployment configurations (e.g., with respect to deployment alternatives) is challenging and must be aligned with the system usage in the production environment. In this regard, Avritzer et al. [2] introduced an approach to generate load tests to automatically assess scalability pass/fail criteria of microservice configuration alternatives. The approach provides a domain-based metric for each alternative that can, for instance, be applied to make informed decisions about the selection of alternatives and conduct production monitoring regarding performance-related system properties, e.g., anomaly detection.

In this chapter, we focus on evaluating how microservice-based architectures deal with the performance attribute in the scenario of a candidate reference architecture for health. For that, we built a performance testing approach upon well-known existing tools not used together for that purpose before. We applied that approach to the OCARIoT project and evaluated the service degradation in terms of memory and CPU usage, response time, and error rate.

4.2.2 Resilience

One of MSA guiding principles is to design for failure, which means that a microservice is able to cope with failures of other microservices and its surrounding software/hardware infrastructure [62]. Although massive efforts have been devoted to the quality assurance of online service systems, in reality, these systems still come across many incidents (i.e., unplanned interruptions and outages), which can decrease user satisfaction or cause economic loss. Recently, online service systems, such as Microsoft Azure and Office 365, have been widely used by millions of users around the world. To assure their quality, practitioners put dedicated efforts, but such online service systems still encounter many incidents (i.e., unplanned interruptions and outages) [14]. These incidents can decrease user satisfaction or cause serious economic loss. For example, the 1-hour downtime for Amazon.com on Prime Day in 2018 (its biggest sale event of the year) caused the loss of up to $100 million [64]. Therefore, resilience is essential to provide availability and reliability to online service systems.

The relevance of resilience has been highlighted by many practitioner books of microservices [44, 47, 65], and studies pointed out key features of MSA systems [16, 17]. In these books and studies, some typical system mechanisms consisting of operations that react to service degradations are mentioned, such as load balancing, circuit breakers, API gateway, bulkheads, etc. These mechanisms are called resilience mechanisms. Some researchers improved these resilience mechanisms for MSA systems in recent years [10, 15, 29, 34, 42, 43, 49].

Together with the spread of DevOps practices and container technologies, MSA has become a mainstream architecture style in recent years. Resilience is a key characteristic in MSA systems and shows the ability to cope with various kinds of system disturbances, which cause degradations of services. In this context, resilience of a MSA system is the ability to maintain the performance of services at an acceptable level and recover the service back to normal, when a disruption causes the service degradation [66].

4.2.2.1 Related Work

Although resilience is an important quality attribute of microservice-based architecture, very few works focus on assuring resilience specifically for microservices. One of the first approaches started based on chaos engineering, which involves experimenting on a distributed system to build confidence in its capability to withstand turbulent conditions in production [13].

In this context, Basiri et al. [5] observed that organizations, such as Amazon, Google, Microsoft, and Facebook, were applying injection failure techniques to test their systems' resilience (through Chaos Monkey, Chaos Kong, Failure Injection Testing). Chaos Monkey [46] is a randomized fault injection tool from Netflix, being used at large scale in production. It is capable of staging unforeseen faults that were not captured by systematic testing and has the ability to kill an entire availability zone or a region of the application. However, the tool lacks support for automatically analyzing application behavior, which is necessary to quickly zero in on implementation bugs. Moreover, random fault injection technique is not efficient, and lots of time and resources will be wasted to explore redundant failure scenarios. It is also unlikely to uncover deep failures involving combinations of different instances and kinds of faults.

Heorhiadi et al. [29] proposed Gremlin, a systematic resilience testing framework that supports to expose fault tolerance bugs in microservice-based applications. It allows the user to write test scripts (recipes), which capture a variety of high-level failure scenarios and assertions to be checked, and then executes them by manipulating the interaction messages between microservices. Long et al. [42] presented IntelliFT, a guided resilience testing technique for microservice-based applications, which aims to expose the defects in the fault-handling logic effectively within a fixed time limit. The characteristic of IntelliFT is that it leverages existing integration tests of the applications under test to explore the fault space and decides whether injected faults can lead to severe failures by designing fitness-guided search technique.

In this chapter, we focus on evaluating how microservice-based architectures deal with the resilience attribute. For that, we built a resilience testing approach where instead of directly injecting faults as Gremlin or IntelliFT, we intentionally caused the outage of a service (or a combination of them) during the execution of existing API tests (from the system under test (SUT)) to detect failures or service degradation. We applied that approach to the OCARIoT project, evaluated the service unavailability, and observed failures related to timeout, server error, network, and unexpected behaviors.

4.3   OCARIoT Architecture

Figure 4.1 introduces the overall idea of the defined software architecture for Health IoT. It is inspired on the best practices of the references mentioned in the introductory section. Taking the benefits of the microservices paradigm, microservices can be implemented in different languages, using different databases. In the case of the OCARIoT platform, we have available components developed in Node.js, Python, and Java for the direct integration of a messaging channel bus for efficient management of microservices. Concerning persistent data in microservices, we also provided libraries for encryption at rest for microservices that use MongoDB and MySQL databases, meeting important requirements from GDPR [26] in Europe. It was also defined as a single entry point for microservices using Express Gateway [20], an open-source API gateway built on Express.js. Also, we have efforts toward high scale and high availability when adopting RabbitMQ [54], one of the most popular open-source message brokers. Finally, the overall privacy and security management of the OCARIoT platform was developed relying in the open-source tools Vault and Consul.

The main identified components are better explained in Table 4.1. The naming of these which confuses with the name of the open-source technology was intentional, emphasizing the main contribution of this chapter toward actual instances and ready-to-use components for a software architecture.

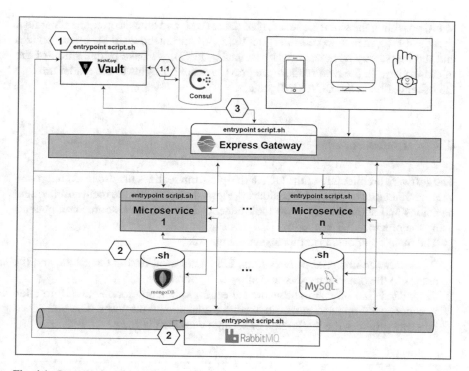

Fig. 4.1 Overall microservices architecture

Table 4.1 Architectural components

Component	Description
Apps, dashboards, IoT gateways	Health IoT tools for aggregating data and synchronization services. The data can be synchronized directly or can be requested by a third-party service
Vault	Offers high-level management policies to secure, store, and control access ensuring security
Consul	Extends the Vault functions creating high availability to manage keys and certificates, among others
Express gateway	Single entry point for interaction of clients and microservices. Realization of the API Gateway and Aggregator patterns and used to manage the service call between the external components and the microservices
RabbitMQ bus	Implementation of a messaging channel, a mechanism used to enable asynchronous communication between microservices

The initialization follows the numbers presented in Fig. 4.1 and defines the flow information that will be presented in the next sections. In (1), Vault generates all the encryption keys and the root token. In (1.1), Consul is initialized as the back-end of

Vault, providing the storage of encrypted data at rest, and other secrets are generated, e.g., databases, messaging channel, etc. In (2), all the databases of the microservices and the messaging bus are initialized. Finally, in (3), we have initialization of the microservices. In the next section, we provide deeper insights to the reader through the instantiation in the OCARIoT project.

4.3.1 Instantiation

The software architecture of the OCARIoT platform realizes the proposed microservices architecture of Fig. 4.2. Considering Fig. 4.4, we explore the main architectural decisions and show the ways we took benefits from the open-source components using the previous IoT scenarios.

The main components in this instantiation are:

1. Wearables: commercial devices (e.g., Fitbit) are used during the pilots, and the access to the proprietary server is allowed by vendors.
2. Embedded Gateway: smart sensors collect important environmental information at schools and updates in the platform for educational purposes. The embedded gateway provides the integration of sensors with the platform.

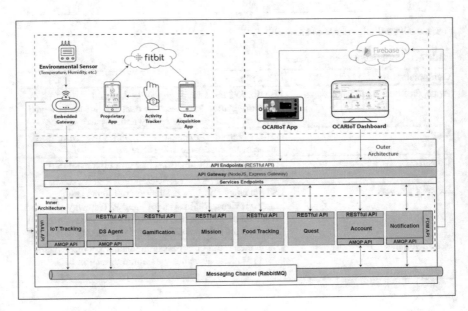

Fig. 4.2 Microservices architecture of the OCARIoT project

3. Data Acquisition App: mobile phone app manages the collection of data from different devices during the pilots and shows key information for the health professionals. Available at github.com/ocariot/da-app.
4. API Gateway: realized using Express Gateway as suggested in the software architecture. Available at github.com/ocariot/api-gateway.
5. Messaging Channel: realized using RabbitMQ as suggested in the software architecture. Available at github.com/ocariot/rabbitmq-client-node.

Eight microservices were defined. Some are not available due to proprietary clauses. Some available are:

1. Account: user management and authentication. Available at github.com/ocariot/account.
2. IoT_Tracking: tracking activities, sleep, environmental data, and measurements. Available at github.com/ocariot/iot-tracking.
3. Data Sync: data synchronization from wearables platforms, allowing token management and revocation and to publish synchronized data in the messaging channel. Available at github.com/ocariot/data-sync-agent.

4.4 Performance Study

Although using a microservice-based application has a lot of advantages, it can bring about major challenges as well. One such challenge includes how to monitor a distributed system; this is because each microservice is heterogeneous and independent in nature. This means that traditional monitoring approaches are not good enough. Monitoring is a critical part of a microservice-based system. It involves knowing how to control it and how to make sure that software is reliable and available and that it performs as expected.

In order to validate the performance of the OCARIoT system, we decided to use the JMeter tool [36], which is a widely used tool for the performance testing of different applications, including microservice ones. In this specific case, JMeter makes requisitions for each service (see Fig. 4.3), and then it can simulate a configurable quantity of simultaneous accesses in order to stress the system.

Figure 4.4 illustrates JMeter tests for the OCARIoT system. On the left side, there are tests for each application service, where each one exercises at least one API endpoint related to its service. On the other side, there is detailed information of how this access is configured, for example, it is set to have simultaneous 600 accesses.

We created tests for all application services; see Fig. 4.5. But we exercised one endpoint as a sample for each one, including the GET method, as shown in Fig. 4.6.

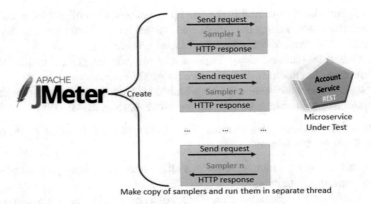

Fig. 4.3 Using JMeter to perform testing microservice applications, source [56]

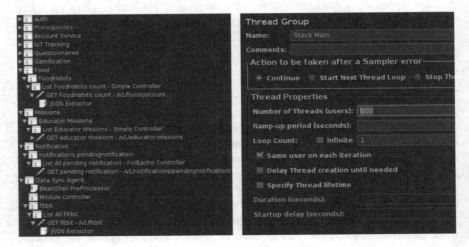

Fig. 4.4 JMeter tests

4.4.1 Approach

Figure 4.7 illustrates our general approach to both stress the OCARIoT system and observe how its resource consumption behaves. The OCARIoT system is running on a virtual machine (VM), and from another machine (HOST), the tester makes requisitions to the OCARIoT API by using JMeter. It is important to remember that this VM is accessible in the cloud.

As illustrated in Fig. 4.8, the monitoring of the OCARIoT platform services is carried out normally through the services Grafana [27], Prometheus [53], cAdvisor [11], and node_exporter [50]. In this, both cAdvisor and node_exporter are responsible, respectively, for collecting the metrics of the containers and the host

Microservice	#Endpoints(paths)
Account	43
IoT Tracking	23
Food	8
Questionnaires	104
Data Sync Agent	7
Gamification	48
Notification	3
Missions	27
TOTAL	263

Fig. 4.5 OCARIoT application services and their corresponding number of endpoints

Microservice	Label	Path	Method
Account	children	/v1/children	GET
IoT Tracking	children.physicalactivities	/v1/children/{child_id}/physicalactivities	GET
Food	FoodHabits	/v1/foodqs/count	GET
Questionnaires	Q1Sociodemographic	/v1/q1sociodemographics/count	GET
Data Sync Agent	fitbit	/v1/fitbit	GET
Gamification	GamificationProfile	/v1/gamificationprofiles/count	GET
Notification	notifications.pendingnotification	/v1/notifications/pendingnotification/{userId}	GET
Missions	Educator Missions	/v1/educator-missions	GET

Fig. 4.6 Services and corresponding endpoints for which we created testers

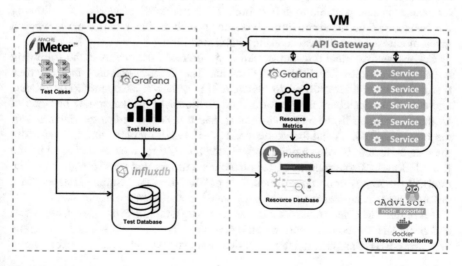

Fig. 4.7 Approach to validate performance

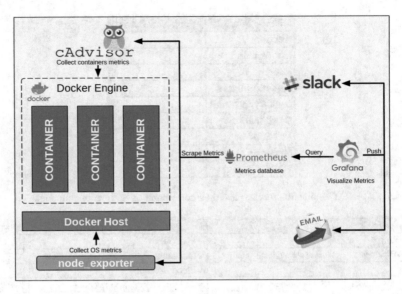

Fig. 4.8 The monitoring of the OCARIoT platform services

where the deployment is performed. The collected data is captured by Prometheus, which has cAdvisor and node_exporter as its data providers. Finally, Grafana connects to Prometheus and monitors the collected data, displaying it in graphs. In Grafana, it is also possible to define limits for the issuance of alerts, thus allowing the issuance of notifications through channels such as Slack and e-mails when a given monitored resource exceeds the established limit.

For the environment test, performed in a different host, we used the following tools: JMeter, InfluxDB [32], and Grafana. The JMeter executes the test plan that makes several requisitions to the OCARIoT services. Next, InfluxDB collects and stores metrics about the performed requisitions. After that, a new instance of Grafana is created in the test environment, and it is connected to the databases of the InfluxDB (HOST) and the Prometheus (VM), resulting in the test analysis from the data collected. Finally, having both (1) the requisitions metrics collected by the InfluxDB and (2) the metrics of resources used in the VM by Prometheus in the moment the requisition is performed, it is possible that the Grafana instance (in a different host) generates the graphics for analysis, as illustrated in Fig. 4.9.

From the VM side, we used some tools, such as Grafana, Prometheus, cAdvisor, and InfluxDB, to monitor both the memory and CPU usage during test execution. Moreover, we also monitored the execution time, and we observed the error rate.

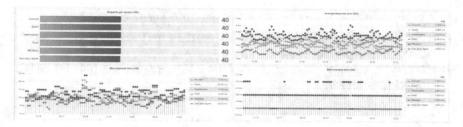

Fig. 4.9 Graphics generated by Grafana

4.4.2   Evaluation

4.4.2.1   Setup

We applied the proposed approach to the OCARIoT system by using the following machine configurations:

For the HOST:

- Local host (local machine—ocariot.test)
- OS: Ubuntu 18.04.4 LTS (Bionic Beaver)
- CPU: 8 cores 3.60 GHz (Intel® Core™ i7-9700K CPU)
- RAM: 16 GB
- HD: 150 GB

For the VM:

- VM01 (new server—ocariot.tk)
- OS: Ubuntu 18.04.3 LTS (Bionic Beaver)
- CPU: 4 cores 2294.560 MHz (Intel Xeon Processor (Skylake, IBRS))
- RAM: 12 GB
- HD: 30 GB

We defined three scenarios of requisitions for validating the performance:

- Simulating 100 requisitions for each test
- Simulating 300 requisitions for each test
- Simulating 600 requisitions for each test

Those amounts of requisitions were chosen based on the estimated number of users that would simultaneously access the system during the pilot. In a typical pilot scenario, there are 132 children, 132 parents, 3 educators, 2 health professionals, and some administrators, roughly 300 users in total. So, we used this typical scenario, and we also defined a lower-bounded one (with 100 requisitions) and an upper-bounded one (with the twice times—600 requisitions).

We also defined two scenarios regarding the environment configuration:

- HOST-HOST: the requisitions are made from the same machine from the one the OCARIoT is deployed;
- HOST-VM: the requisitions are made from a different machine from the one the OCARIoT is deployed.

4.4.2.2 Results

Considering the three scenarios of requisitions and the two scenarios regarding the environment configuration, we evaluated the response time, both memory and CPU usage, and both the error rate per requisitions and per service.

4.4.2.2.1 Response Time X Number of Requisitions

We evaluated the response time of all requisitions considering the three scenarios of requisitions for HOST-HOST and HOST-VM; see Fig. 4.10. As expected, (i) the greater the number of requisitions, the more the time spent for the two scenarios of environment configuration, and (ii) the HOST-VM scenario takes more time than the HOST-HOST, for all three scenarios of requisitions. This happens because in the HOST-HOST scenario, all the evaluation runs in the local machine, and so it is faster.

4.4.2.2.2 Memory Usage X Number of Requisitions

We evaluated the memory usage of all requisitions considering the three scenarios of requisitions for HOST-HOST and HOST-VM; see Fig. 4.11. And as we can observe, in most cases, the memory usage is greater for HOST-HOST because both the tests and OCARIoT system are running in the same machine.

4.4.2.2.3 CPU Usage X Number of Requisitions

We evaluated the CPU usage of all requisitions considering the three scenarios of requisitions for HOST-HOST and HOST-VM; see Fig. 4.12. And as we can observe, in most cases, the CPU usage is greater for HOST-HOST because both the tests and OCARIoT system are running in the same machine. It is important to note that the CPU usage refers to how much each service consumed from the total in use of the processor.

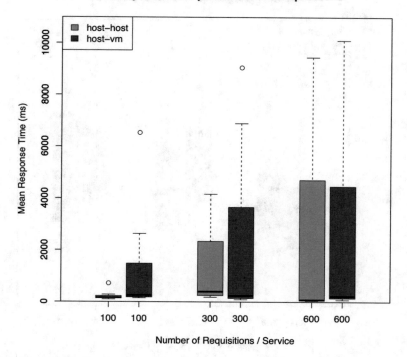

Fig. 4.10 Plots the response time per number of requisitions of each service test

4.4.2.2.4 Error Rate X Number of Requisitions

We evaluated the error rate for all requisitions considering the three scenarios of requisitions for HOST-HOST and HOST-VM. And as we can see in Fig. 4.13, (i) the greater the number of requisitions, the higher is the error rate for the two scenarios of environment configuration, and (ii) the HOST-VM scenario has a greater error rate than the HOST-HOST one, for all three scenarios of requisitions, except for the 300 requisitions scenario.

4.4.2.2.5 Error Rate x Service

We evaluated the error rate per service considering the two scenarios of configuration environment for all requisitions scenarios.

- For 100 requisitions, in the HOST-HOST scenario, no service failed; just Account, IoT_Tracking, and Notification failed for HOST-VM scenario, as we can see in Fig. 4.14.

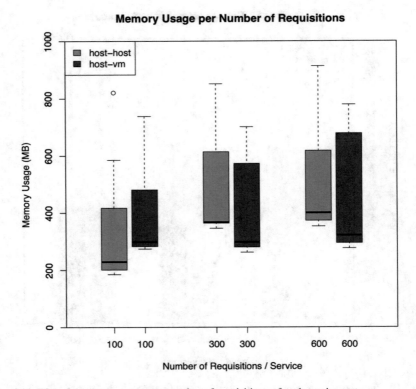

Fig. 4.11 Plots the memory usage per number of requisitions of each service test

- For 300 requisitions, in the HOST-HOST scenario, some services started to fail, Account, IoT_Tracking, and Notification. In the HOST-VM scenario, Account, IoT_Tracking, Gamification, and Notification failed, as we can observe in Fig. 4.15

- For 100 requisitions, in the HOST-HOST scenario, no service failed; just Account, IoT_Tracking, and Notification failed for HOST-VM scenario, as we can see in Fig. 4.16.

4.5 Resilience Study

Microservices applications operate on a constantly changing infrastructure environment, and sometimes, portions of those environments may encounter failures. For instance, a server that is running a specific service may crash or become unavailable, network may stop traffic, or a database may have problems. Microservices applica-

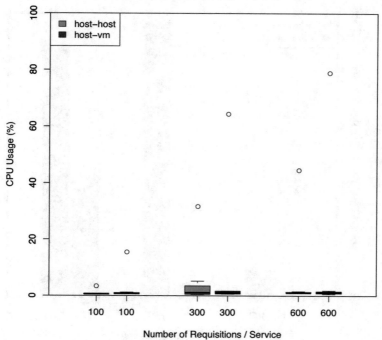

Fig. 4.12 Plots the CPU usage per number of requisitions of each service test

tions must be resilient in the face of infrastructure failures. A desirable approach to evaluating the system resilience is to test whether it can continue operation if the underlying resources fail.

In order to validate the resilience of the OCARIoT system, we used both the infrastructure and application services, in total as illustrated in Fig. 4.17, including the eight application services and their respective database services, the RabbitMQ, Redis DS Agent, API Gateway, and Redis API Gateway, 20 services in total.

4.5.1 Approach

Figure 4.18 presents our approach resilience testing; the general idea is to remove some services of the system and observe how it behaves. The results must indicate critical services, sensible parts of the system, typical errors, etc. This approach is based on SPLat [38, 57], a technique for testing configurable systems, and here we adjusted it to consider services instead of features, and we added all infrastructure

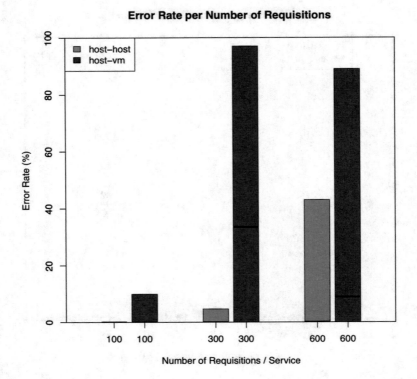

Fig. 4.13 Plots the error rate per number of requisitions of each service test

to deal with a microservices architecture. The approach receives as input the microservice system, a list of services, and a set of existing system tests.

4.5.2 Evaluation

4.5.2.1 Setup

4.5.2.1.1 Environment Configuration

We applied the proposed approach on the OCARIoT system, and we have some observations regarding the environment configuration and the tests. For the environment configuration, the services RabbitMQ, API Gateway, and Redis API Gateway, with their dependencies, are mandatory for the system execution, and so they cannot be disabled. Therefore, they are fixed for all combinations generated by the approach.

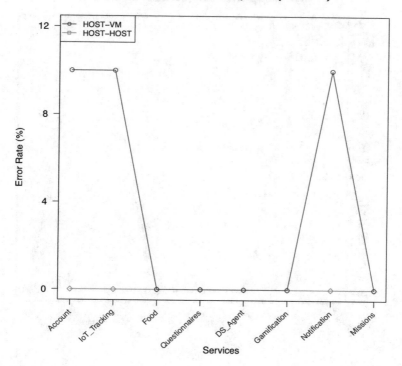

Fig. 4.14 Plots the error rate per service for 100 requisitions

4.5.2.1.2 Tests Used

Regarding the tests used, all the tests are system tests based on the API Gateway which validates the OCARIoT platform; we reused some existing tests. Each test may depend on another system functionality. Thus, during the test setup, it is common to perform other operations for a successful execution, which ones may include other service operations. Due to those dependencies, a test may need more than a service of the OCARIoT platform in order to execute in a successful manner.

From all previous API system tests, we observed that they touch seven or eight services, where only two correspond to application service (Account that is present in all tests and another one) and the others are infrastructure services. Three of those services are fixed (RabbitMQ, API Gateway, and Redis API Gateway), which means they always will be present. This way, we chose some tests which touch 4 services or more, in total 23 tests. This test set exercises all services of the OCARIoT platform.

For the 23 tests, our approach generated 432 combinations of services in total; 404 combinations failed when run with its corresponding test, and 28 passed. Table 4.2 illustrates those statistics and informs the application service being tested

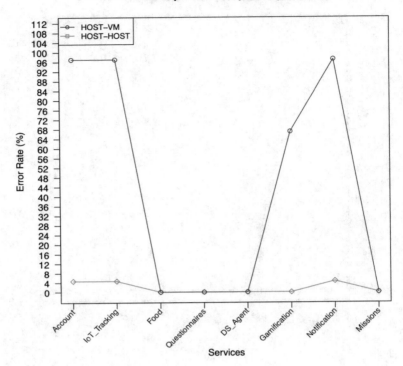

Fig. 4.15 Plots the error rate per service for 300 requisitions

(in column Service) by each test case and the total number of services touched in column #Services. For the amount of services touched, one corresponds to the application service being tested, and the others are infrastructure tests. It is important to observe that the Account service does not appear in Table 4.1 because all tests depend on it, so it is touched by all tests.

Note that in Table 4.2, the test case from 1 to 16 and 18 had only one combination of services that passed, which corresponds to the combination with all services available. The test cases 17 and 19–22 had two combinations of services that passed due to a partial dependence from one of the services, consequently, making possible the successful execution of the test cases.

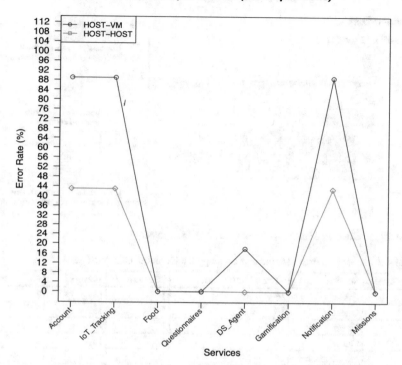

Fig. 4.16 Plots the error rate per service for 600 requisitions

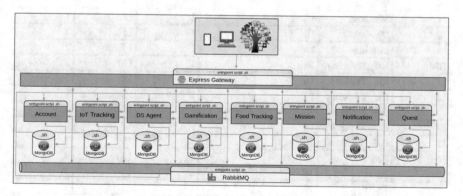

Fig. 4.17 The OCARIoT microservices architecture including the infrastructure services

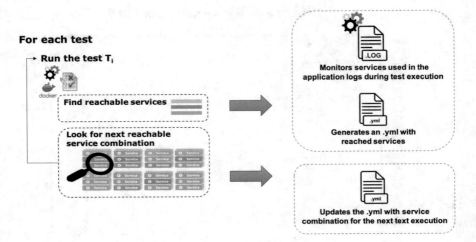

Fig. 4.18 Microservices architecture of the OCARIoT project

Table 4.2 General statistics for the approach application in the OCARIoT test

TestCaseID	Service	#TotalCombinations	#Passing	#Failing	#Services
0	Quest	16	1	15	7
1	Quest	16	1	15	7
2	Quest	16	1	15	7
3	Quest	16	1	15	7
4	Notification	16	1	15	7
5	Notification	16	1	15	7
6	Missions	16	1	15	7
7	Missions	16	1	15	7
8	Missions	16	1	15	7
9	Missions	16	1	15	7
10	IoT_Tracking	16	1	15	7
11	IoT_Tracking	16	1	15	7
12	IoT_Tracking	16	1	15	7
13	IoT_Tracking	16	1	15	7
14	Gamification	16	1	15	7
15	Gamification	16	1	15	7
16	Food	16	1	15	7
17	Food	16	2	14	7
18	Food	16	1	15	7
19	ds-agent	32	2	30	8
20	ds-agent	32	2	30	8
21	ds-agent	32	2	30	8
22	ds-agent	32	2	30	8

4.5.2.2   Results

4.5.2.2.1   Distribution of Unavailable Services x Error Type

We evaluated the distribution on the amount of services unavailable when each kind of error happened; see Fig. 4.19. And in maximum, five services are unavailable when Time exceeded happens, but in major cases, there are two or three services unavailable.

4.5.2.2.2   Number of Failures x Error Type

We measured the number of combinations that failed per error type. And according to Fig. 4.20, most failures are concentrated in both the errors 401 Unauthorized and Time exceeded.

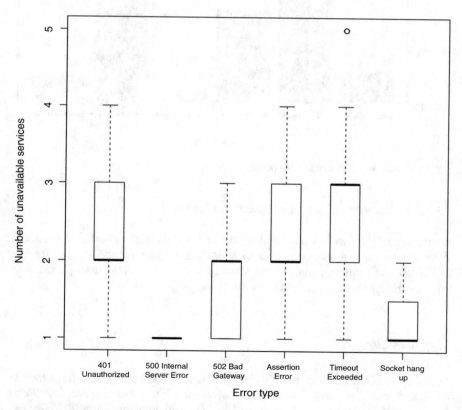

Fig. 4.19 Plots the unavailable services per error type

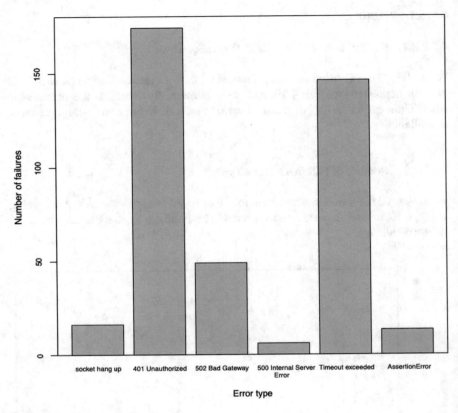

Fig. 4.20 Plots the number of failures per error type

4.5.2.2.3   Number of Failures x Unavailable Service

We measured the services unavailable when each failure happened; see Fig. 4.21. With this evaluation, it is possible to identify the more critical service for the OCARIoT platform and analyze the services with more failures and planning to improve the number of replicas for the more critical services.

4.6   Conclusions

This chapter offered a brief overview of reference architectures for health, which is a critical domain, and contributed with a new approach of evaluating non-functional requirements for a very common scenario for the health domain currently: IoT-based and microservice-based architecture.

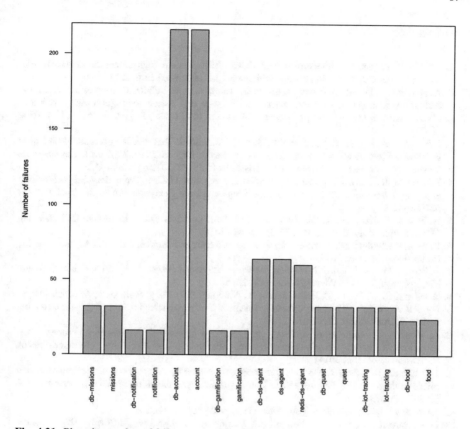

Fig. 4.21 Plots the number of failures per unavailable services

We conducted an empirical study and observed how a microservice-based architecture deals with some relevant non-functional requirements, such as performance and resilience, for the OCARIoT project.

With respect to performance, we built a performance testing approach and applied it to the OCARIoT project to evaluate service degradation in terms of memory and CPU usage, response time, and error rate.

Concerning resilience, we built a resilience testing approach that intentionally causes the outage of a service (or a combination of them) during the execution of existing API tests (from the system under test (SUT)) to detect failures or service degradation. We applied that approach to the OCARIoT project, evaluated service unavailability, and observed failures related to timeout, server error, network, and unexpected behaviors.

References

1. ATOS. IT reference architecture for healthcare. https://atos.net/wp-content/uploads/2016/06/atos-itah-architecture-for-healthcare-whitepaper.pdf, Accessed June 2021
2. A. Avritzer, V. Ferme, A. Janes, B. Russo, A. van Hoorn, H. Schulz, D. Menasché, V. Rufino, Scalability assessment of microservice architecture deployment configurations: a domain-based approach leveraging operational profiles and load tests. J. Syst. Softw. **165**, 110564 (2020)
3. P. Barbosa, A. Figueiredo, S. Souto, E. Gaeta, E. Araujo, T. Teixeira, An open source software architecture and ready-to-use components for health iot, in *2020 IEEE 33rd International Symposium on Computer-Based Medical Systems (CBMS)* (2020), pp. 374–379
4. P. Barbosa, D. Santos, C. Lucena, L. Bastida, J.F. Ferreira, G. Cea, The ocariot data acquisition app, in *2020 IEEE 33rd International Symposium on Computer-Based Medical Systems (CBMS)* (2020), pp. 409–414
5. A. Basiri, N. Behnam, R. De Rooij, L. Hochstein, L. Kosewski, J. Reynolds, C. Rosenthal, Chaos engineering. IEEE Softw. **33**(3), 35–41 (2016)
6. L. Bass, P. Clements, R. Kazman, *Software Architecture in Practice*, 3rd edn. (Addison-Wesley Professional, Boston, 2012)
7. L. Bass, I. Weber, L. Zhu, *DevOps: A Software Architect's Perspective*. SEI Series in Software Engineering (Addison-Wesley, New York, 2015)
8. S. Blackman, C. Matlo, C. Bobrovitskiy, A. Waldoch, M.L. Fang, P. Jackson, A. Mihailidis, L. Nygård, A. Astell, A. Sixsmith, Ambient assisted living technologies for aging well: a scoping review. J. Intell. Syst. **25**, 01 (2015)
9. A. Bondi, *Foundations of Software and System Performance Engineering: Process, Performance Modeling, Requirements, Testing, Scalability, and Practice* (Addison-Wesley Professional, Boston, 2014)
10. J. Brilhante, R. Costa, T. Maritan, Asynchronous queue based approach for building reactive microservices, in *Proceedings of the 23rd Brazillian Symposium on Multimedia and the Web* (2017), pp. 373–380
11. cAdvisor. https://github.com/google/cadvisor, Accessed Mar 2021
12. D. Calvaresi, D. Cesarini, P. Sernani, M. Marinoni, A.F. Dragoni, A. Sturm, Exploring the ambient assisted living domain: a systematic review. J. Ambient Intell. Human. Comput. **8**, 04 (2017)
13. Chaos Community, Principles of Chaos Engineering. https://principlesofchaos.org/, Accessed Mar 2021
14. J. Chen, S. Zhang, X. He, Q. Lin, H. Zhang, D. Hao, Y. Kang, F. Gao, Z. Xu, Y. Dang, et al., How incidental are the incidents? Characterizing and prioritizing incidents for large-scale online service systems, in *2020 35th IEEE/ACM International Conference on Automated Software Engineering (ASE)* (IEEE, Piscataway, 2020), pp. 373–384
15. M. Cinque, R. Della Corte, R. Iorio, A. Pecchia, An exploratory study on zeroconf monitoring of microservices systems, in *2018 14th European Dependable Computing Conference (EDCC)* (IEEE, Piscataway, 2018), pp. 112–115
16. N. Dragoni, S. Giallorenzo, A.L. Lafuente, M. Mazzara, F. Montesi, R. Mustafin, L. Safina, *Microservices: Yesterday, Today, and Tomorrow* (Springer International Publishing, Cham, 2017), pp. 195–216
17. N. Dragoni, I. Lanese, S.T. Larsen, M. Mazzara, R. Mustafin, L. Safina, Microservices: How to make your application scale, in *International Andrei Ershov Memorial Conference on Perspectives of System Informatics* (Springer, Berlin, 2017), pp. 95–104
18. S. Eismann, C.-P. Bezemer, W. Shang, D. Okanović, A. van Hoorn, Microservices: A performance tester's dream or nightmare? in *Proceedings of the ACM/SPEC International Conference on Performance Engineering*, ICPE '20 (Association for Computing Machinery, New York, 2020), pp. 138–149

19. C. Esposito, A. Castiglione, K.R. Choo, Challenges in delivering software in the cloud as microservices. IEEE Cloud Comput. **3**(5), 10–14 (2016)
20. Express Gateway. Microservices and Serverless to Production Insanely Fast. https://www.express-gateway.io/, Accessed Mar 2021
21. P.D. Francesco, I. Malavolta, P. Lago, Research on architecting microservices: Trends, focus, and potential for industrial adoption, in *2017 IEEE International Conference on Software Architecture (ICSA)* (2017), pp. 21–30
22. L. Garcés, A reference architecture for healthcare supportive home systems from a systems-of-systems perspective. https://teses.usp.br/teses/disponiveis/55/55134/tde-16102018-111654/en.php, Accessed June 2021
23. L. Garcés, A. Ampatzoglou, F. Oquendo, N. Elisa, Reference architectures and reference models for ambient assisted living systems: a systematic literature review. http://repositorio.icmc.usp.br/handle/RIICMC/6564, Accessed June 2021
24. F.M. Garcia-Moreno, M. Bermúdez-Edo, J. Garrido, E. Rodríguez García, J.M. Pérez-Mármol, M.J. Rodríguez Fórtiz, A microservices e-health system for ecological frailty assessment using wearables. Sensors **20**, 3427, 06 (2020)
25. Gartner Company. https://www.gartner.com/en/information-technology/trends/top-strategic-technology-trends-iot-brnd-gb-pd?utm_source=google&utm_medium=cpc&utm_campaign=RM_NA_2020_ITTRND_CPC_LG1_2021-TSTT-GB-PD&utm_adgroup=115089184712&utm_term=%2Bgartner%20%2Biot&ad=484688563377&matchtype=b&gclid=CjwKCAjwgOGCBhAlEiwA7FUXkgXQl4KTJaBxT5DDsdjqJDRbZ9SjptfY02lEkNuBAG-PmxIzvXml1hoC8YoQAvD_BwE, Accessed Mar 2021
26. GDPR. General Data Protection Regulation. https://gdpr\discretionary-info.eu/, Accessed Mar 2021
27. Grafana. The analytics platform for all your metrics. https://grafana.com, Accessed Mar 2021
28. R. Heinrich, A. van Hoorn, H. Knoche, F. Li, L. Ellen Lwakatare, C. Pahl, S. Schulte, J. Wettinger, Performance engineering for microservices: Research challenges and directions, in *Proceedings of the 8th ACM/SPEC on International Conference on Performance Engineering Companion*, ICPE '17 Companion, (Association for Computing Machinery, New York, 2017), pp. 223–226
29. V. Heorhiadi, S. Rajagopalan, H. Jamjoom, M.K. Reiter, V. Sekar, Gremlin: Systematic resilience testing of microservices, in *2016 IEEE 36th International Conference on Distributed Computing Systems (ICDCS)* (2016), pp. 57–66
30. N. Herbst, S. Kounev, R. Reussner, Elasticity in cloud computing: What it is, and what it is not, in *10th International Conference on Autonomic Computing (ICAC'13)* (2013), pp. 23–27
31. M. Ianculescu, A. Alexandru, G. Neagu, F. Pop, Microservice-based approach to enforce an ioht oriented architecture, in *2019 E-Health and Bioengineering Conference (EHB)* (2019), pp. 1–4
32. InfluxDB. InfluxDB: Purpose-Built Open Source Time Series Database. https://www.influxdata.com, Accessed Mar 2021
33. P. Jamshidi, C. Pahl, N.C. Mendonça, J. Lewis, S. Tilkov, Microservices: the journey so far and challenges ahead. IEEE Softw. **35**(3), 24–35 (2018)
34. J. Jenkins, G. Shipman, J. Mohd-Yusof, K. Barros, P. Carns, R. Ross, A case study in computational caching microservices for HPC, in *2017 IEEE International Parallel and Distributed Processing Symposium Workshops (IPDPSW)* (IEEE, Piscataway, 2017), pp. 1309–1316
35. Z.M. Jiang, A.E. Hassan, A survey on load testing of large-scale software systems. IEEE Trans. Softw. Eng. **41**(11), 1091–1118 (2015)
36. JMeter. Apache JMeter. https://jmeter.apache.org/, Accessed Out 2020
37. D. Kehagias, D. Tzovaras, E. Mavridou, K. Kalagirou, M. Becker, Implementing an open reference architecture based on web service mining for the integration of distributed application and multi-agent systems, in *ADMI'10: Proceedings of the 6th International Conference on Agents and Data Mining Interaction* Lecture Notes in Computer Science (2010), p. 5980

38. C.H.P. Kim, D. Marinov, S. Khurshid, D. Batory, S. Souto, P. Barros, M. D'Amorim, SPLat: Lightweight dynamic analysis for reducing combinatorics in testing configurable systems, in *Proceedings of the 2013 9th Joint Meeting on Foundations of Software Engineering*, ESEC/FSE 2013 (Association for Computing Machinery, New York, 2013), pp. 257–267

39. H. Knoche, Sustaining runtime performance while incrementally modernizing transactional monolithic software towards microservices, in *Proceedings of the 7th ACM/SPEC on International Conference on Performance Engineering*, ICPE '16 (Association for Computing Machinery, New York, 2016), pp. 121–124

40. P. Leitner, C.-P. Bezemer, An exploratory study of the state of practice of performance testing in java-based open source projects, in *Proceedings of the 8th ACM/SPEC on International Conference on Performance Engineering*, ICPE '17 (Association for Computing Machinery, New York, 2017), pp. 373–384

41. J. Lewis, M. Fowler, Microservices a definition of this new architectural term. https://martinfowler.com/articles/microservices.html, Accessed Mar 2021

42. Z. Long, G. Wu, X. Chen, C. Cui, W. Chen, J. Wei, Fitness-guided resilience testing of microservice-based applications, in *2020 IEEE International Conference on Web Services (ICWS)* (2020), pp. 151–158

43. F. Montesi, J. Weber, From the decorator pattern to circuit breakers in microservices, in *Proceedings of the 33rd Annual ACM Symposium on Applied Computing* (2018), pp. 1733–1735

44. I. Nadareishvili, R. Mitra, M. McLarty, M. Amundsen, *Microservice Architecture: Aligning Principles, Practices, and Culture* ("O'Reilly Media", Sebastopol, 2016)

45. E.Y. Nakagawa, M. Guessi, J.C. Maldonado, D. Feitosa, F. Oquendo, Consolidating a process for the design, representation, and evaluation of reference architectures, in *2014 IEEE/IFIP Conference on Software Architecture* (2014), pp. 143–152

46. Netflix Open Source Platform. Chaos Monkey. https://netflix.github.io/chaosmonkey/, Accessed Mar 2021

47. S. Newman, *Building Microservices*, 1st edn. (O'Reilly Media, Sebastopol, 2015)

48. P.B. Nichol, Microservice ecosystems for healthcare (2017). https://www.cio.com/article/3159071/microservice-ecosystems-for-healthcare.html, Accessed Mar 2021

49. Y. Niu, F. Liu, Z. Li, Load balancing across microservices, in *IEEE INFOCOM 2018-IEEE Conference on Computer Communications* (IEEE, Piscataway, 2018), pp. 198–206

50. Node Exporter. https://github.com/prometheus/node_exporter, Accessed Mar 2021

51. W. H. ORGANIZATION, E-health. https://gateway.euro.who.int/en/themes/e-health/, Accessed Mar 2021

52. W. H. ORGANIZATION. mHealth New horizons for health through mobile technologies. https://www.who.int/goe/publications/goe_mhealth_web.pdf, Accessed Mar 2021

53. Prometheus. From metrics to insight. https://prometheus.io, Accessed Mar 2021

54. RabbitMQ. Messaging that just works. https://www.rabbitmq.com/, Accessed Mar 2021

55. F. Rademacher, J. Sorgalla, S. Sachweh, Challenges of domain-driven microservice design: a model-driven perspective. IEEE Softw. **35**(3), 36–43 (2018)

56. D. Rajput, *Hands-On Microservices - Monitoring and Testing* (Packet Publishing, Birmingham, 2018)

57. S. Souto, M. D'Amorim, R. Gheyi, Balancing soundness and efficiency for practical testing of configurable systems, in *2017 IEEE/ACM 39th International Conference on Software Engineering (ICSE)* (2017), pp. 632–642

58. M. Tazari, F. Furfari, J. Ramos, E. Ferro, The persona service platform for aal spaces, in *Handbook of Ambient Intelligence and Smart Environments* (Springer, Berlin, 2010), p. 5

59. J. Tummers, H. Tobi, C. Catal, B. Tekinerdogan, Designing a reference architecture for health information systems. BMC Med. Inf. Decision Making **21**, 55–69 (2021)

60. T. Ueda, T. Nakaike, M. Ohara, Workload characterization for microservices, in *2016 IEEE International Symposium on Workload Characterization (IISWC)* (2016), pp. 1–10

61. UniversAAL Consortium. Universaal iot European project. https://ec.europa.eu/eip/ageing/standards/healthcare/e-health/universaal-platform_en.html, Accessed June 2021

62. A. Van Hoorn, A. Aleti, T.F. Düllmann, T. Pitakrat, Orcas: Efficient resilience benchmarking of microservice architectures, in *2018 IEEE International Symposium on Software Reliability Engineering Workshops (ISSREW)* (IEEE, Piscataway, 2018), pp. 146–147
63. F. Wartena, J. Muskens, L. Schmitt, M. Petrovic, The reference architecture of a personal telehealth ecosystem, in *12th IEEE International Conference on e-Health Networking, Applications and Services (Healthcom* (2010)
64. S. Wolfe, Amazon's one hour of downtime on prime day may have cost it up to $100 million in lost sales. https://www.businessinsider.com/amazon-prime-day-website-issues-cost-it-millions-in-lost-sales-2018-7, Accessed Mar 2021
65. E. Wolff, *Microservices: Flexible Software Architecture* (Addison-Wesley Professional, Boston, 2016)
66. K. Yin, Q. Du, W. Wang, J. Qiu, J. Xu, On representing and eliciting resilience requirements of microservice architecture systems. CoRR **abs/1909.13096** (2019)

Chapter 5
Reference Architectures for Automotive Software

Thomas Bauer, Donald Barkowski, Adam Bachorek, and Andreas Morgenstern

Abstract The development of the system and software architectures of modern passenger cars is a complex and demanding task, performed by OEMs and countless suppliers. Ever-shorter time-to-market cycles and an increasing number of multimedia features and assistant systems create new challenges in every product cycle. Manifold standards, design approaches, modeling notations, and tools have been developed to tackle these challenges, first and foremost AUTOSAR [8]. In this chapter, we provide a comprehensive overview and comparison of historical and current architecture design approaches on the system and software level with their advantages and drawbacks. Relevant process and product standards such as ISO 26262 [33] and Automotive SPICE [60] will be presented and discussed. View-based architecture modeling frameworks have been developed, like AADL [24], the SEI view types [16], and the SPES approach [42, 44], in order to consider the different views and abstraction levels of architecture models, e.g., the system context, the system feature with its data flow, and the mapping to concrete hardware and software solutions. In addition, we discuss the impact of emerging trends such as flexible component deployment, automotive ecosystem infrastructures such as *Car2Car* and *Car2X*, and the integration of machine learning components into the architecture design and corresponding design approaches.

5.1 Introduction

Software-intensive systems have become integral parts of all technical domains, including the automotive industry. The proportion of software in automotive systems has increased greatly in the recent decades regarding the size of program code

---

T. Bauer · D. Barkowski · A. Bachorek (✉) · A. Morgenstern
Fraunhofer Institute for Experimental Software Engineering IESE, Kaiserslautern, Germany
e-mail: thomas.bauer@iese.fraunhofer.de; donald.barkowski@iese.fraunhofer.de;
adam.bachorek@iese.fraunhofer.de, http://www.iese.fraunhofer.de;
andreas.morgenstern@iese.fraunhofer.de

E. Y. Nakagawa, P. Oliveira Antonino (eds.), *Reference Architectures for Critical Domains*, https://doi.org/10.1007/978-3-031-16957-1_5

and the number of requirements, components, and their interconnections [3, 20]. Nowadays, most innovations in the automotive domain are achieved through software, and the main part of automotive production costs is spent on software development, integration, and quality assurance [27, 59].

In complex software-intensive systems such as vehicles, systematic design and development approaches have become crucial for achieving high quality from the constructive perspective and facilitate analytical quality assurance measures, product release, and maintenance. And a major factor influencing the quality of a software-defined product like a modern vehicle is a proper software architecture [20].

"Software architecture is the set of principal design decisions made about the systems" [56]. These sets of design decisions are usually manifested within various architecture artifacts, as captured in the following definition: "Software architecture is the structure or structures of the system, which comprise software elements, the externally visible properties of those elements, and the relationships among them" [16].

However, the architecture design of systems and software is closely intertwined with the development processes. Dedicated process and development standards for the automotive domain have been introduced, which provide recommendations and standard solutions for the architecture design at the software and system level. The architecture design in development standards is usually mapped to particular process phases, which contain activities for designing system and software architectures and assuring their quality.

The outline of this chapter is as follows: Sect. 5.2 summarizes the beginnings and the evolution of system and software architectures in the automotive domain. Current development approaches for automotive systems and software such as model-based engineering solutions are described in Sect. 5.3. Relevant standards and guidelines such as AUTOSAR, ISO 26262, and Automotive SPICE are presented in Sect. 5.4. Section 5.5 describes emerging architecture design solutions such as continuous software engineering, resilient architectures for integrating AI components, and control units that process large amounts of data. The chapter concludes with a summary in Sect. 5.6.

5.2 From the Origins to the Present of Automotive System and Software Architectures

Vehicles have evolved from purely mechanical devices to highly connected and distributed cyber-physical systems with large portions of software [54]. This section provides an overview of the evolution stages in automotive architecture design on the system and software level. We will start with an introductory part that gives a high-level overview of these changes from purely mechanical devices to the software-driven systems we see today and continue with a deeper look at the E/E and software architecture evolution.

5.2.1 Historical Outline

Electronics entered the automotive segment in the 1970s with the introduction of electronic ignition, electronic fuel injection, or central locking. Safety-critical functions were related to pure mechanical parts and did not involve any software or electronics. Software was designed as monoliths without any communication with the other software-controlled parts of the vehicle [54].

In the 1980s, additional electronic devices enabled the realization of new software-based control functions such as anti-lock braking and electronic gearboxes. First in-car computers and digital displays allowed the implementation of basic software-based infotainment functions, such as the introduction of indication instruments in the driver cockpit for the time and distance traveled or calculation of the fuel consumption [54].

In the 1990s, electronics with software for novel safety-related control functions were introduced and integrated, such as adaptive cruise control (ACC) [18]. This led to discussions on the liability of software-controlled products and the creation of standards and guidelines for the systematic engineering of safety-critical automotive systems [54]. Additionally, further consumer-related infotainment, entertainment, and comfort features were introduced to vehicles, such as audio devices and navigation systems.

This evolution continued into the 2000s, when major innovations in the automotive industry started being realized by software [18]. Novel advanced driver assistance systems (ADAS) were introduced, providing increased automated decision support and control, which was implemented by a distributed set of electronic control units (ECUs) connected by dedicated communication protocols [54]. In that decade, the AUTOSAR standard as a platform-based approach emerged with the vision of harmonizing the components developed by manufacturers, integrators, and suppliers based on a common standard and aimed at decreasing the overall development effort along the whole automotive supply chain.

In the 2010s, new paradigms for system design were introduced to support the higher needs regarding connectivity and autonomy to enable car-to-car (C2C) and car-to-x (C2X) communication and autonomous driving functions [27, 54]. The design shifted from software-controlled mechanical devices to technical mobility platforms, which facilitated the market entrance of IT technology-driven companies such as Tesla.

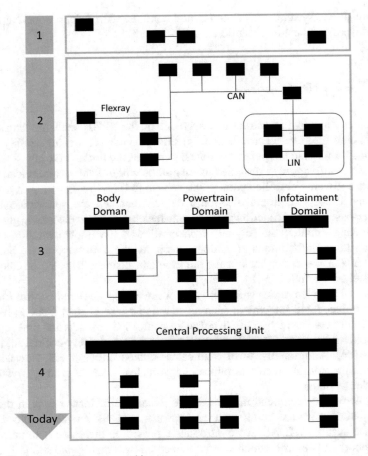

Fig. 5.1 Evolution of E/E system architectures

5.2.2 Evolution of E/E System Architecture

First and foremost, the changes in architectures in the automotive domain can be seen in the electrical and electronic architecture as visualized in Fig. 5.1.[1]

The first evolutional step comprises independent ECUs connected to sensors and actuators, each of them realizing an isolated functionality only. Usually, no interconnection between ECUs existed, and if data needed to be transported from

---

[1] Note that while the figure might create the impression that there have been isolated steps in the development of automotive E/E architectures, we want to highlight that the steps should be interpreted as evolutionary steps as history has mostly seen a mixture of these architecture styles.

one ECU to the other, hardwired connections or simple serial connections were used [62].

The next evolution was the introduction of bus systems, most importantly the CAN bus [55] developed in the 1980s, which became state of the practice in the 1990s. Besides CAN, other specialized communication protocols like FlexRay [39] and LIN [50] were introduced and connected to the main vehicle CAN bus via dedicated controllers. The physical location of ECUs was often dictated by the cable length as one major driver of E/E architecture cost. While the figure seems to indicate that this kind of E/E architectures is outdated, it is still state of the practice in domains like construction machines where only a limited number of ECUs (typically less than ten) need to be connected. In such cases, a single CAN bus is often sufficient [62].

Triggered by the aforementioned software-driven innovations in the 2000s, the E/E architectures of modern passenger cars have seen an explosion of the number of ECUs from a dozen in the 1990s up to 60 or even a hundred ECUs in the 2000s [48]. This highly distributed system led to an enormous increase in software complexity to the point where this complexity was no longer feasible. The next evolutionary step was the introduction of so-called domain-driven architectures [48] in the 2010s. The dominating paradigm here is the domain, like the body domain, the powertrain domain, or the infotainment domain. Each domain is responsible for closely related features, and within each domain, ECUs collaborate to realize higher-level features like advanced driver assistance. Every domain has its own separate bus system; e.g., the infotainment domain might be connected by a classic Ethernet network, while the powertrain domain typically uses a CAN bus to ensure that real-time requirements are met. Within each domain, sensor acquisition and actuator control are performed by individual low-performance ECUs, whereas higher-level functionality like sensor fusion or decision-making is done by the so-called domain controllers at the top of each domain. Ideally, domains are isolated as far as possible. This fosters, e.g., security in the infotainment domain with its high attack surface for threats, which is isolated from the safety-critical parts of the powertrain and body domains. Today, dual- or quad-core systems are already available on the market for vehicle manufacturers, which are used especially for the domain controllers. In the future, this trend will continue, and the number of cores will rise, which brings us to the fourth evolutionary step. Multi-core controllers are already revolutionizing current development standards and strategies as can be seen, e.g., by Audi's ZFA (Zentrales Fahrer Assistenzsystem) developed together with NVIDIA or Tesla's HW3. Tesla's HW3 [17], for example, is a highly integrated central processing unit including, among others, a main processor, a graphic processing unit, and dedicated neural processing units for deep neural networks—all on one integrated circuit. These highly integrated circuits offer computational power comparable to (or exceeding) the computational power of modern business PCs. Looking at the overall software architecture, it seems that this consolidation helps to reduce the overall complexity as more functionality is offered on the same control unit, reducing external communication. However, this paradigm change also introduces new problems: When more and more functionality is deployed to the same ECUs, these functionalities can easily interfere in terms of, e.g., CPU load, a problem usually referred to as freedom from interference. Therefore, software technologies like hypervisors are already part of standards like AUTOSAR Adaptive [8].

5.2.3 Evolution of Software Architecture

With the introduction of simple control units and data processing units to cars, the development of automotive-specific software started. Given that the first control units ran in isolation and independently and provided disjoint functions, the first software-based solutions were strictly local, were technically isolated, and did not communicate with each other [18]. Until the early 1990s, a typical vehicle had a dozen nodes, each running a few kilobytes of compiled software. The software applications were developed in machine code or C for performance and flexibility, with an emphasis on minimizing resource consumption of the limited hardware [18]. Recognizing the difficulties and drawbacks of C, especially for engineers and developers with limited software expertise, dedicated programming guidelines were developed such as MISRA-C by the Motor Industry Software Reliability Association [30].

With the introduction of communication buses and increasing connection of sensors, control units, and actuators in the vehicle, distributed software functions were developed to provide more sophisticated features. These functions are highly dependent on each other, as they share resources and access control units and actuators at the same time. In the 2000s, premium cars contained more than 2000 software-based functions [18], which addressed different domains including engine and transmission control and comfort and infotainment features.

Automotive software is typically organized in different layers, i.e., the automotive software stack covers low-level firmware and hardware-related functions, operating systems, framework and communication services, and high-level application functions. The distribution and connection of functions required the systematic design of software architectures, leading to hierarchical and view-based design approaches and the increasing use of models on different levels [18].

In the automotive past, development was ECU-centric, i.e., suppliers developed the software for an ECU either from scratch or on top of manufacturer-specific operating systems. Recent years have seen a change from these manufacturer-specific architectures toward AUTOSAR. The main idea is to decouple the software from the hardware by using a strong middleware layer that abstracts hardware capabilities and makes them available to functions and services through standardized application programming interfaces (APIs). For example, AUTOSAR offers a basic layer that abstracts from the underlying hardware, like microcontrollers and CPUs. On top of this basic layer, the AUTOSAR runtime environment (RTE) implements a common API for communication between application software components, regardless of whether they are deployed on the same ECU or on different ECUs. This has enabled the development of hardware-independent application functions (AUTOSAR application software) that can be executed on any AUTOSAR-compatible environment. The next generation of AUTOSAR, which is currently under development, is called "AUTOSAR Adaptive." It addresses the needs of modern cars like vehicle-to-X (V2X) connections.

According to [27], the software architecture of a typical vehicle of the newest generation is composed of several domains from infotainment to engine control, plus autonomous driving functions. The integration of third-party applications from different software companies with less background in mechanical and electrical engineering has increased the variety of development languages, operating systems, and software designs. With regard to outsourcing and integration, many automotive companies use third-party code in several layers of the software stacks. This approach leads to a significant reduction of development time and costs and increases innovation capabilities by enabling the integration and update of software parts. New suppliers have entered the automotive domain to provide and exploit their software development expertise from other sectors. For example, operating systems and application software for mobile devices and smartphones are being adapted and integrated into the entertainment and infotainment systems of automobiles, and real-time operating systems from semiconductor manufacturers have been used and tailored to implement autonomous driving functions [27].

5.3 Current Development and Engineering Approaches for Software-Intensive Automotive Systems

Current approaches for the architecture design of automotive systems and software use specific development processes and dedicated system and software engineering practices that rely on the use and exploitation of different models. Further details on both aspects will be described in the following subsections.

5.3.1 Software Development in Automotive Projects

Automotive systems and software development processes have been designed in a way that parts of cars are produced by a chain of suppliers and are more or less only assembled by the original equipment manufacturer (OEM) [19]. Thus, a large proportion of the engineering and production activities have been outsourced in order to optimize cost and risk distribution. Process interfaces for the exchange of defined documents between OEM and supplier have been defined.

V model-like development processes are primarily used, which consists of parallel construction and quality assurance activities. An example development process is shown in Fig. 5.2, which has been adapted from [19]. The system is specified, constructed, and implemented in a top-down manner. The outputs of

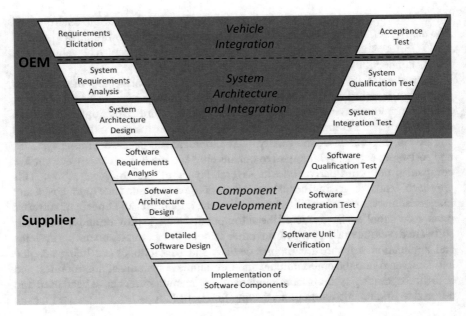

Fig. 5.2 Typical development process for automotive systems with OEM and supplier (Adapted from [19])

every construction activity are verified by appropriate quality assurance activities. In the early process stages, analysis activities (such as requirements inspections or static interface analysis) are conducted. Testing is performed when executable artifacts (such as software units) become available. Software units are integrated into larger software systems, control units, and integrated networks of ECUs in several integration steps following a bottom-up strategy. In model-based development, the architecture and design stages may additionally yield executable models, which can be used to enable early virtual validation [14].

On the one hand, OEMs are responsible for requirements specifications and high-level architecture design for the construction activities. OEMs provide detailed specification, the architecture design of the surrounding subsystem, and guidelines and restrictions for the construction of the components developed by suppliers [5].

On the other hand, deliverables, i.e., the integrated components with their documentation and development and quality reports, are thoroughly checked on the manufacturer's side during the acceptance and integration test stages. The development process concludes with further integration and validation stages.

Suppliers develop components based on manufacturer specifications and information in dedicated component design and implementation phases and assure component quality through appropriate analysis and test activities.

With software becoming the main driver for innovation, the roles and responsibilities of companies are changing [5]. In the beginning, the supplier produced and delivered independent parts with disjoint and unrelated functions (such as engine control or entertainment), and the OEM conducted stepwise integration testing of supplier results. The development of complex and distributed software functions led to the challenge of feature interactions caused by sharing communication infrastructure and controlling the same components and actuators. An early example of a feature is central locking, which covers the actual door locks, seat control, and exterior light control. Therefore, the importance of design stages and integration test stages has significantly increased.

The architecture design has to answer the question of how separate software components deployed on different ECUs interact to provide distinct user functions. This increases the importance of architecture verification, which is used to assess and assure the appropriateness of the designed system and software architecture for realizing the distributed functions and facilitating their implementation [18]. Bringing together the implemented software components and making sure that they interact correctly according to the designed architecture is called integration testing, which is the counterpart on the quality assurance path of the development process.

While the integration of subsystems is always a challenging task for developers, architects, and testers of complex systems, the situation in automotive software engineering is even more complicated. The main driver are the different development processes on the suppliers' side and the high degree of freedom in implementing functions and components based on the specifications received by the OEM. Therefore, in acceptance and integration tests, the OEM usually only has black-box specifications of the components and subsystems to be integrated, which complicates modifications and debugging.

While the value of systematic software development processes and process models such as ISO 26262 [34] and the software process improvement and capability determination (SPICE) [32] is increasingly recognized by companies in the automotive industry, major challenges remain at the interface between OEMs and suppliers. Critical issues here are the quality and precision of requirements documents that are exchanged and the protection of intellectual properties for both sides.

5.3.2 Model-Based Systems and Software Engineering

The development of modern systems is becoming increasingly difficult and challenging. Domains such as automotive and avionics demand high integrity levels between hardware and software to ensure proper execution of their systems. A commercial airplane, for example, contains systems that control ground proximity, navigation, and engine commands, among others. A modern car contains various advanced driver assistance systems with high demands regarding real time and safety. Because of that, it is important to ensure that each aspect of the system is properly described and understood. One means to address this problem is model-based design [23].

Model-driven system development (a.k.a. model-based systems engineering) is a system development approach based on the refinement of models. This refinement of models usually happens on different abstraction levels until such a level of detail is achieved that the system can be implemented immediately or, ideally, extracted automatically from the models. A set of integrated modeling techniques and tools is usually provided to support all substantial development disciplines, starting with model-based requirements engineering, via model-based design and model-driven implementation (which can be partially automated by extracting code from models) to the certification of these systems (using modeling techniques such as fault trees). Model-driven system development is an important technique for managing the complexity of modern systems.

Model-driven software development is part of the overall model-driven system development, which incorporates different techniques across the entire spectrum of software development activities, including model-driven requirements engineering, model-driven design, code generation from models, model-driven testing, model-driven software evolution, and more. One prominent example of model-driven (software) development is the increasing use of MATLAB/Simulink in the automotive domain [22]. Nowadays, most of the software for controlling the physical parts of a modern car, such as valves, is developed with models from which executable code is automatically generated using code generators. The reason for that is the higher abstraction level offered by these tools, which is closer to the problem space and hence reduces development effort and coding errors.

5.3.2.1 Model-Based Design and Architecture View Frameworks

As already outlined above, a framework for model-based architecture design has to incorporate all the assets in the development process, from the requirements down to the (embedded) code on the control units. In the software architecture community, architecture views are the established technique for organizing these development assets. An architecture view is "a representation of one or more structural aspects of an architecture that illustrates how the architecture addresses one or more concerns held by one or more of its stakeholders" [49]. In this regard, some view-based architecture frameworks like Kruchten's 4+1 view model [35] or the SEI viewpoints [29] have been developed to support the specification of software-based systems. However, most of these frameworks are very much influenced by the computer science community and are thus not specific enough for the needs of the automotive domain. But there are approaches that have been successfully used to this end, which will be described in the following paragraph.

A well-known approach for the specification of embedded systems architecture is the Architecture Analysis and Design Language (AADL) [24], which offers tailored support for addressing dependability aspects like safety and security in architecture specifications and is intended to capture architecture concepts from different levels of abstraction. AADL has been widely used in the development of safety-critical systems, such as the SAVI initiative (which includes companies like Airbus, Boeing, and Embraer), the US Army, and many other industries in Europe and Asia, including the automation industry. EAST-ADL [21] is an architecture description language designed in the context of several European research projects that has been used for architecting automotive embedded systems. The language defines architecture views that support specifying the structure and behavior of vehicle features and their realization via software and hardware and does all of that with precise traceability between the elements.

5.3.2.2 The SPES Modeling Framework for Model-Based Design

Another approach is the SPES methodology, which was developed during the SPES (Software Platform Embedded Systems) 2020 initiative [44], a joint research project funded by the German government between academia and industry partners from different domains like avionics, automotive, health care, and energy. The SPES approach is already being applied in automotive production as the tool PREEVision [61] from Vector offers tailored support for architecting embedded systems based on the SPES 2020 methodology. The SPES modeling framework organizes the development artifacts of model-driven system development into four architecture viewpoints:

- **Requirements Viewpoint:** This view aims at supporting the requirements engineering process in eliciting, documenting, and managing the system requirements. In SPES, the elicitation of requirements starts with the identification of the system context, such as users, stakeholders, and external systems that somehow interact with the system. These entities are documented in a system/context diagram of the requirements viewpoint, which shows the system as a black box and documents the interaction of the system with its environment. This diagram complements traditional requirements engineering techniques (like use case scenarios) and helps in eliciting functional and quality requirements, business drivers, and constraints (e.g., legal constraints), which are all documented in the requirements viewpoint. Moreover, in the requirements view, we identify customer features with techniques like feature trees.
- **Functional Viewpoint:** In the SPES methodology, the context diagram, the use case scenarios, and the features from the requirements viewpoint are used as the starting point to identify functionality delivered by the system. The first step is usually to break down the system features into smaller functions. Afterward, it involves the identification of the input/output behavior of those identified functions, e.g., by means of functional data flow diagrams. Hence, the functional viewpoint is the place where dependencies between functions are identified and where a refinement of user functions into sub-functions takes place.
- **Logical Viewpoint:** Once the functional model has been established, the next step is to identify which of the functionalities are to be implemented by software or hardware (or as a mixture). Hence, the logical model describes how the functionality of the system (as identified in the functional perspective) should be decomposed into a network of communicating and cooperating logical (i.e., usually high-level) components. The logical viewpoint is the first place where

design decisions should be made and is hence solution-oriented, whereas the functional viewpoint is ideally only problem-oriented.

- **Technical Viewpoint:** In this viewpoint, the hardware and software elements are detailed into implementation entities that realize the logical components. Besides the detailed software design, this view includes the Hardware Network View, which describes networks of hardware elements such as buses, sensors, and actuators, and the Deployment View, which shows the deployment strategy of software components to hardware entities.

While the description given above seems to stress a waterfall-like process from the requirements viewpoint to the technical viewpoint, the SPES methodology is actually more iterative. Usually, one starts by eliciting requirements on a high abstraction level, which are then formalized in the functional model and realized at the logical/technical level. Each of the identified components at the logical level can itself be regarded as a system under discussion, with its own more concrete requirements, functions, as well as logical and technical solutions.

5.3.2.3   PREEVision: A Tool for the Model-Driven Design of Automotive Systems

The tool PREEVision [61] from Vector is a tool for the model-driven development of automotive systems that shares a lot of similarities with the SPES approach. Actually, Vector was a consortium member of the SPES project. While the requirements viewpoint matches exactly and the technical layers of PREEVision can be seen as an extension of the technical viewpoint of the SPES methodology, there is one big difference in the functional and logical viewpoints. In PREEVision, there is a shared logical function architecture layer containing both logical building blocks and functions. On the one hand, this allows modeling essentially the same properties as in the functional and logical viewpoints of SPES (but now in one layer). On the other hand, it avoids a problem that we have seen in a couple of consulting projects we performed with customers from industry and academia: While the distinction between the functional viewpoint and the logical viewpoint seems to be clear in principle, people tend to mix up the two concepts. Hence, it often happens during the evolution of a model that the functional and the logical viewpoints end up representing similar information. If we merge the two viewpoints from the start, we can avoid such problems. Figure 5.3 shows the SPES viewpoints and the corresponding modeling layers in PREEVision.

5.4   Standards and Guidelines

For the development of automotive systems and software, different standards and guidelines have been developed to optimize engineering processes and ensure product safety. The standards share the assumption that a well-structured process

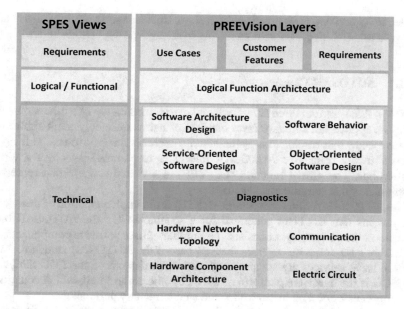

Fig. 5.3 SPES viewpoints vs PREEVision modeling layers

delivers high-quality products. In the following subsections, relevant standards and company-specific guidelines for the automotive domain such as AUTOSAR, ISO 26262, and Automotive SPICE will be introduced with a focus on the architecture-related parts.

5.4.1   AUTOSAR

AUTOSAR (AUTomotive Open Systems ARchitecture) defines a software platform and a middleware standard for automotive embedded systems [7]. It is being developed jointly by a large consortium of automotive manufacturers, suppliers, and tool vendors. The members of the AUTOSAR consortium cooperate in the development and standardization of the AUTOSAR platform, but offer competing implementations of software stacks and development tools. The main goal of AUTOSAR is to enable the development of hardware-independent application functions (AUTOSAR application software) that can be executed in any AUTOSAR environment. AUTOSAR application software uses AUTOSAR interfaces to communicate with other software modules. The AUTOSAR RTE (runtime environment) implements a common API for communication between application software components, regardless of whether they are deployed on the same ECU or on different ECUs. AUTOSAR defines requirements for base software components to deliver ECU and MCU abstraction. Therefore, different software modules can be deployed to different ECUs without having to change the application code.

5.4.1.1   AUTOSAR Classic

AUTOSAR is split into three layers, which are executed on top of a microcontroller [10]. The application software layer consists of hardware-independent application software code that implements value-added functions for customers. This application software code uses AUTOSAR interfaces to communicate over a virtual function bus. The virtual function bus (VFB) is a virtual concept that represents communication at runtime in an abstract way.

The AUTOSAR runtime environment (RTE) is the implementation of this virtual function bus that has been generated for a specific ECU. The AUTOSAR basic software as the bottom layer consists of a number of base software components that implement common base services that are part of the AUTOSAR standard. Some of these basic services are standardized, and some depend on the ECU hardware. The ECU is the hardware platform of the electronic control unit, which consists of a microprocessor or a microcontroller and supplementary peripherals.

The AUTOSAR applications in the application layer should be limited to interfacing only with the RTE; no direct calls to other applications shall be made, and no direct calls to hardware-related functionality shall be used. Global variables shared between applications must not be used. This ensures portability, but at the cost that legacy code that does not comply with this paradigm needs to be ported or rewritten. As a dirty workaround of this situation, the complex device drivers (CDD) type exists: Here, basically, all rules of AUTOSAR software design can be broken, at the expense of these modules not being portable.

The architecture of AUTOSAR Classic clearly targets highly embedded ECUs with limited resources, as it is optimized for efficiency by sacrificing flexibility [10]. The following two examples illustrate this:

- The AUTOSAR operating system (OS), which is based on OSEK OS [8], has limited flexibility, e.g., with statically defined tasks only.
- The RTE is generated as static code, which is highly efficient in terms of resource consumption but requires all applications to be compiled into a big monolith that can only be changed or updated as a whole, even if the distinct functions need not be as closely coupled and could be updated separately from a functional point of view.

5.4.1.2   AUTOSAR Adaptive

As we will point out in more detail in Chap. 5.5.3, a trend is emerging to condense functionality in high-performance ECUs. For these, saving resources does not play such an important role, and a higher degree of flexibility is required. AUTOSAR

Adaptive aims to close this gap, with its first release in March 2017 (labelled R17-03). The current version at the time of writing is R20-11 [12]. Its architecture shares some resemblance with the AUTOSAR Classic architecture, but a few things have fundamentally changed:

- Service-oriented communication serves as the basis of service-oriented architecture (SOA).
- The default language for applications is C++11.
- The hardware base can now be a real machine as well as a virtual machine running on a hypervisor.
- The OS, as the lowest level of the ARA (AUTOSAR Runtime for Adaptive Applications), is based on the POSIX-51 standard, which is a subset of POSIX-54 with 287 interfaces available.
- The ARA offers several base functions via APIs, e.g., for logging or persisting data.
- Additionally, some of the ARA services are available as dynamically routed services.
- Inter-application communication is realized as a SOME/IP [13].
- Each application is an independent POSIX process/executable. Applications are hooked into the ARA through a POSIX interface and invocation of ARA APIs. They communicate with other applications and ARA services via service-oriented communication.

Service-oriented architecture is far more flexible than the RTE since service discovery happens at runtime. Combined with the fact that applications are stand-alone binary executables, this enables dynamic installation, removal, and update of applications in the system, which is imperative for supporting over-the-air updates. The ARA provides the *ucm* (Update and Configuration Manager) service for managing installed applications.

Hence, AUTOSAR Adaptive realizes many technologies like service-oriented communication, the POSIX-API, and usage of modern C++, which have already been state of the practice in the development of information systems for a couple of years. This is no surprise given the fact that the problems that need to be solved in the development of modern vehicles share a lot of similarity with "classic" information systems.

5.4.1.3 Co-existence of AUTOSAR Platforms

While AUTOSAR Adaptive is the response to new trends, AUTOSAR Classic is expected to play an important role also in the long run, as highly embedded ECUs with high demands on boot time, power consumption, and cost are not expected to die out anytime soon. Examples of this are engine control or door control ECUs. AUTOSAR Classic and AUTOSAR Adaptive have been designed from the start to interoperate smoothly, with communication taking place on the basis of the SOME/IP protocol. From the system architecture side, a gateway

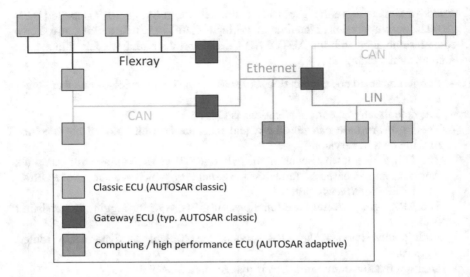

Fig. 5.4 Integration of AUTOSAR adaptive and AUTOSAR classic ECUs

ECU is required to mediate between the Ethernet/TCP-based service-oriented communication of AUTOSAR Adaptive and the packet-oriented communication over buses like CAN [55], LIN [50], or FlexRay [39] typically found in highly integrated ECUs. Figure 5.4 illustrates such a mixed architecture for a vehicle's ECU network.

To avoid double specification of common parts of AUTOSAR Classic and AUTOSAR Adaptive, this part of the documentation has been carved out as the "Foundation," with separate additional documentation for the two platforms. Since 2019, updates for all three releases have been issued time-synchronously, giving all three documents a unified release number. This caused a break in the AUTOSAR Classic release numbering, making version R19-11 the successor of version 4.4.0.

5.4.1.4   AUTOSAR in Practice

As already pointed out, AUTOSAR has grown to be a generally adopted standard, and most European, American, and Japanese OEMs nowadays don't allow direct contractors to integrate components into their vehicles which are not based on AUTOSAR. This makes it mandatory for suppliers to work on interfaces that are defined based on the AUTOSAR standard or to deploy an AUTOSAR stack within their products. The AUTOSAR standard defines the file exchange format for certain system configurations (e.g., CAN bus matrix, RTE configuration, MCAL configuration, etc.) as an XML file scheme (arxml files). The standard itself is not related to any specific tooling, but the AUTOSAR configurations are so complex that handling of those files without proper tool support is unfeasible. Following the paradigm "common standard, concurring implementations," many different solutions emerged to configure AUTOSAR systems; see, for example, here [51] for a concise list. Typically, different tools and vendors can be combined, thanks to the specification of the interchange format, e.g., BSW and RTE can be configured and generated with tools from different vendors.

5.4.1.5   Practical Challenges Concerning AUTOSAR

A practical problem for the daily use emerges from AUTOSAR tools creating a monolithic configuration affecting the entire system. Even though some tools create multiple arxml files for individual configurations, these single files are so commingled (e.g., by cross-referencing each other by UUIDs) that they must be seen as one monolithic configuration.

On the one hand, this creates challenges because a complex tool –for which to use often only very few people are trained or skilled– is substantial to implementing features across the entire system. This requires a high performance and flexibility in executing requested configuration changes, which can easily become a bottleneck in large-scale developments.

On the other hand, even though the arxml files are XML files and theoretically changeable with external tools, in practice, their complexity makes any out-of-tool edit so error-prone that it should be avoided. So when software development is done on a Git repository, the AUTOSAR config must be kept the same on all branches, as merging back or rebasing dedicated changes is only feasible for very simple changes. This is orthogonal to the typical pattern of using model-year or feature branches to drive specific aspects of the development in an isolated manner.

5.4.2   ISO 26262

ISO 26262 is a technical standard for the development of road vehicles [33]. It is based on IEC 61508 [31] and refines process requirements for the functional safety-aware development of software-controlled systems in the automotive domain. Some of the characteristics have become relevant for non-safety-related systems and therefore in conventional development processes as well. The general approach is as follows: For the system to be developed, the hazards are systematically identified, and their risks are determined. Safety goals and safety requirements are derived and assessed regarding their criticality. ISO 26262 distinguishes four criticality levels for safety-critical functions, ASIL-A to ASIL-D, where ASIL-D represents the highest degree of automotive hazard and ASIL-A the lowest. There is another level called QM (for Quality Management level), which represents hazards that do not dictate any safety requirements. ISO 26262 proposes concrete level-specific recommendations for the construction and quality assurance stages and measures to be applied to reduce and minimize the residual risk of critical failures and hazards below an acceptable threshold.

The standard is composed of 11 parts focusing on different process aspects. It proposes a set of development processes for hardware, software, and integrated system level, each consisting of several stages with defined interfaces, outcomes, and document flows. ISO 26262 describes the structure and stages proposed for the development of the system (part 4 [33]) and the software level (part 6 [34]). Dedicated architecture design activities are defined for the system level in the technical safety concept stage and for the software level in the separate software architecture design stage. For each process stage and each integrity level, a set of concrete recommendations and methods is given for (1) systematically developing and designing the work products and (2) analytically verifying the quality of the work products.

5.4.2.1   ISO 26262:4 Recommendations for System Architecture Design

Part 4 contains the recommendations on the system level [33]. The system architecture design is part of the technical safety concept stage. The goal is to design a system architecture that satisfies the safety requirements and the non-safety-related requirements on the system level as well as defining the technical safety concepts. Additionally, the architecture design shall prevent faults and incorporate the necessary safety-related design measures on the system design level. The stage may consist of several layers and decomposition steps. The main outcomes of the architecture design stage are [33]:

– system architecture design specification
– hardware-software interface specification
– stage-specific analysis and verification reports

For the system architecture design specification, the section defines a set of general design principles, which include the hierarchical design of the system architecture, the avoidance of unnecessary complexity of the system components and their interfaces, as well as the demand for maintainability and verifiability [33]. The architecture design also covers the allocation to hardware and software components and the definition of interfaces and interactions between them [33]. Relevant operating modes, configuration parameters, dependencies, and shared and exclusive resources are defined in the hardware-software interface specification.

The outcomes of the system architecture design stages are verified for compliance and completeness with regard to the technical safety concept and the safety-related system requirements by appropriate verification methods. These comprise static analysis methods and dynamic validation methods. ISO 26262 part 4 recommends the following methods [33]: For ASIL-A, less strict design walkthroughs are highly recommended, while from ASIL-B, more formal design inspections have to be applied. Dynamic validation by simulation and prototyping are mandatory from ASIL-C.

5.4.2.2   ISO 26262:6 Recommendations for Software Architecture Design

Part 6 contains the development and validation recommendations on the software level, including the stage of software architecture design [34]. This stage aims at developing an appropriate software architecture design that satisfies the safety-related and non-safety-related requirements and supports the implementation of the software design. The design stage receives inputs from software safety requirements and provides specifications for the subsequent software unit design and implementation.

The main outcome of this stage is the design specification of the software architecture, which defines software architecture elements and their interactions in a hierarchical structure, covering static aspects like interfaces and structural decomposition and dynamic aspects like process sequences and timing behavior [34].

The goal of the phase is to develop a software architecture design that is consistent, comprehensive, maintainable, verifiable, modular, and of low complexity. Part 6 defines a set of general principles for architecture design [34]. On the one hand, general recommendations on the notation type for specifying and modeling architecture designs are given. The standard distinguishes between natural, informal, semi-formal, and formal languages [34]. The basic assumption is that the cost for applying a modeling language increases with the degree of formality. Therefore, ASIL-A and ASIL-B rely on informal design languages, i.e., languages that enable descriptions in figures and diagrams with incomplete syntax. For ASIL-C and ASIL-D, semi-formal modeling approaches, i.e., languages with complete syntax but incomplete semantics, are highly recommended. Examples are SysML/UML or Simulink/Stateflow. Formal approaches, i.e., approaches with complete syntax and complete semantics, are listed but never highly recommended for any level. Additionally, natural language is accepted and mandatory for all ASILs for topics and explanations that cannot be efficiently described using more formal notations.

Furthermore, concrete design principles are given. Most of them deal with reducing and managing the complexity of architecture design elements, for example, by restricting algorithmic and interface complexity and communication intensity within and between software components [34]. A further aspect is software performance, which is covered by appropriate strategies for scheduling tasks and usage of shared resources. The recommendations for appropriate hierarchical design, algorithmic complexity, and performance properties are mandatory for all ASILs [34]. From ASIL-B, cohesion and coupling constraints have to be considered. ASIL-D requires fulfilling the complete set of principles.

Additionally, guidelines and recommendations for fault detection and failure-handling mechanisms are provided [34]. Both aspects have a great impact on software architecture design and will affect design decisions on different levels. Fault detection mechanisms include monitoring of program execution and temporal properties and checks for plausibility, out-of-range, and access permission. Fault-handling mechanisms comprise different approaches for the stepwise reduction of services, recovery, data correction, and redundancy. In Sect. 5.4.3, we will discuss how these measures are realized within the AUTOSAR standard.

The outcomes of the software architecture design stages are verified for compliance and completeness with regard to the safety-related software requirements and provide evidence for the suitability of the design based on appropriate verification methods.

According to [34], the list of recommendations comprises mostly static analysis methods and some dynamic validation approaches. For ASIL-A, less strict design walkthroughs are highly recommended, while from ASIL-B, more formal design inspections have to be applied. Additionally, analyses of control flow, data flow, and scheduling are recommended for ASIL-A and ASIL-B and mandatory from ASIL-C. Formal verification plays a minor role only in terms of formal notations and is not recommended for the lower criticality levels A and B. The dynamic validation approaches simulation and prototyping are recommended for ASIL-B and ASIL-C and mandatory for the highest level.

5.4.3 AUTOSAR and ISO 26262

The safety-related functionality of AUTOSAR and the functional safety standard ISO 26262 have been developed in parallel with mutual stimulation. As an industry standard, AUTOSAR's main objective is not safety. Nonetheless, AUTOSAR supports the development of safety-related systems by offering safety measures and mechanisms. Hence, the software architecture development process described in ISO 26262 and the architecture concepts in AUTOSAR are complementary methods that can improve the safety of the developed systems. In the following, we will discuss some of the safety measures in AUTOSAR, but we refer the interested reader to the original AUTOSAR documentation [9] for details.

Modern ECUs contain a lot of independent software components, not all of them with the same ASIL ratings. According to ISO 26262, this means that either all components have to be developed according to the highest ASIL level on the ECU or freedom from interference has to be ensured for software components with a higher ASIL rating with regard to components with a lower ASIL rating. With respect to freedom from interference, ISO 26262 distinguishes the following aspects, memory, timing, execution, and exchange of information, while AUTOSAR provides countermeasures for faults in the respective aspect.

AUTOSAR provides freedom from interference for memory-related faults through the concept of an OS application. Within each OS application, tasks and AUTOSAR runnables (which are basically C-functions) share the same memory space but cannot access the memory regions of other OS applications. Hence, every OS application has its own memory region without interference from other OS applications. Note that memory partitioning cannot be guaranteed by software alone and hence AUTOSAR assumes that the microcontroller has a memory protection unit or similar hardware features as outlined in ISO 26262 part 6.

To tackle timing faults, e.g., blocking of execution, deadlocks, or livelocks between software elements, AUTOSAR provides a basic software component called the Watchdog Manager [11]. To be able to supervise these timing faults, the Software Watchdog Manager usually interacts with a Hardware Watchdog component. The Watchdog Manager offers basically three functionalities. The first one is alive supervision. This requires defining checkpoint (i.e., program locations) within a runnable; the Watchdog Manager then checks periodically whether the checkpoint has been reached within a given limit. Essentially, this is realized via callback functions that the supervised entity has to call whenever it reaches one of the two checkpoints. As a consequence, the Watchdog Manager can check whether a supervised entity is run too frequently or too rarely. By defining two checkpoints within a program location, we can achieve deadline supervision: Here, the Watchdog Manager ensures that the time between the two checkpoints is within a specified range. The last timing monitoring feature that is also recommended by ISO 26262 in part 6 is logical supervision. While the aforementioned alive and deadline supervision are measures against deadlocks and livelocks, logical supervision mitigates failures of the microcontroller or the hardware clock. Logical supervision is achieved by defining a control flow graph for every supervised entity (refer, e.g., Figures 8 or 9 of [11]). The Watchdog Manager performs logical supervision by checking that the execution order that is observed while running the supervised entity conforms to the control flow graph.

In addition to functional safety measures such as those discussed in this section, the development of safety-relevant software is also supported by the architecture and the design principles underlying AUTOSAR: ISO 26262, part 6, for example, demands the use of established design principles, which is supported by the AUTOSAR layered architecture. Another principle is the use of naming conventions, which is satisfied by the AUTOSAR application interface definition. We can find many more of these examples; in fact, some implementations of AUTOSAR like Vector's MICROSAR Stack are certified according to the highest ASIL-D.

However, we also want to highlight that the AUTOSAR standard alone is not sufficient to support the development of safety-critical systems as it does not define, e.g., the use of systematic approaches for risk analysis and management like HARA. Hence, as already outlined in the introduction to this section, AUTOSAR and the ISO 26262 standard complement each other to support the construction of safety-critical systems.

5.4.4 Automotive SPICE

Automotive Software Process Improvement and Capability dEtermination [60] (ASPICE) is a tailored version of the international standard ISO/IEC 15504 [32]. It aims at improving and standardizing the development processes of suppliers in the automotive industry. Many car manufacturers of distinction, including VW,

Audi, BMW, Daimler, Fiat, and Ford (to name but a few), form the AUTOSIG (AUTOmotive Special Interest Group), which has been driving the development of this standard since 2001. As of 2017, version 3.1 is the most current version, with version 4.0 already in the making. The standard itself is freely available at [6]. It is of very high importance for companies involved in the automotive industry if they intend to work for European or American manufacturers, who demand a certain ASPICE capability level to even consider business.

ASPICE consists of a process assessment model (*PAM*) as a guideline for assessors to evaluate a company's processes and a process reference model (*PRM*) describing the cornerstones of a standard-conformant development process [60]. Basically, the *PRM* is based on the V model and breaks down the complex system development process into distinct processes. For each of these processes, the quality can be assessed and expressed by a capability level. In the standard, this is referred to as the process dimension versus the capability dimension. The capability can be seen as a grade, and the weakest of the measured capabilities defines the overall grade of the company.

The ASPICE standard gives an overview of the total process landscape and illustrates its grouping into three categories [60]:

- *Primary lifecycle processes* (covering process groups for *system engineering* (SYS), *software engineering* (SWE), *acquisition* (ACQ), and *supply* (SPL))
- *Organizational lifecycle processes* (covering process groups for *management* (MAN), *reuse* (REU), and *process improvement* (PIM))
- *Supporting lifecycle processes* (SUP)

Typically, not all processes will be assessed and evaluated. A subset form the "VDA scope," the processes where an assessment is demanded by automotive manufacturers, which includes [60]:

- *System engineering*: system requirements analysis (SYS.2), system architecture design (SYS.3), system integration and integration test (SYS.4), and system qualification test (SYS.5)
- *Software engineering*: software requirements analysis (SWE.1), software architecture design (SWE.2), software detailed design (SWE.3), software unit verification (SWE.4), software integration and integration test (SWE.5), and software qualification test (SWE.6)
- *Management*: project management (MAN.3)
- *Acquisition processes*: supplier monitoring (ACQ.4)
- *Supporting processes*: quality assurance (SUP.1), configuration management (SUP.8), problem resolution management (SUP.9), and change request management (SUP.10)

This scope may be narrowed down; e.g., supplier monitoring (ACQ.4) can be omitted if one tier below no supplier is required [43].

Based on the process overview, one can easily guess which processes mainly impact the architecture: SYS.3 on the system level and SWE.2/SWE.3 on the software level. The standard does not impose the usage of certain tools or architectural patterns, nor does it tell you which process (agile or not) you have to follow. It gives advice on what artifacts need to be created with what level of detail and how their consistency and correctness shall be ensured. For the software architecture, for example, the following items are demanded (referred to as "base practices" in the standard [60]):

– Static software design, broken down hierarchically to the point where detailed design takes over
– Allocation of software requirements to architecture elements
– Interface definition for every interface used (internal and external)
– Dynamic software design, defining timing and interaction of the blocks of static design
– Resource consumption planning for each architecture element at one hierarchy level
– Evaluation of alternative software architectures

The required work products and their attributes on the architecture level impose a new aspect on software architecture: In practice, the software architecture is more or less treated as a nice-to-have in many cases, leading to the situation that it does not exist at all or is abandoned at an early development stage when other tasks get more momentum. If the process is assessed according to ASPICE, this incompleteness and lack of detail are not acceptable, as the capability level of the respective processes will be severely downrated. So even an insufficient level of detail can turn into a technical debt that directly harms the business. OEMs will not tolerate this and demand thoroughly tracked countermeasures.

5.4.5   Company-Specific Guidelines

ASPICE and ISO 26262 leave many degrees of freedom as to how certain software quality goals can be achieved [34, 60]. So OEMs tend to pay more attention to achieving a unified level of quality measures among the suppliers. As an example, some details of the Volkswagen Group Basic Software Requirements (in German: "Konzern Grundanforderungen Software," KGAS) will be presented here [40]. For supplier companies, these are provided as a mandatory requirement specification.

The MISRA coding standard [41] is widely adopted in the automotive industry. But while ASPICE, SWE.4 BP2, only mentions this as an example of static code validation rules and ISO 26262, 6-8.4, Table 6, only has a side note for it ("For the C language, MISRA C . . . covers many of the principles listed" [34]), the KGAS very specifically demand MISRA C to be applied for every piece of source code that is written in C [40].

Another example is the level of detail at which interfaces must be specified at the software architecture level. The KGAS requirements are quite precise here: Every interface must have a static description, including types, value ranges, technical structure, offset, initial values, etc.—basically a formal description down to the source level. It also clearly states that this also applies to any public variable, which must be treated as interfaces. ASPICE, SWE.2 BP3, is more vague here, with "Identify, develop and document the interfaces of each software element" [60]. In the literature [43], hints are given that more precision in this matter is desirable and that all data elements transferred over an interface should be listed and specified. ISO 26262 Chapter 6-7.4.5 states on this matter: "The software architectural design shall describe: ... the static design aspects of the software architectural elements; and ... the external interfaces of the software components; and ... the global variables" [34], but does not give any deeper advice on the level of detail.

5.5 Emerging Approaches and Future Development

The continuous evolution of automobiles from mechanically powered wheeled motor vehicles mainly used for plain transportation since their appearance in the late nineteenth century, via multimedia-enabled infotainment systems with hybrid powertrains, to purely electrified software-based IT computing nodes aimed at ever-increasing comfort by means of autonomy is clearly evident. Every historical step in this progress was necessarily accompanied by the introduction of more and more sophisticated engineering approaches, development methods, and architectural designs. After detailing initial best practices and current standards with respect to architecture-related techniques and tooling in the automotive domain, the following sub-chapter is meant to give a brief overview of upcoming trends shaping the future of automotive systems in these regards.

5.5.1 Continuous Software Engineering and DevOps

Recent years have seen significant changes in system development processes in the automotive domain. Agile development approaches like SCRUM are already being implemented in automotive software development departments. However, we see growing interest in continuous software engineering techniques in the same area of industry as well. For example, Tesla is realizing changes much faster than other automotive companies do. In one particular case, a Tesla customer sent a Twitter message to Elon Musk, suggesting to automatically move the car seat back and raise the steering wheel once the gear box is in park. Elon Musk answered 24 min later, promising that the feature will be included in one of the next software updates [15]. The requested feature was released by Tesla less than 2 months later and deployed over-the-air. Realizing cases like this is only possible by incorporating continuous engineering practices and will hence disrupt existing software development processes in the automotive domain. There is a common misunderstanding that continuous software engineering is a synonym for continuous integration or continuous delivery. Additionally, continuous software engineering

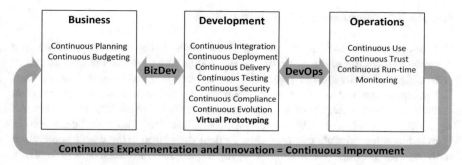

Fig. 5.5 General overview of continuous engineering activities (Adapted from sources [4] and [26])

incorporates aspects intrinsically related to business strategy, development, and operations ranging from market and product monitoring to architecture analysis, redesign, verification, and deployment [26]. As shown in Fig. 5.5, these other aspects include continuous planning, continuous deployment, continuous evolution, continuous trust, and continuous experimentation. Therefore, these sources also refer to continuous engineering as *Continuous**. As an example of continuous evolution, we can again consider Tesla. The whole fleet of Tesla cars is running the autopilot software in the background, constantly collecting data that is shared with the company to improve the next version of the autopilot [57].

One particular challenge of applying continuous engineering practices in the automotive domain is to ensure safety despite the challenge of a continuously evolving system. The literature discusses that, in continuous software engineering, the traditional V model is no longer sequential but is rather based on iterative execution of activities on the left side of the V (Decomposition and Definition) and on the right side (Integration and Validation) [52]. One important technique to support those activities are hence virtual prototypes, which can be used not only to validate existing software components but also to guide decision-making during architecture design [4].

Despite these challenges, we nevertheless see a big trend of continuous engineering practices being adopted in the automotive industry. Tesla is one of the forerunners, but other companies like BMW have also changed their development processes, turning them into a truly integrated BizDevOps process [45]. Regarding the software architecture, there are various challenges with respect to continuous engineering. Most importantly, the software architecture for continuous engineering must be prepared for change due to the enormous number of evolutionary steps. It must support independent teams that can develop, test, and deploy their parts independently. A well-known concept for addressing these topics is the microservice architecture, which we will discuss in more detail in the following subsection.

5.5.1.1 The Microservices Architecture Style

The microservices architecture style has its roots in big web applications like Amazon and Netflix at the beginning of the 2000s. In a nutshell, the microservices style defines an architecture composed of loosely coupled and independent services. For example, an e-commerce application can be decomposed into the product catalog service, the search service, the ordering service, and the support service. As depicted in Fig. 5.6, one distinguishing aspect of microservices is that each service is an independent module that realizes a vertical slice through the whole application with the user interface (UI), the business logic (BL), and the data that is completely independent from the other services. With this architecture, we achieve complete independence of the user-conceivable features. It is, for example, possible to realize a new advanced search feature within the search engine including UI, BL, and data layer without sacrificing, e.g., the product catalog.

One major pillar of the microservices architecture is containerization. Every service is integrated into its own docker container. One added benefit of docker containers is that they remove the dependency on shared libraries, as every service can have its own set of libraries. This allows, e.g., one service to use a newer version of a library with the functionality it needs without affecting the other services at all. Another major ingredient of the microservices architecture is the use of language-independent communication protocols like HTTP-Rest or ActiveMQ. One service should only communicate with the other services via these protocols using fixed APIs. A major benefit of the aforementioned protocols is that they realize asynchronous communication, which avoids blocking as far as possible.

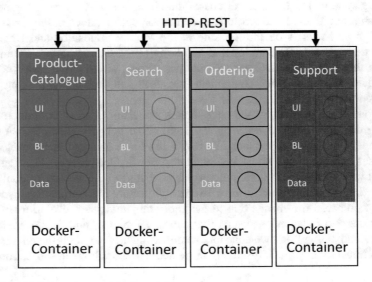

Fig. 5.6 The microservices architecture style

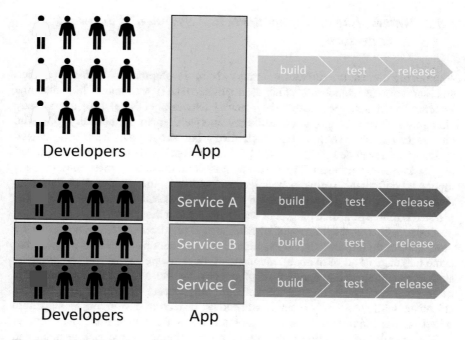

Fig. 5.7 DevOps with microservices

For example, in our e-commerce application, a user will still be able to finish their ordering process even if the product catalog is temporarily unavailable.

So we already saw that microservices offer a lot of benefits. But how does this relate to continuous engineering and DevOps? To truly benefit from the microservices architecture, an organizational change is also needed. While it is common in traditional software engineering projects with a so-called monolithic app to have a UI team, a (backend) team for the business logic, and a database team, the microservices architecture calls for a different team structure. In a microservices-based development cycle, a team is responsible for a whole service, e.g., for the user interface, the business logic, and the data layer. The added benefit is that each team can build, test, and release its own service independent of other teams. Thanks to microservices and DevOps, Amazon is deploying about one new feature every second (Fig. 5.7).[2]

---

[2] AWS Summit 2016: KJ Wu & Ting Chun Hu, "DevOps on AWS—A look at our tools/processes and Trend Micro's DevOps story".

5.5.2 Integrating AI Components into System and Software Architecture

Another big trend in the automotive industry is the development of highly automated and autonomous vehicles. Artificial intelligence (AI) techniques like machine learning (ML) and specifically deep neural networks (DNNs) [46] are already changing software development in the automotive domain dramatically [53]. The change is not only about a new technology but about how these ML-enabled systems are developed and validated [37]. Traditionally, requirements are elicited by requirements engineers. The software/system architect uses these requirements inputs to define the software architecture, which is then realized by software developers and tested by verification engineers [18]. Of course, in reality, this process is more spiral-like instead of waterfall-like, but there are already established processes with a clear handover of artifacts such as requirements from one step to the next, and, more importantly, all mentioned stakeholders have learned to speak the same language as all of them are members of the software engineering community. In contrast to this, the major task of developing the actual ML component is often done by experts outside the software engineering discipline, e.g., by data scientists, with completely separate workflows: Instead of developing an algorithm based on the requirements and the architecture as done in a traditional setting, a data scientist has to choose the right learning engine for the task at hand and prepare enough good examples from which the learning algorithm can infer the desired behavior. Hence, one source of complexity is the integration of different workflows. Moreover, integrating ML components seems to be more challenging than integrating hand-crafted components due to mismatches in assumptions made by the different involved disciplines. We as architects bringing all the pieces together have to find techniques for dealing with this problem. Finding solutions for these problems is an open research question [37] faced not only by the automotive industry but by all software industries adopting machine learning.

However, for the automotive industry, maybe the biggest challenge is the assurance of safety in ML-enabled systems as traditional safety techniques like HARA (Hazard Analysis and Risk Assessment) are not sufficient to deal with the adaptability and uncertainty of machine learning components. One means of dealing with that approach from an architectural point of view is a safety bag, as described in the IEC 61508 safety standard [28]:

> A safety bag is an external monitor implemented on an independent computer to a different specification. This safety bag is solely concerned with ensuring that the main computer performs safe, not necessarily correct, actions. The safety bag continuously monitors the main computer. The safety bag prevents the system from entering an unsafe state. In addition, if it detects that the main computer is entering a potentially hazardous state, the system has to be brought back to a safe state either by the safety bag or the main computer.

Actually, a safety bag is a very generic concept (or an architecture tactic) to ensure the safety of a system. One potential realization of this concept is the Simplex architecture as given in [38] and shown in a simplified version in Fig. 5.8. Here, the supervised system (our ML component) is supervised by a secondary system (often

Fig. 5.8 The Simplex architecture

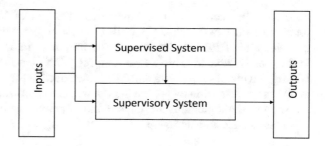

called safety supervisor) that receives the same inputs and observes the outputs generated by the ML component. The main idea of the Simplex architecture is separation of concerns: While the AI component is still in charge of performing the actual task, the supervisor component has to evaluate whether the decisions of the ML component are "safe." A typical example for automated vehicles would be trajectory planning. The desirable requirement for the ML component would be to find a smooth and efficient trajectory in motion planning that considers traffic rules, efficiency, and comfort. This is obviously much more complex than checking a given trajectory for freedom from collisions. The latter can be performed by the supervisor component, which then has to perform, e.g., an emergency braking maneuver. While the Simplex architecture is appealing in theory due to its simplicity, there are a lot of challenges in actually realizing this kind of safety supervisors. For further reading, we refer the interested reader to [25, 47], for example.

5.5.3 Future Vehicular System and Software Architectures

These days, the automotive industry is witnessing tremendous changes in its landscape, including more impacts on key aspects of mobility, than ever before. As indicated previously, this is due to manifold innovations and the integration of enabling technologies from the IT and consumer electronics domain, which leads to a constant increase in the size and complexity of corresponding system architectures, not only in terms of vehicular hardware but also in terms of the required software and engineering concepts. So far, this emerging complexity has particularly manifested itself in the ever-growing structures of electronic control units (ECUs), which are interconnected with a plethora of sensors and actuators via countless wiring harnesses and which communicate via software-controlled network facilities. Even if the latter will remain the case for quite some time, especially in the context of multi-sensor data fusion as required by higher levels of driving autonomy [54], upcoming developments do, however, indicate a trend toward significantly more powerful, dynamically operated devices aggregating hitherto isolated functionality of single-purpose system components. Whereas this kind of gradually increasing centralization embodied by domain controllers primarily applies to physical system architectures in terms of the hardware component topology of a single vehicle, the distribution aspect behind functional electrical and electronic (E/E) architectures in the imminent future will be rather extended in favor of distributed vehicle-to-everything (V2X)-based mobility concepts. These will rely on cloud-driven data and AI-enabled decision-making services that are still evolving but have already proven their potential to constitute the key aspects for the realization of autonomous driving and mobility management far beyond advanced driver assistance and automated traffic monitoring functions on a global scale.

5.5.3.1 Hierarchical Architectures

In contrast to the evolutionary way in which flat E/E architectures have been conceived so far in the automotive sector, the next generation of architectures will increasingly rely on hierarchical designs that allow for the differentiation of functionalities, responsibilities, and objectives of system components within these multi-level structures. On the one hand, this is due to the advantage of the resulting resource efficiency when applying unified development methods on a class of components rather than on single heterogeneous instances that require individual treatment because of solution-specific restrictions imposed by component suppliers. On the other hand, a level-based classification of components, with each class responsible for aggregated functionalities, facilitates system-wide optimization against system requirements that goes beyond merely finding local optima like the most effective deployment of partitioned software functions onto separate hardware components.

As another means to counteract the complexity of modern automotive systems partly arising from the limited extensibility of legacy solutions for inter-device communication based on the point-to-point sender/receiver paradigm, future system architectures will make use of multi-hop and multi-layered protocol stack-based network technologies. To maintain scalability, corresponding gateway components will be dedicated to the abstraction of the communication infrastructure based on the de-/encapsulation of any-level protocol data to unify the interaction between the manifold sources and destinations of hardware-level raw data and application-level service data alike. In terms of security and safety, access to data and routing of data flows will be restricted by firewall concepts known from IT system solutions. A contemporary example for this trend is the hierarchical E/E architecture applied by BMW [58]. On the top level, high-performance central computing platforms manage the main software functions while fulfilling the highest requirements in terms of security and safety. On the second level, integration ECUs represent another component class used to deploy critical functions that require direct access to sensors and actuators by bridging those computing platforms with commodity ECUs on level 3. The latter component class together with standard sensors and actuators assigned to the bottom level is also commonly used for implementing less critical simple functions (cf. Fig. 5.9). For the integration of components on all these levels, a central communication server is meant to seamlessly convert protocol-

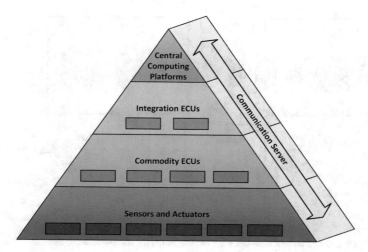

Fig. 5.9 Automotive component classification based on the concept of hierarchical structuring and cross-layer communication

specific data between commonplace wired bus networks like CAN, FlexRay, LIN, and Ethernet along with wireless communication technologies expected in future V2X-based deployment setups.

5.5.3.2 Service-Oriented Architectures

Global players in the digital markets like Amazon, Microsoft, and Google and their IT solutions are paving the way for automotive ecosystems of interconnected devices with high-performance processors, the software of which will build upon seamless hierarchical architecture designs. As a consequence of the technological trends in question, automotive original equipment manufacturers (OEMs) and suppliers have started to face new challenges in coping with the associated rise of service-oriented architectures also in view of their business models. It is the rapid evolution of opportunities arising from digitalization and electrification that makes future-proofing technologies indispensable in order to sustain market advantage, which is a whole new challenge by itself. In this regard, new reference architectures along with optimized processes, enhanced methods, and sophisticated tooling will be necessary to handle the trending upgrade of classic system architectures to upcoming electric, distributed, and autonomous platform designs [58]. The immanent urgency of this demand is reflected in the combined endeavors of otherwise competing industry partners collaborating within corporate consortia on common standards like AUTOSAR Adaptive, as described in Sect. 5.4.1.

In this regard, the software design style of service-oriented architecture (SOA) constitutes the foundation for the upcoming provision and reuse of automotive

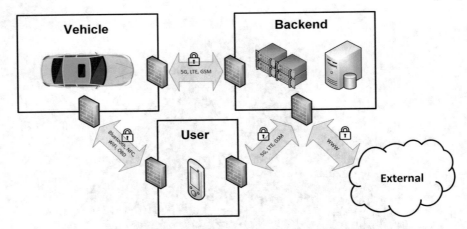

Fig. 5.10 Distributed and service-oriented architectures for the automotive domain

functions irrespective of their complexity. An automotive system built upon the SOA principles will profit from abstracted services available across the board in that their independence will make development, testing, and distribution of corresponding automotive functions significantly more efficient. In the near future, automotive system architectures will no longer be limited to the hardware components that physically reside in an autonomous vehicle, but will consist of further peripheral and backend components on which automotive functions will depend. Considering imminent autonomous driving scenarios, where driving-related actions will no longer be decided by the human driver but rather by an AI-enabled software, these decisions will not even have to be made in-car anymore but potentially at a remote intelligence service center (see Fig. 5.10). This will turn today's human drivers into ordinary passengers who can spend the time thus freed up for purposes other than having to pay constant attention to road traffic.

5.5.3.3 Distributed Architectures

The aforementioned evolution of centralized in-vehicle architectures toward decentralized multi-layer architectures as required to support distributed system topologies is already starting to have a corresponding influence on the way the associated kinds of cyber-physical systems are designed, developed, and maintained. In terms of software development practices as already adopted to a certain extent by leading automotive manufacturers, there are several major trends affecting their prospective characteristics and pushing the underlying architecture designs into certain directions from an overall system perspective. Up to now, vehicular software was rather considered an isolated entity with marginal impact on the surroundings beyond the explicit interaction its hardware runtime platform had with the physical environment. In contrast, the software implementations to come will increasingly make use of the hardware platform's processing and connectivity features to virtually interact not only with other traffic participants but also with any other part of the proximate environment it is actually embedded in.

As of today, modern cars no longer appear to be self-contained systems but rather part of a larger unity of networked entities allowing for a multitude of service opportunities and diverse deployment scenarios. The integration of in-car multimedia components with mobile smartphone applications like Android Auto, Apple CarPlay, and even non-mobility-related software already enables advanced infotainment features like driving behavior assessments, personalized trip plan suggestions, and immersive multimedia-based augmented reality experiences. In the near future, however, the necessary kind of always-on connectivity based on cloud access technologies will further evolve from initial in-car infotainment scenarios via vehicle-to-vehicle (V2V) interactions facilitating local traffic management like intersection coordination and collision prevention to enhanced vehicle-to-infrastructure (V2I) communications fostering mechanisms for regional traffic flow monitoring with traffic jam detection and prevention. Finally, once a pervasive communication infrastructure is in place, the next evolutionary step of automotive mobility toward vehicle-to-everything (V2X)-enabled systems of systems, where cars will turn into computing edges of a globally scoped inter-communication network, is just a matter of time. Together with AI-based techniques that will soon reach a satisfactory level of dependability in terms of prediction quality, V2X-based precognition services will enable a kind of collective consciousness on a worldwide scale that will change the way we perceive mobility as one of the most important aspects of modern life today. However, V2X communications also imply heavy demands in terms of high bandwidth, low latency, and energy-aware massive machine interconnection and data exchange. Therefore, upcoming communication standards like the fifth generation of mobile broadband cellular networks (5G) are being ratified with exactly this kind of resource-related issues in mind. They specify corresponding technical properties that will not only meet such high requirements but will even accelerate the ever-increasing demand for loosely coupled heterogeneous subsystems of vehicles, infrastructure facilities, and data services while stimulating new possibilities not even thought of yet [1, 2]. Besides the automotive domain, the application fields of V2X are numerous, and practitioners have only just started to investigate the potentials of the associated enabling technologies.

5.5.3.4 Event-Driven Architectures

Considering the sheer size that systems of smart cyber-physical systems may potentially reach, we need to look beyond contemporary architecture patterns, development concepts, and validation tools to cope with the involved challenges. In terms of decomposition, such systems need to be modular and adaptive in order to meet application requirements that will most probably be changing on a regular basis in future realizations. These requirements will specifically affect on-board processing and data transfer mechanisms, which need to become high-performance capabilities in order to cope with large amounts of data. In particular, the concept of vehicular edge computing with cars acting as an integral part of a collective overlay computing system implies special requirements in terms of information management to be met by the architecture design. It is the large amount of online data that such systems are expected to capture, store, and process in the near future for the correct operation of self-abilities like decision-making in the context of any autonomous driving behavior. Though AI- and ML-based approaches to situation prediction as the basis for decision-making and resource optimization can be applied relatively quickly for an already learned model compared to the learning process for building that model itself, the parametrical input for such a model, however, depends on sensor data fusion techniques that might have an impact on data quality in terms of the decision to be made. In any case, this renders fully meshed data exchange as part of contemporary system architectures non-viable despite ever-growing networking capacities. Relevant data needs to be provided by relevant sources and retrieved by relevant destinations in a scalable way without unnecessary replication and redundancy. In this regard, event-driven architectures (EDAs) are suited very well due to their inherent asynchronous data exchange paradigm, which allows for loosely coupled system components and services. As such, EDAs also complement SOAs rather well in that corresponding triggers can activate services via incoming events. Complex event processing, in turn, denotes a set of concepts and techniques for supporting real-time situations in terms of data generation and response timing.

The increased complexity of such systems is in contrast to the fact that only simplicity and scalability are the key aspects with regard to the desired sustainability of automotive software systems, as history from other domains has taught us. Additionally, it has to be taken into account that these end systems are no longer going to remain unchanged after delivery, as used to be the case for cars in the past, but will undergo regular updates depending on the booked functionality that needs to be added, modified, or removed. Over-the-air upgrades will allow keeping the basic firmware and the local application software repository up-to-date without even having to visit a car dealer or repair workshop. This, in turn, requires a flexible service-oriented communication infrastructure for on-demand application retrofitting. Depending on the level of autonomy and the self-adaptation algorithms, the amount of required sensor data also varies. To that effect, there is a trend toward using dynamic operating systems like Linux with POSIX support for autonomous driving-related features beyond multimedia and navigation applications in order to handle sensor data appropriately.

After all, the deliberate combination of the different architecture types discussed in this section, which has partly been picked up by standardized approaches to system architecting like AUTOSAR over the course of time, helps to decouple the development of hardware components from the development of software components and thus supports the application of recurring and iterative principles to the agile development of both. Also, [54] observed that with the increased amount of software included especially in safety-critical parts of a system, there is an increased focus on traceability, non-functional properties, and security requirements. In this context, an intuitive way to assure not only functional but also non-functional quality aspects of complex systems in general will be to apply continuous engineering approaches as discussed in Sect. 5.5.1. Besides a traceable and transparent requirements engineering process, seamlessly integrated architecture design on the system and component level, and the application of agile implementation techniques, the continuous engineering process will also need to include virtual validation and integration mechanisms with each system component considered on appropriate levels of abstraction. To this end, future simulation-based validation solutions will have to support two major feature scopes:

1. Domain-specific simulation modeling and design of individual system components based on adaptable levels of abstraction
2. Platform coupling and co-simulation of heterogeneous and distributed simulation components for the purpose of holistic validation scenarios

That is, on the one hand, a potential solution shall provide a comprehensive portfolio of ready-to-use simulation models fitting the target domain with appropriate granularity of detail along with the facilities to develop and adapt further models as required. On the other hand, it shall provide facilities for the integration of upstream, downstream, and co-simulation tooling in order to build and assess holistic testing scenarios. While most simulation tools focus on a specific system evaluation aspect like network communication, high-level functional behavior, or low-level hardware states (cf. Fig. 5.11), and others provide support for co-simulation between heterogeneous simulation model providers and the integration of those, only exceptional solutions support both. One such example is the Virtual Continuous Integration Platform (VCIP) [14], an instantiable validation solution based on an event-driven simulation framework with support for nestable models of computation and communication named FERAL. It includes out-of-the-box simulation models for common ICT system components such as those used

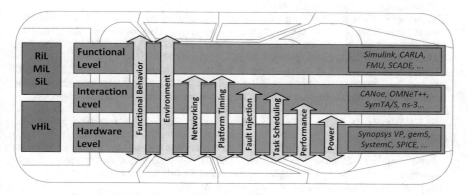

Fig. 5.11 Simulation abstraction levels for major ICT system component aspects within the scope of common validation solutions

especially in the automotive sector and can be coupled with prevalent co-simulators via adjustable integration connectors for the purpose of design space exploration and testing of holistic simulation scenarios [36].

5.6 Conclusions

In this chapter, we have provided a comprehensive overview and comparison of historical, current, and future architecture design approaches for the automotive domain on the system and software level. We described the evolution of system and software architectures from their beginnings with simple software-based functions and few controllers to the current state of the practice with complex networks of control units, system-spanning distributed functions, and automated, model-based systems and software engineering approaches. Furthermore, we discussed the demands and recommendations of relevant process and product standards for system and software architecture design, such as ISO 26262, AUTOSAR, and Automotive SPICE. Finally, we presented novel emerging trends and technologies such as continuous software engineering, design changes for automotive systems with AI components, and hierarchical, service-oriented, and event-driven architecture design approaches.

References

1. 5GAA-Working-Group1, C-V2X Use Cases and Service Level Requirements Volume I (2020). https://5gaa.org/wp-content/uploads/2020/12/5GAA_T-200111_TR_C-V2X_Use_Cases_and_Service_Level_Requirements_Vol_I-V3.pdf. Accessed 31 Jan 2021
2. 5GAA-Working-Group1, C-V2X Use Cases Volume II: Examples and Service Level Requirements (2021). https://5gaa.org/wp-content/uploads/2020/10/5GAA_White-Paper_C-V2X-Use-Cases-Volume-II.pdf. Accessed 31 Jan 2021
3. V. Antinyan, Revealing the complexity of automotive software, in *Proceedings of the 28th ACM Joint Meeting on European Software Engineering Conference and Symposium on the Foundations of Software Engineering*. ESEC/FSE 2020 (Association for Computing Machinery, New York, 2020), pp. 1525–1528
4. P.O. Antonino, M. Jung, A. Morgenstern, F. Faßnacht, T. Bauer, A. Bachorek, T. Kuhn, E.Y. Nakagawa, Enabling continuous software engineering for embedded systems architectures with virtual prototypes, in *Proceedings of the Software Architecture – 12th European Conference on Software Architecture, ECSA 2018, Madrid, September 24–28, 2018*, vol. 11048, ed. by C.E. Cuesta, D. Garlan, J. Pérez. Lecture Notes in Computer Science (Springer, Berlin, 2018), pp. 115–130
5. S. Apostu, O. Burkacky, J. Deichmann, G. Doll, Automotive software and electrical/electronic architecture: implications for OEMs (2019). https://www.mckinsey.com/industries/automotive-and-assembly/our-insights/automotive-software-and-electrical-electronic-architecture-implications-for-oems. Accessed 31 Jan 2021
6. Automotive Special Interest Group and the Quality Management Center in the German Association of Automotive Industry (VDA QMC), Automotive spice. http://www.automotivespice.com. Accessed 30 Aug 2021

7. AUTOSAR, Autosar web page. https://www.autosar.org/. Accessed Jan 31 2021
8. AUTOSAR, Specification of operating system (2015). https://www.autosar.org/fileadmin/user_upload/standards/classic/4-2/AUTOSAR_SWS_OS.pdf. Accessed 31 Jan 2021
9. AUTOSAR, Overview of functional safety measures in autosar (2016). https://www.autosar.org/fileadmin/user_upload/standards/classic/4-3/AUTOSAR_EXP_FunctionalSafetyMeasures.pdf. Accessed 31 Jan 2021
10. AUTOSAR, Autosar layered software architecture (2017). https://www.autosar.org/fileadmin/user_upload/standards/classic/4-3/AUTOSAR_EXP_LayeredSoftwareArchitecture.pdf. Accessed 31 Jan 2021
11. AUTOSAR, Autosar specification of wathchdog manager (2017). https://www.autosar.org/fileadmin/user_upload/standards/classic/4-3/AUTOSAR_SWS_WatchdogManager.pdf. Accessed 31 Jan 2021
12. AUTOSAR, Explanation of adaptive platform software architecture (2020). https://www.autosar.org/fileadmin/user_upload/standards/adaptive/20-11/AUTOSAR_EXP_SWArchitecture.pdf. Accessed 31 Jan 2021
13. AUTOSAR, SOME/IP protocol specification (2020). https://some-ip.com/standards.shtml. Accessed 31 Jan 2021
14. A. Bachorek, F. Schulte-Langforth, A. Witton, T. Kuhn, P. Antonino, Towards a virtual continuous integration platform for advanced driving assistance systems, in *IEEE International Conference on Software Architecture Companion (ICSA-C 2019)* (2019)
15. J. Bariso, A tesla customer complained on twitter. less than 30 minutes later, elon musk promised to fix it. https://www.inc.com/justin-bariso/elon-musk-promises-to-implement-customer-suggestio.html. Accessed 31 Jan 2021
16. L. Bass, P. Clements, R. Kazman, *Software Architecture in Practice*, 3rd edn. (Addison-Wesley Professional, Boston, 2012)
17. B. Bos, Tesla's new HW3 self-driving computer — it's a beast. https://cleantechnica.com/2019/06/15/teslas-new-hw3-self-driving-computer-its-a-beast-cleantechnica-deep-dive/. Accessed 8 Feb 2021
18. M. Broy, I.H. Kruger, A. Pretschner, C. Salzmann, Engineering automotive software. Proc. IEEE **95**(2), 356–373 (2007)
19. O. Burkacky, J. Deichmann, B. Klein, K. Pototzky, G. Scherf, Cybersecurity in automotive case – mastering the challenge (2020). https://www.mckinsey.com/industries/automotive-and-assembly/our-insights/cybersecurity-in-automotive-mastering-the-challenge. Accessed 31 Jan 2021
20. O. Burkacky, J. Deichmann, S. Frank, D. Hepp, A. Rocha, When code is king: mastering automotive software excellence (2021). https://www.mckinsey.com/industries/automotive-and-assembly/our-insights/when-code-is-king-mastering-automotive-software-excellence. Accessed 31 Aug 2021
21. P. Cuenot, P. Frey, R. Johansson, H. Loenn, Y. Papadopoulos, M.-O. Reiser, A. Sandberg, D. Servat, R.T. Kolagari, M. Toerngren, et al., The EAST-ADL architecture description language for automotive embedded software, in *Model-Based Engineering of Embedded Real-Time Systems*, vol. 6100, ed. by H. Giese, G. Karsai, E. Lee, B. Rumpe, B. Schaetz. Lecture Notes in Computer Science (Springer, Berlin, 2007), pp. 297–307
22. F. Deissenboeck, B. Hummel, E. Juergens, B. Schaetz, S. Wagner, J. Girard, S. Teuchert, Clone detection in automotive model-based development, in *2008 ACM/IEEE 30th International Conference on Software Engineering. ICSE'08*, Los Alamitos (IEEE Computer Society, Washington, 2008)
23. P. Feiler, D. Gluch, *Model-Based Engineering with AADL: An Introduction to the SAE Architecture Analysis & Design Language*, 1st edn. (Addison-Wesley Professional, Boston, 2012)
24. P. Feiler, D. Gluch, J. Hudak, The architecture analysis and design language (AADL): an introduction. Technical Report. CMU/SEI-2006-TN-011, Software Engineering Institute, Carnegie Mellon University, Pittsburgh (2006)
25. P. Feth, Dynamic Behavior Risk Assessment for Autonomous Systems. Ph.D. Thesis, Kaiserslautern University of Technology (2020)

26. B. Fitzgerald, K.-J. Stol, Continuous software engineering: a roadmap and agenda. J. Syst. Softw. **123**, 176–189 (2017)
27. R. Fletcher, A. Mahindroo, N. Santhanam, A. Tschiesner, The case for an end-to-end automotive-software platform (2020). https://www.mckinsey.com/industries/automotive-and-assembly/our-insights/the-case-for-an-end-to-end-automotive-software-platform. Accessed 31 Jan 2021
28. H. Gall, Functional safety IEC 61508/IEC 61511 the impact to certification and the user, in *The 6th ACS/IEEE International Conference on Computer Systems and Applications, AICCSA 2008*, Doha, March 31–April 4, 2008 (IEEE Computer Society, Washington, 2008), pp. 1027–1031
29. D. Garlan, F. Bachmann, J. Ivers, J. Stafford, L. Bass, P. Clements, P. Merson, *Documenting Software Architectures: Views and Beyond*, 2nd edn. (Addison-Wesley Professional, Boston, 2010)
30. L. Hatton, Safer language subsets: an overview and a case history, MISRA C. Inf. Softw. Technol. **46**(7), 465–472 (2004)
31. International Electrotechnical Commission (IEC), Functional safety of electrical/electronic/programmable electronic safety-related systems – part 2: requirements for electrical/electronic/programmable electronic safety-related systems. Standard IEC 61508-2:2010
32. International Organization for Standardization (ISO), Information technology – process assessment. Standard ISO/IEC 15504 (2011)
33. International Organization for Standardization (ISO), Road vehicles — functional safety — part 4: product development at the system level. Standard ISO 26262-4:2018 (2018)
34. International Organization for Standardization (ISO), Road vehicles — functional safety — part 6: product development at the software level. Standard ISO 26262-6:2018 (2018)
35. P. Kruchten, The 4+1 view model of architecture. IEEE Softw. **12**(6), 42–50 (1995)
36. T. Kuhn, T. Forster, T. Braun, R. Gotzhein, Feral – framework for simulator coupling on requirements and architecture level, in *Eleventh ACM/IEEE International Conference on Formal Methods and Models for Codesign (MEMOCODE)* (2013)
37. G.A. Lewis, S. Bellomo, A. Galyardt, Component mismatches are a critical bottleneck to fielding AI-enabled systems in the public sector. CoRR abs/1910.06136 (2019)
38. S. Lui, Using simplicity to control complexity. IEEE Softw. **18**(4), 20–28 (2001)
39. R. Makowitz, C. Temple, Flexray – a communication network for automotive control systems, in *2006 IEEE International Workshop on Factory Communication Systems* (2006), pp. 207–212
40. R. Messnarz, M. Sehr, I. Wüstemann, J. Humpohl, D. Ekert, *Experiences with SQIL – SW Quality Improvement Leadership Approach from Volkswagen*, vol. 748 (Springer, Berlin, 2017) pp. 421–435
41. MISRA-Consortium, MISRA C:2012: guidelines for the use of the C language in critical systems. https://www.misra.org.uk/. Accessed 30 Aug 2021
42. A. Morgenstern, P.O. Antonino, T. Kuhn, P. Pschorn, B. Kallweit, Modeling embedded systems using a tailored view framework and architecture modeling constraints, in *Companion Proceedings of the 11th European Conference on Software Architecture, ECSA 2017, Canterbury, September 11–15, 2017*, ed. by R. de Lemos (ACM, New York, 2017), pp. 180–186
43. M. Müller, K. Hörmann, L. Dittmann, J. Zimmer, Automotive SPICE in der Praxis (2016). dpunkt.verlag
44. K. Pohl, H. Hönninger, R. Achatz, M. Broy (eds.) *Model-Based Engineering of Embedded Systems, The SPES 2020 Methodology* (Springer, Berlin, 2012)
45. F. Ramsak, R. Waltram, Our journey to 100% agile and a bizdevops product portfolio (2019). https://www.youtube.com/watch?v=f50e5YGuFG4&feature=youtu.be. DevOps Enterprise Summit 2019, Las Vegas
46. S. Raschka, *Python Machine Learning* (Packt Publishing, Birmingham, 2015)
47. J. Reich, D. Schneider, I. Sorokos, Y. Papadopoulos, T. Kelly, R. Wei, E. Armengaud, C. Kaypmaz, Engineering of runtime safety monitors for cyber-physical systems with digital

dependability identities, in *Proceedings of the Computer Safety, Reliability, and Security – 39th International Conference, SAFECOMP 2020, Lisbon, September 16–18, 2020*, vol. 12234, ed. by A. Casimiro, F. Ortmeier, F. Bitsch, P. Ferreira. Lecture Notes in Computer Science (Springer, Berlin, 2020), pp. 3–17

48. D. Reinhardt, M. Kucera, Domain controlled architecture – a new approach for large scale software integrated automotive systems, in *PECCS* (2013)
49. N. Rozanski, E. Woods, *Software Systems Architecture: Working with Stakeholders Using Viewpoints and Perspectives* (Addison-Wesley Professional, Boston, 2005)
50. M. Ruff, Evolution of local interconnect network (LIN) solutions, in *2003 IEEE 58th Vehicular Technology Conference. VTC 2003-Fall (IEEE Cat. No. 03CH37484)*, vol. 5 (2003), pp. 3382–3389
51. O. Scheid, Autosar tool (2016). https://automotive.wiki/index.php/AUTOSAR_Tool. Accessed 31 Jan 2021
52. C. Shamieh, *Continuous Engineering for Dummies* (John Wiley & Sons Inc., Hoboken, 2014)
53. P. Shayler, M. Goodman, T. Ma, Applications of neural networks in automotive engine management systems. IFAC Proc. **30**(18), 899–905 (1997). IFAC Symposium on Fault Detection, Supervision and Safety for Technical Processes (SAFEPROCESS 97), Kingston upon Hull, UK, 26–28 August 1997
54. M. Staron, *Automotive Software Architectures* (Springer Publishing Company, Incorporated, New York, 2017)
55. C.P. Szydlowski, Can specification 2.0: protocol and implementations, in *Future Transportation Technology Conference & Exposition* (SAE International, Warrendale, 1992)
56. R.N. Taylor, N. Medvidovic, E.M. Dashofy, *Software Architecture: Foundations, Theory, and Practice* (Wiley Publishing, Hoboken, 2009)
57. The Tesla Team, Upgrading autopilot: Seeing the world in radar. https://www.tesla.com/de_DE/blog/upgrading-autopilot-seeing-world-radar?redirect=no. Accessed 31 Jan 2021
58. M. Traub, A. Maier, K.L. Barbehön, Future automotive architecture and the impact of it trends. IEEE Softw. **34**(3), 27–32 (2017)
59. A. Tschiesner, A. Cornet, H. Deubener, P. Schaufuss, Race 2050 – a vision for the european automotive industry (2019). https://www.mckinsey.de/publikationen/2019-01-08-race-2050-publikation#. Accessed 31 Jan 2021
60. VDA QMC Working Group 13/Automotive SIG, Automotive spice process reference model process assessment model. https://www.automotivespice.com/fileadmin/software-download/AutomotiveSPICE_PAM_31.pdf. Accessed 30 Aug 2021
61. Vector, Website of the PREEvision tool. https://www.vector.com/int/en/products/products-a-z/software/preevision/. Accessed 30 Aug 2021
62. W. Zimmermann, R. Schmidgall, *Bussysteme in der Fahrzeugtechnik*, 5th edn. (ATZ/MTZ-Fachbuch. Vieweg, Wiesbaden, 2014)

Chapter 6
Reference Architecture for Commercial Avionics Software

Conrado Pilotto and Pablo Oliveira Antonino

Abstract Avionics are the electronic systems used onboard aircraft to perform a broad range of functions, such as communication, navigation, and flight control. Modern commercial avionics are designed according to the integrated modular avionics (IMA) reference architecture. This chapter explores the key elements involved in the development and certification of commercial avionics software, emphasizing its role in the overall system design and aircraft safety assessment.

6.1 Introduction

Avionics, a portmanteau of the words aviation and electronics, refers to the electronic systems used on aircraft, satellites, and spacecraft. Avionics include a broad range of systems, from displays, communication, and navigation to any other electronic equipment used by aircraft to perform individual functions, such as engine management, collision avoidance, and flight control.

Today, avionics are a major contributor to the overall functionality, complexity, and cost of modern aircraft. Recent estimations show that avionics comprise up to 40% of the total costs for commercial aircraft and more than 50% for military aircraft. In this context, software plays an important role. The continuous demand for additional functionality and safer operation has led to the number of aircraft functions controlled by software increasing exponentially over the last 35 years [6, 7].

The design of avionics software on board modern commercial aircraft follows the Integrated modular avionics (IMA) architecture. IMA focuses on modularity and integration in order to aggregate multiple aircraft functions on the same execution

C. Pilotto (✉)
AEL Sistemas (Elbit Systems Group), Porto Alegre, Brazil
e-mail: cpilotto@ael.com.br

P. O. Antonino
Fraunhofer IESE, Kaiserslautern, Germany
e-mail: pablo.antonino@iese.fraunhofer.de

© The Author(s), under exclusive license to Springer Nature Switzerland AG 2023
E. Y. Nakagawa, P. Oliveira Antonino (eds.), *Reference Architectures for Critical Domains*, https://doi.org/10.1007/978-3-031-16957-1_6

platform. Due to the inherent consequences of resource sharing, IMA systems are extremely complex. As a result, the development, integration, and certification of commercial avionics software must follow a strict process aligned with the overall system design and the aircraft certification plan—all of which must be communicated to, and overseen by, international Airworthiness Authorities (AAs).

In this setting, this chapter explores the fundamental concepts involved in the development and certification of commercial avionics software, emphasizing its role in overall system design and aircraft safety assessment.

6.2   The Aircraft Context

The aircraft context is very different from the ground-based context in which most equipment operates. In turn, avionics end up costing up to ten times more than equivalent equipment designed to work in traditional industrial settings. Hence, to understand and develop avionics systems, it is essential to understand the design constraints and architectural drivers imposed by their operating environment.

Avionics are vital to the successful and safe operation of commercial flights. A failure in an avionics system can have potentially catastrophic effects on the aircraft, crew and passengers, third-party property, and the environment. Unquestionably, the cost of such failures can be devastating, in both monetary and human terms. Consequently, Reliability, Availability, Maintainability, and Safety (RAMS) have been the major drivers for the civil avionics industry since the introduction of the first avionics systems in the mid-1950s.

Another major driver for the civil avionics industry is the physical environment. Although the crew and the passengers are not subject to the same environmental conditions, some avionics devices installed in the equipment bays face very different and demanding requirements. For example, temperature conditions must take into account freezing situations, such as flying at high altitudes, but also blazing hot days, like soaking in the Middle Eastern sun for several hours. In addition to this, there are also severe vibration, acceleration, and electromagnetic compatibility requirements, to name but a few.

The third major driver for avionics equipment is weight. Weight is a key aspect of aircraft design and operation, as the total aircraft weight is correlated directly with its efficiency and performance characteristics. Thus, when an aircraft is designed, the idea is to make it as light as its structural strength will allow. Increasing the weight requires the wings to produce more lift, which, in turn, requires the structure to support additional static and dynamic loads. This requires a heavier construction, which increases drag; drag increases fuel consumption, which reduces the total payload available for passengers and cargo. Clearly, weight can cause a snowball effect, which is why the total weight of the aircraft, including the weight of avionics equipment, is always kept to a minimum.

Lastly, as part of a larger aviation industry comprising aircraft manufacturers and operators, the civil avionics sector is also driven by commercial and business aspects. From this perspective, there is a constant demand for portability, reusability, modularity, and interoperability of equipment, in order to promote faster maintenance cycles, reduce the number of aircraft on the ground, and increase the revenue from additional flights. At the same time, from the passengers' perspective, there is a growing expectation for gate-to-gate connectivity and faster transfer times.

In summary, the avionics context is extremely complex. On the one hand, there are intricate technical constraints; on the other hand, there is a constant demand for increased functionality in a fast-changing market. Overall, avionics architectures need to be carefully managed and balanced to meet both technical and business requirements while complying with safety and regulatory processes [8].

6.3   The Evolution of Avionics Architectures

Over the last decades, the avionics industry has primarily used two prominent, distinct reference architectures for the development of civil avionics systems, namely, the federated architecture and the Integrated modular avionics (IMA) architectures. Generally speaking, these are opposing architectural models. The former focuses on the self-contained, distributed, independent allocation of aircraft functions, whereas the latter uses highly integrated, partitioned environments that host multiple functions on shared computing platforms. In theory, the same system can be designed using either model; however, the resulting implementation, integration, and certification efforts will vary greatly depending on which model is used. Ultimately, this decision comes from the company engaged in the design and manufacture of the complete aircraft platform, also called airframer or Original equipment manufacturer (OEM), and is a direct result of the design constraints and architectural drivers applicable to that specific aircraft's type design, as discussed in Sect. 6.2.

6.3.1   Federated Reference Architecture

Traditionally, all avionics systems followed the federated architecture model. In this model, each function constitutes a self-contained subsystem comprising its own dedicated computers, sensors, and actuators. Consequently, each function has guaranteed processing time and deterministic access to Input/output (I/O) resources, all of which ensures controlled latency and predictable jitter [9, 20].

Figure 6.1 shows an example of a system designed according to the federated architecture model. Despite a large number of interconnections between different pieces of equipment, the federated architecture model promotes controlled resource sharing and clear interfaces between different aircraft functions, which allow for a simple design and an incremental integration process.

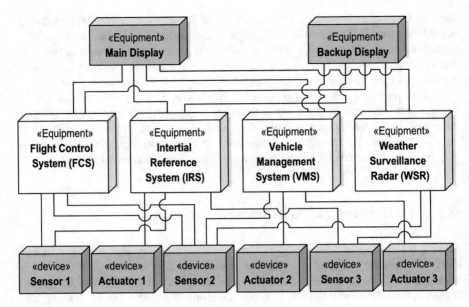

Fig. 6.1 Example system using the federated architecture model

Until the late 1990s, most civil aircraft were based on a federated architecture. However, during the past decades, there has been an expanding demand for more functionality, performance, and safety. This increase in the total number of aircraft functions has pushed the federated architecture to its limit. On the one hand, the extensive point-to-point wiring between communicating systems associated with the prohibitive Size, Weight, and Power (SWaP) requirements from so many individual systems hit the aircraft's envelope restrictions. On the other hand, the low portability and modularity of each function, which required new computers for each new aircraft type, increased upgrade costs for the airframers and made spare parts storage and obsolescence management costs even more significant for the airlines [6].

6.3.2 Integrated Modular Avionics (IMA) Reference Architecture

In order to address the problems with the traditional federated architecture model, the aviation industry decided to start integrating multiple functions on the same computer. Honeywell took the first steps in this direction with the design of the Airplane Information Management System (AIMS) for the Boeing 777. Shortly after, Airbus started to use a similar approach during the development of the A380. This new architecture was named Integrated modular avionics (IMA). Today, IMA is a mature concept and constitutes the state-of-the-art architecture for new

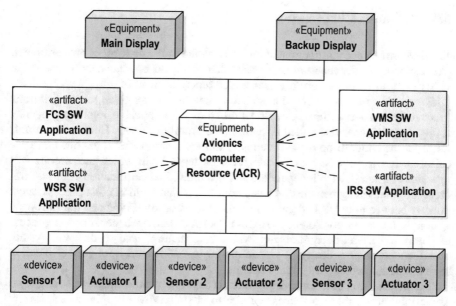

Fig. 6.2 Example system using the IMA model

commercial avionics development, including air transport, regional, and business aircraft [11].

The IMA architecture model focuses on modularity and standardization in order to aggregate multiple aircraft functions on the same execution platform and high-speed multiplexed networks to replace point-to-point computer intercommunication. IMA systems decrease SWaP requirements, allow extensive reuse of software and hardware components, increase the portability of applications across different platforms, provide commonality of aircraft equipment, and reduce the impact of future airframe functionality changes [23].

Figure 6.2 shows the same system from the federated architectures example but implemented according to the IMA model. As can be noted, all the individual pieces of equipment implementing aircraft functions have been replaced by a single generic computer platform that hosts the individual aircraft functions in the form of software applications. Additionally, all the point-to-point connections have been replaced by a packet-switched interconnection.

Despite its benefits and apparent simplicity, IMA systems are extremely complex due to the inherent consequences of resource sharing. These systems-of-systems create non-functional dependencies between aircraft functions that, when managed incorrectly, can lead to unintended interactions and common mode failures.

6.4 Avionics Certification

The development of commercial avionics is rooted in the concept of airworthiness. Airworthiness is the measure of an aircraft's ability to operate within acceptable safety margins while performing its intended functions in all foreseeable conditions.

For an aircraft (and onboard avionics) to operate in any given territory, it must first receive an airworthiness certification from the applicable regulatory agency ruling that airspace, also called Airworthiness Authority (AA). Hence, the aircraft OEM, or the entity responsible for an aircraft modification after it has been initially certified, has to request a certificate for each territory in which the aircraft will operate. In general, each independent AA has individual certification criteria. Still, there are bilateral agreements between some AAs that facilitate this process, most notably between the US Federal Aviation Administration (FAA) and the European Union Aviation Safety Agency (EASA). Despite that, each certification process can impose different requirements, which can, in turn, lead to different system architectures. Consequently, it is paramount to understand how the certification regulations can affect the system's design.

The certification of avionics equipment is a complex topic and has a strong legal aspect; therefore, this work does not aim to be exhaustive. In this regard, it only briefly describes the top-level requirements, processes, and expectations of the FAA.

6.4.1 Regulatory Basis

In the United States, all the rules defined by the federal government's executive departments are published under the Code of Federal Regulations (CFR). The CFR is organized into 50 titles and covers a wide range of subjects. In this context, the US Federal Aviation Administration (FAA) is the governmental agency that regulates all aspects of civil aviation in that nation and over its surrounding international waters. The FAA operates primarily through the publication and enforcement of the so-called Federal Aviation Regulation (FAR). The FAR is published under CFR Title 14 (Aeronautics and Space) and is organized by sections known as Parts. In general, the FAR Parts associated with avionics development are:

- Part 21—Certification Procedures for Products and Parts
- Part 23—Airworthiness Standards: Normal, Utility, Acrobatic, and Commuter Category Airplanes
- Part 25—Airworthiness Standards: Transport Category Airplanes
- Part 27—Airworthiness Standards: Normal Category Rotorcraft
- Part 29—Airworthiness Standards: Transport Category Rotorcraft

The FAR provides different methods for approving the design, manufacturing, and installation of electronic equipment installed on board a commercial aircraft. Usually, most avionics suppliers will be involved, to some extent, in either a Type certificate (TC), an Supplemental type certificate (STC), or a Technical Standard Order (TSO) [11].

6.4.1.1   Type certificate (TC)

The TC is the basic framework for the airworthiness certification of commercial aircraft and onboard avionics systems. In short, the TC is a document by which the FAA states that the certification applicant has demonstrated the compliance of an aircraft manufacturing design (type design) with all applicable airworthiness requirements specified in its applicable FAR Part.

Although the TC is under the direct responsibility of the OEM, avionics suppliers involved in such projects must be prepared to support the aircraft certification process by providing all the certification data associated with the systems they develop. Not only that, they must understand and receive from the OEM the applicable certification requirements for their system based on the aircraft design and their system's role in its operation. In this sense, it is essential to note that the same system can play different roles in different aircraft—e.g., in one, it can be the primary instrument, while in another, it can be the backup. For this reason, reusing certification artifacts of the same avionics system between different aircraft might not be straightforward.

6.4.1.2   Supplemental type certificate (STC)

The STC is a regulatory instrument used to approve modifications to the original design of an existing aircraft, including changes or upgrades of existing avionics equipment. An STC is the typical process used to install new avionics systems on aircraft that already have an associated TC.

Similar to the Type certificate (TC), the Supplemental type certificate (STC) is governed by a certification base, i.e., the list of regulatory requirements with which the applicant must demonstrate compliance. However, contrary to the former, the latter is more concerned with the design alteration and the impact that the new system has on the aircraft's installation, weight and balance, structural characteristics, electrical load, human factors, safety, and other airworthiness aspects.

Additionally, in contrast to a TC, an STC is usually granted to an organization other than the aircraft OEM. In most cases, the applicant for a Supplemental type certificate (STC) is the owner of an aircraft (i.e., an airliner) or an avionics supplier involved in an aircraft modernization project.

6.4.1.3   Technical Standard Order (TSO)

The TSO is a regulatory instrument used to approve standard products, parts, and other devices on board civil aircraft. They range from a variety of avionics systems, such as flight-deck displays, navigation equipment, and communication radios, to other typical articles, such as seat belts and oxygen masks. In general terms, a TSO is a generic specification published by the FAA that defines the Minimum Performance Standards (MPS) for each system type. These include, for example, the minimum set of requirements for environmental testing; the required level of design assurance for software and hardware parts; the operating instructions and equipment limitations; installation, calibration, and maintenance procedures; the data required to be submitted by the applicant seeking approval; and any other regulatory aspect applicable for a given type of product. Considering the effort required to prepare such specifications, the FAA only publishes a TSO for widely used products. In this sense, it is unlikely that tailored solutions or novel products will be considered under a TSO. Regardless, TSOs are important since they improve consistency across avionics suppliers and ease the certification process of the complete aircraft.

Note, however, that a TSO authorization (TSOA) does not grant permission for the installation of the article in an aircraft. Although the TSOA can be used to support an installation approval, such approval must be granted through other regulatory instruments that are not necessarily under the equipment manufacturer's responsibility (e.g., a TC or STC).

6.4.2   Guidance Material

Interpreting and understanding the FAR is not a straightforward task. In general, FAR requirements are pervasive and provide room for varying interpretations. So, to clarify the agency's expectations, the FAA publishes guidance material in the form of Advisory Circulars (ACs).

ACs are publications that provide information and guidelines that are considered acceptable means of compliance with the airworthiness regulation. In other words, they define means—although not the only means—for showing compliance with the FAR.

The guidelines published in the ACs are not, under any circumstances, prescriptive or binding to the certification process. Certification applicants are eligible to propose alternative means in the certification plans they submit to the FAA. Still, these guidelines are a result of extensive FAA and industry experience and, over the years, have been successfully adopted by a number of different certification projects.

Usually, ACs refer to industry guidance published by organizations such as the Society of Automotive Engineers (SAE) and the Radio Technical Commission for Aeronautics (RTCA) as recommended design practices. Because of that, some ACs and the industry publications they refer to have become de facto avionics standards.

6.5   Airworthiness Requirements for Commercial Avionics

The airworthiness requirements for transport category airplanes are defined in CFR Title 14 Part 25, simply referred to as FAR Part 25. In this context, the key requirement for designing an avionics system on board commercial aircraft is Sec 25.1309.

- CFR Title 14—Aeronautics and Space
  - Chapter I—Federal Aviation Administration, Department of Transportation
    - Sub-chapter C—Aircraft
      - Part 25—Airworthiness Standards: Transport Category Airplanes
        - Subpart F—Equipment
          - General
            - Sec 25.1309 Equipment, Systems, and Installations

(a) The airplane equipment and systems must be designed and installed so that:

   (1) Those required for type certification or by operating rules, or whose improper functioning would reduce safety, perform as intended under the airplane operating and environmental conditions.
   (2) Other equipment and systems do not adversely affect the safety of the airplane or its occupants or the proper functioning of those covered by sub-paragraph (a)(1) of this paragraph.

(b) The airplane systems and associated components, considered separately and in relation to other systems, must be designed and installed so that:

   (1) Each catastrophic failure condition

      (i) is extremely improbable;
      (ii) does not result from a single failure;

   (2) Each hazardous failure condition is extremely remote;
   (3) Each major failure condition is remote.

(c) Information concerning unsafe system operating conditions must be provided to the crew to enable them to take appropriate corrective action. A warning indication must be provided if immediate corrective action is required. Systems and controls, including indications and annunciations, must be designed to minimize crew errors which could create additional hazards.

6.5.1   Advisory Circular (AC) 25.1309

Among other guidance, AC 25.1309 [1] recognizes three important industry publications as suitable methods of showing compliance with the airworthiness requirements in Sec 25.1309.

First, AC 25.1309 recognizes ARP 4761 [5] and ARP 4754 [4] as suitable methods for performing the safety assessment and developing civil aircraft and onboard systems and equipment. Second, it recognizes DO-160 [13] as a suitable method for defining the environmental conditions and test procedures required for such equipment.

ARP 4754, in turn, further recognizes other industry guidelines for specific aspects of the avionics development cycle, namely, DO-297 [16] for the design and certification of IMA systems; DO-178 [14] for the development and verification process of airborne software; and DO-254 [15] for the development and verification process of airborne electronic hardware. Similarly, these publications also refer to other publications for detailed information on each of their particular domains. Figure 6.3 shows the most important publications recognized by AC 25.1309 and the documents they refer to.

Effectively, AC 25.1309 defines an ontology of practices, methods, and techniques that, when followed in all essential aspects, form a suitable process for designing and certifying civil avionics systems on board civil aircraft.

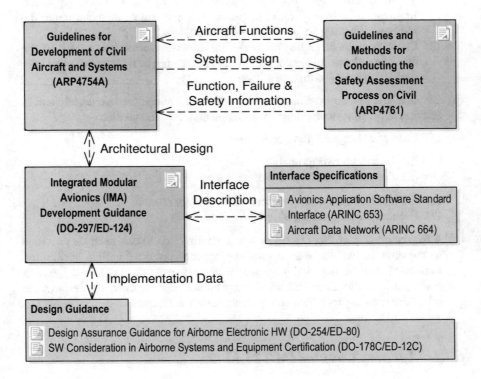

Fig. 6.3 Relationship of industry practices

6.6   Integrated Modular Avionics (IMA) Concepts

The intrinsic resource sharing of IMA architectures introduces additional concerns regarding the avionics design process, from both technical and managerial points of view. Furthermore, because aircraft functions are not incrementally verified as they were in the federated architecture, the integration and certification processes of IMA systems become more complex and bring additional challenges [6].

In order to guide the development, integration, and certification of IMA systems, the RTCA published DO-297 [16]. This document provides guidance for developers, system integrators, certification applicants, and all others involved in the approval and continued airworthiness of IMA systems. This guidance material addresses several aspects, such as functional performance, aircraft safety and security, design process, fault containment, health monitoring, and robust partitioning.

6.6.1   Robust Partitioning

According to the DO-297, one of the key characteristics of an IMA system is robust partitioning. Robust partitioning provides means for assuring the required level of isolation between independent aircraft functions accessing the same shared resources in the presence of design errors and hardware failures [9]. Its objective is to provide the same level of functional isolation that is physically provided in the federated architecture model. In this regard, robust partitioning is defined in two dimensions: temporal and spatial partitioning [20].

Temporal partitioning consists of assuring a function's access to a prescribed set of hardware resources for a defined period of time and the consistency of its execution order during each execution cycle. It is usually achieved through deterministic scheduling of the processor and the communication channels [9].

Spatial partitioning consists of the protection of the function's program, data, and dedicated I/O resources in a way that any persistent storage locations can be written to only by one function and any temporary storage location used by a function is saved when control is transferred. The usual means for achieving this are a high-integrity Real-time operating system (RTOS), a Memory management unit (MMU), and separated virtual memory spaces [9].

In order to manage robust partitioning, DO-297 refers to two specifications. The first, ARINC 664 [3], deals with the partitioning of the physical and logical resources associated with the communication network. The second, ARINC 653 [2], deals with the partitioning and integration of the software applications.

6.6.2 APEX Interface

The ARINC 653 specification, entitled "Avionics Application Software Standard Interface," defines the interface requirements between avionics software applications and the underlying RTOS executing on an IMA system. The core concept of this specification is called the APplication/Executive (APEX) interface [12].

The APEX interface allows creating platform-independent software units that can abstract from the underlying RTOS and execute on the same hardware platform as other units developed and certified independently and with varying Design Assurance Level (DAL). It is the only RTOS interface specification that supports the safety-critical, real-time, and deterministic properties required for avionics equipment certification [12]. Because of that, it is used extensively on new civil and military aircraft (e.g., Boeing 787 Dreamliner in 2009, Airbus A330 MRTT and Northrop Grumman X-47B in 2011), as well as in space vehicles (e.g., NASA Orion Multi-Purpose Crew Vehicle) [22].

At the platform level, the APEX defines all the data structures that permit the configuration of the IMA platforms according to requirements defined for the system integration process.

6.6.3 System Integration

System integration is the group of activities required to incorporate a set of avionics functions, realized by different software applications, into one or more execution platforms. This process includes all system configuration aspects required to convey the system's functional and safety assessment requirements, including the list of applications to be hosted, their required resource allocation, and the overall performance of the platforms [10].

During the system integration process, shared resources are allocated through contracts established between the platform's RTOS and the software applications. These contracts are defined in the form of constraints that assure the safety, integrity, and availability of the required resources for each software application [10].

In ARINC 653, the system integration contracts are specified through XML configuration tables. These tables define the application requirements in terms of memory access, processor utilization, and communication ports [10]. This scheme enables the IMA system integrator to ensure that the demands of each application are consistent with the platform performance and that their sum does not exceed the total platform capacity.

6.7   ARINC 653 Specification

The ARINC 653 specification [2] defines an execution environment for the software included as part of an IMA system. This environment is defined through a general-purpose interface named APEX that is established between the RTOS of an avionics computer and the software applications (aircraft functions) deployed on it.

The APEX interface defines the list and the behavior of all RTOS services used by the application software to control the scheduling of its processing units, operate its communication ports, and manage the status of its internal elements. Furthermore, it specifies the structure of all the data that is exchanged statically (via configuration tables) or dynamically (via services) between the parties.

In order for the APEX interface to be as generic as possible and to be, ultimately, used on a broad range of systems, its specification only defines the minimum functionality that is required from the RTOS and provided to the application software. It is not the intent of the ARINC 653 specification to define any implementation requirements that might be necessary to realize the APEX interface nor to drive any system-level requirements that might be required to fulfill any of its properties. To that extent, the specification of the APEX interface is High-order language (HOL) independent, which allows systems developed in different programming languages and with compilers to adhere to it.

6.7.1   Goals

The goal of the APEX interface is to define a standardized, general-purpose interface for the development of avionics software within the IMA architecture model, which allows the use of hardware and software components from a wide range of suppliers, thus encouraging competition and reducing the cost of system development and ownership. In order to accomplish this, the interface was designed with the following objectives [2]:

1. To provide the minimum set of services required to fulfill IMA requirements, allowing the interface to be easily developed and utilized.
2. To be extendable, allowing the interface to accommodate extensions due to future system updates and maintain compatibility with legacy software.
3. To satisfy the common real-time requirements of Ada 83, Ada 95, and Catalogue of Interface Features and Options for the Ada Runtime Environments (CIFO), allowing these models to use the interface in accordance with their criticality levels.
4. To decouple software from the underlying hardware architecture, allowing hardware changes to be transparent to the application.
5. To be HOL independent, allowing the interface to be implemented by different languages and providing flexibility in the selection of compilers and development tools.

6.7.2 Quality Requirements

Adherence to the APEX interface brings the following benefits [21]:

1. Portability—Due to the decoupling of the software from the hardware platform, the interface facilitates the portability of software applications between different computers and aircraft with minimal certification impact.
2. Reusability—Due to the standardized services, the interface allows the development of reusable applications.
3. Integration of Multiple Criticalities—Due to the partitioning of application software, the interface allows co-allocating components developed according to different DAL.
4. Modularity—Due to benefits (1), (2), and (3), the interface allows the composition of systems using reusable components and minimizes the software impact caused by changes in the overall system.

In addition to the technical benefits described above, the APEX interface brings the following advantages to avionics industry stakeholders [21]:

1. For airframe manufacturers, the APEX interface allows the specification of a common interface for all aircraft software they purchase, the flexibility to add new capabilities to existing platforms, and benefits from the increased maturity of products as a result of well-defined interfaces being used.
2. For avionics equipment suppliers, it enables the concurrent design of application software, promotes software reuse across programs, and reduces time-to-market.
3. Finally, for real-time operating system providers, it allows an open marketplace to supply interoperable equipment and clear requirements for RTOS design.

6.7.3 Specification Compliance

The ARINC 653 specification defines an interface that is required from the RTOS and provided to the application software. Therefore, there are two types of compliance with this standard: application compliance and implementation compliance.

A conformant application must demonstrate application compliance. This is achieved through an analysis showing that all application system calls are limited to the services defined in ARINC 653 Part 1 (Required Services).

A conformant RTOS must demonstrate implementation compliance. This is achieved through the execution of the test suite defined by ARINC 653 Part 3 (Conformity Test Specification). This test specification includes implementation-independent pass/fail criteria intended to verify the correct implementation of all required system services, data structures, and behavioral aspects described in ARINC 653 Part 1 (Required Services). An RTOS may implement additional and non-standard services, but must ensure that conformant applications execute as expected.

6.7.4   Configuration Considerations

The ARINC 653 specification defines an environment that allows portability, reuse, and modularity of software components. This flexibility requires an authoritative role, named system integrator, responsible for the integration of all software applications into a module that satisfies both the functional requirements of the system and the availability and safety requirements of each aircraft function.

In order to enable the correct integration of the software components, application developers must provide to the system integrator the following information about each partition:

1. Timing requirements (period and duration)
2. Memory requirements (memory usage and access rights)
3. Communication requirements (messages sent and received)

Based on this information, the system integrator can allocate partitions to specific core modules in a way that their availability and integrity requirements can be satisfied.

The result of this system integration process is a set of configuration tables that specify the module integration requirements. These tables are used by the RTOS during system initialization to perform the configuration and partitioning of the system resources and enable the correct operation of each partition.

6.7.4.1   Configuration Specification

In order to provide a standard mechanism for the specification of the system configuration tables, the ARINC 653 specification defines an intermediate representation of the configuration data. This intermediate representation allows the system integrator to describe the integration requirements in a standard format that can later be transformed into the required RTOS-specific format.

The ARINC 653 specification uses eXtensible Markup Language (XML) files for the intermediate representation of the configuration data and an XML schema to define the required data structure of the XML instance files.

6.7.4.2   ARINC 653 XML Schema

The ARINC 653 XML schema describes the structure of the XML configuration data parameters and defines the reference standard according to which ARINC 653 XML instance files are defined. It must be possible to configure a compliant RTOS using only the information specified in this schema and for it to operate in a manner compliant with the ARINC 653 specification.

The schema specification only covers the configuration of the ARINC 653 core module. Larger systems may require additional data to configure other aspects of the platform (e.g., sensors, data bus communications). For this reason, the schema can be extended by RTOS suppliers to include additional data items required for a particular implementation.

The ARINC 653 XML schema is presented in Appendix H of the ARINC 653 specification [2].

6.7.4.3 XML Processes

It is the system integrator's responsibility to build XML instance files that are conformant to the XML schema. ARINC 653 specifies five major steps that are required for producing ARINC 653 configuration files, as shown in Fig. 6.4.

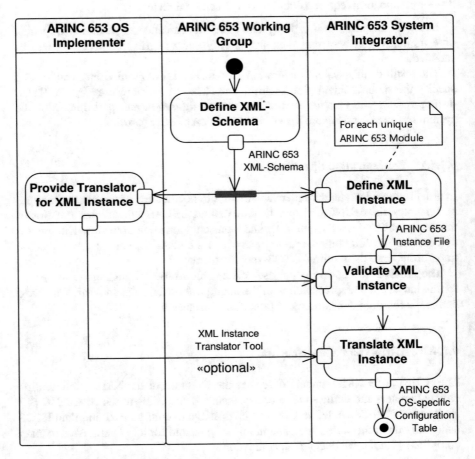

Fig. 6.4 XML instance file generation process

1. The ARINC 653 Working Group (WG), through the ARINC 653 specification, defines the ARINC 653 XML schema.
2. The ARINC 653 RTOS supplier develops a tool that, based on the ARINC 653 XML schema, translates an XML instance file into the implementation-specific format used by the RTOS implementation.
3. The system integrator uses the information provided by the application developers to produce an XML instance file that is conformant to the ARINC 653 XML schema and captures the availability and integrity requirements for the module that is being integrated.
4. The system integrator verifies that the generated XML instance file complies with the ARINC 653 XML schema definition.
5. The system integrator can optionally use a conversion tool provided by the RTOS supplier to translate the XML instance file into the format utilized by the RTOS implementation.

6.8 Reference Architecture

This section describes the architectural elements defined in the ARINC 653 specification. These elements define the reference architecture for all software developed and integrated within the scope of IMA systems. All information presented herewith is based on the architecture considerations and the interface specification presented in the ARINC 653 specification [2].

6.8.1 General Concepts

6.8.1.1 Partitions

In an IMA system, the purpose of the core module is to enable the execution of one or more software applications in a way that each one is unaware and unaffected by the execution of the others. This isolation can only be achieved with proper functional partitioning of avionics functions and application-shared resources. This partitioning prevents fault propagation across functions, eases the verification and validation of each application, and allows an incremental certification process.

The unit of partitioning in an ARINC 653 system is called a partition. Externally, a partition relates to the concept of a program in a single application environment: It includes code and data sections that are loaded into an individual address space. Internally, a partition is similar to a multi-task application. Its structure consists of a set of concurrent processes that share access to the processor resources and have attributes that affect their scheduling, synchronization, and execution.

6.8.1.2 Software Decomposition

The software included as part of an IMA system can be decomposed into partitions, system-specific functions, and the Operating system (OS) kernel.

Additionally, the RTOS may include a software abstraction layer to translate the HOL specification of the APEX interface into its proprietary system calls. This abstraction layer, as well as the interface requirements between system partitions and system-specific functions, is outside the definitions of the ARINC 653 specification. The definition of these interfaces is directly dependent on the RTOS implementation, on the virtualization capabilities provided by the hardware platform, and even on the extension mechanisms provided by the software compiler. In any case, they must still comply with system's robust partitioning requirements.

6.8.1.2.1 Application Partitions

Application partitions are the partitions containing the avionics functions supported by the system. The software that is executed inside a partition is developed and verified according to the DAL defined by the system safety assessment and is restricted to using only APEX system calls.

6.8.1.2.2 System Partitions

System partitions are the partitions that must access services that are not provided by the APEX interface, but are still constrained by the same temporal and spatial partitioning mechanisms as the application partitions—they are usually associated with hardware-dependent functions. System partitions are optional in an IMA system and are tightly dependent on the core module implementation.

6.8.1.2.3 Operating System Kernel

OS kernel is the software that implements the APEX interface and enforces the partitions' processing times, memory access rights, and usage of shared resources.

6.8.1.2.4 System-Specific Functions

System-specific functions include hardware interfaces such as device drivers, software uploading, maintenance data download, software debug ports, and built-in test functions.

6.8.1.2.5   Pseudo-Partitions

Pseudo-partitions are any devices, subsystems, or other software applications which can communicate with a hosted ARINC 653 Partition, but it is external to the module in which this partition resides. From a module's perspective, any partitions residing on other module is considered a pseudo-partition.

6.8.1.3   Implementation Guidelines

The APEX interface is, in its simplest form, only the specification of a list of RTOS services that must be provided to the application developers. RTOS providers can choose any mechanism for providing such services, but the most direct way is to define a conformant Application Programming Interface (API). Other alternatives, such as the development of appropriate compilers and assemblers that translate application code according to the prescribed APEX services, are more expensive and lead to inflexibility and potential problems with future extensions.

Usually, avionics software development is performed using either Ada or C programming languages. Therefore, the APEX interface defines HOL specifications for both of them. Each specification comprises the complete interface definition from the application's viewpoint and provides services with the same semantics. Nevertheless, due to the unavoidable differences between strong-typed languages, like Ada, and weak-typed ones, like C, the syntax of some services may be different.

Regardless of any differences, applications executing on a core module do not necessarily need to be developed according to the same HOL specification.

6.8.1.4   Hardware Considerations

Certain aspects of the APEX interface might be affected by the processor architecture. Considering this, RTOS providers need to account for specific hardware constraints when switching from one platform to another. On the other hand, to ensure portability of the applications, software developers must develop code that is hardware-independent and makes no assumptions about the implementation of the APEX interface by RTOS.

Nevertheless, the segregation of multiple partitions in a shared environment requires specific support from the execution platform, specifically from the hardware processor in which the software applications are executed. In order to correctly implement the APEX interface, the following hardware assumptions must be considered in the design of the hardware platform:

1. The processor provides the ability to restrict the access to different memory spaces and I/O ports for each partition (e.g., MMU and separated virtual memory spaces).

2. The processor has access to time resources to implement time services. Additionally, the time interrupt used to control the partition scheduling is deterministic.
3. The processor provides a mechanism for transferring the control flow back to the RTOS in case a partition performs an invalid operation.

6.8.2 Reference Architecture Overview

The APEX interface has been designed to be used in an Avionics Computer Resource (ACR)—a generic shared computation resource that is able to interface with a variety of aircraft systems.

An ACR can contain one or more core processors. Each core processor that hosts a unique ARINC 653 execution context constitutes an ARINC 653 module. If a computer contains multiple core processors, each unit that executes a partition is considered an independent module. Figure 6.5 shows the typical architecture of a core processor and an integrated ARINC 653 module.

Partitions can be allocated to different core processors, but cannot be distributed over multiple modules.

Communication between partitions is carried out independent of the partitions' physical allocation. Messages exchanged between partitions are specified only in terms of source and destination ports and do not contain information regarding the location of the involved parties concerning processors or modules.

The allocation of partitions to specific modules, their scheduling attributes, and the routing of messages between partition ports is outside the responsibility of the application developer. These aspects are handled during system integration and are defined through the RTOS configuration tables.

6.8.3 Functional Description

In ARINC 653, the RTOS implements a separation kernel between the applications (i.e., the partition space) and the core environment (i.e., the module space). At the partition level, the RTOS manages the partition processes and their intrapartition communication facilities. At the module level, it manages the partition resources and the interpartition communication within and across module boundaries.

At any point in time, the RTOS is either in the initialization, operational, or idle state. During the power-up procedure, it enters the initialization state. After completing the boot sequence, it transitions to the operational state, where it remains until power-off or until an error-handling action forces it to move to the idle state.

In order to preserve the robust partitioning of the application software and the aircraft functions, the RTOS kernel services are decomposed according to their level of operation.

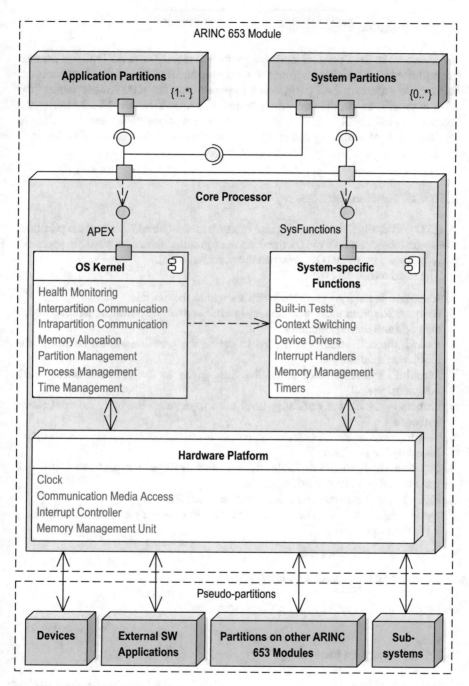

Fig. 6.5 ARINC 653 module architecture

6.8.3.1 Partition Management

As discussed in Sect. 6.8.1, aircraft functions that reside on an ARINC 653 module are partitioned with respect to time and space into a partitioning unit called partition. In order to enforce robust partitioning requirements, the RTOS must manage the different partitions residing on a module and guarantee their correct scheduling and memory region access rights. This ensures that partitions developed according to varying levels of criticality can execute in the same module without affecting each other.

6.8.3.1.1 Partition Attributes

ARINC 653 defines the minimum set of attributes required to manage a partition. These attributes can be fixed (defined via configuration tables) or variable (dynamically managed by the RTOS based on the partition state).

The fixed attributes are:

1. Identifier: the unique partition identifier within the module.
2. Memory Requirements: the memory boundaries for the partition, with appropriate code and data segmentation.
3. Period: the activation period used to define the partition allocation inside the module scheduler.
4. Duration: the amount of execution time given to the partition during each activation period.
5. Criticality Level: the criticality level used to develop the partition application software.
6. Communication Requirements: the properties of the communication ports established by the partition.
7. Partition Health Monitor Table: the mapping between the partition errors and their associated error-handling actions.
8. Entry Point: the start address for partition execution.
9. System Partition: the indication that the partition is not restricted to using only APEX services.

The variable attributes are:

1. Lock Level: the current lock level of the partition.
2. Operating Mode: the current operational mode of the partition.
3. Start Condition: the reason for the partition restart.

6.8.3.1.2 Temporal Partitioning

Temporal partitioning is achieved by deterministically scheduling the core module partitions over time.

The module scheduler is generated from a static analysis of the individual time and resource availability requirements of each partition, in a way that the resulting periodic activation order satisfies the overall partitioning requirements for the entire module.

The analysis of the partitions' activation is performed based on the period specified for each partition (fixed attribute). The least common multiple of all these periods is used to the define the scheduler's major frame, which represents the time interval that is periodically repeated throughout the system's runtime and over which the partition activation windows are allocated. The partition activation windows define when each partition is allowed to execute and are specified by their offset from the major frame start time and their total duration.

Figure 6.6 illustrates the temporal partitioning model of the ARINC 653 specification.

The ARINC 653 scheduling model guarantees a deterministic execution order for each partition and correct and uninterrupted access to the required resources during their activation periods. The key features of this model are:

1. The scheduling unit is a partition.
2. A partition does not have a scheduling priority.

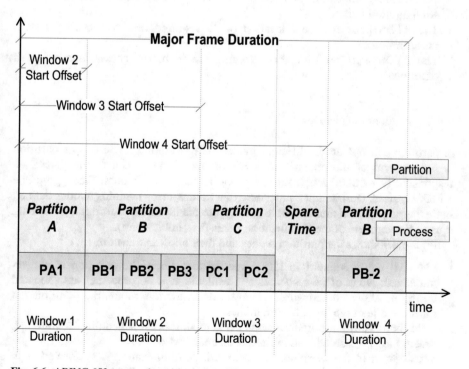

Fig. 6.6 ARINC 653 temporal partitioning model

3. At least one partition window is allocated to each module partition.
4. The scheduling algorithm is fixed, periodic, and statically defined based on the system configuration tables.
5. The scheduling of the module's partitions is controlled exclusively by the RTOS.

6.8.3.1.3 Spatial Partitioning

Spatial partitioning is achieved by restricting partition memory accesses to pre-defined memory regions.

The allocation of memory regions to specific partitions must be based on the analysis of the individual partition requirements regarding which data must be available and their size and access rights. This analysis must consider the different address space segments (e.g., text and data), application-shared memories, and I/O-mapped registers.

The key features of this model are:

1. One partition at most has write access to a particular area of memory.
2. The memory allocation is fixed and statically defined based on the system configuration tables.
3. The RTOS performs the allocation of all required resources during system initialization.
4. The RTOS is responsible for enforcing the memory access rights of each partition.

6.8.3.1.4 Operating Modes

A partition can operate in different modes. The operating mode of one partition is independent of the operational mode of the others, and it is the partition's responsibility to transition from one mode to the other through the appropriate APEX services. Despite this, in the case of a failure, error-handling actions defined in the partition health monitor table can set it to the idle state or restart it by forcing it to go through one of the initialization states (i.e., cold, warm).

Figure 6.7 shows the partition modes and their allowed transitions.

- Idle: All partitions start in idle mode. In this mode, the partition is not yet initialized: None of its resources are available, and no processes are executed during its allocated activation windows. From the idle mode, the partition can transit to one of the initialization modes.
- Cold Start: Partition initialization is performed. Process scheduling is inhibited, preemption is disabled, and initialization code is executed.
- Warm Start: In the warm start mode, partition initialization is performed as in the cold start mode. The purpose of having different modes is to indicate to the RTOS that there is no need to perform a full initialization from the hardware

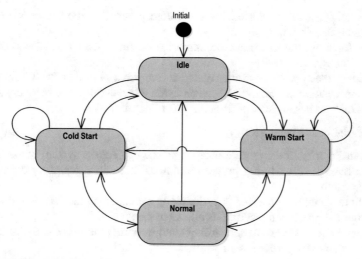

Fig. 6.7 Partition operating modes

perspective (e.g., copy the code from Flash to RAM). This mode is system-specific and heavily relies on the hardware platform's capability requirements.
- Normal: In the normal mode, all partition resources are available, and all processes are allowed to execute during partition activation windows.

6.8.3.2   Process Management

A process is a programming unit that is deployed to a partition. It contains executable object code, data regions, stack pointer, program counter, and scheduling attributes such as priority and deadline. A partition contains one or more processes that, when executed concurrently, realize its function within the IMA system.

6.8.3.2.1   Process Attributes

ARINC 653 defines the minimum set of attributes required to manage a process. These attributes can be fixed (defined during partition initialization) or variable (dynamically managed by the partition during runtime).

The fixed attributes are:

1. Name: the unique process identifier in the partition.
2. Entry Point: the start address for process execution.
3. Stack Size: the maximum stack size for the process.
4. Base Priority: the default process priority.

5. Period: the activation period for a periodic process or the indication that the process is aperiodic.
6. Time Capacity: the maximum amount of time the process can take to finish its execution cycle.
7. Deadline: the type of deadline related to the process (either "soft" or "hard"). This information can be used by the partition when taking error recovery actions. This attribute has no impact from the RTOS point of view.

The variable attributes are:

1. Current Priority: the dynamic process priority to access system resources. Set to the base priority during process initialization and managed by the partition during runtime.
2. Deadline Time: the time that is periodically evaluated by the RTOS to determine whether the process is meeting its allocated time.
3. Process State: the current scheduling state in which the process is. Valid states are dormant, ready, running, or waiting.

6.8.3.2.2 Process Control

A process is not visible outside its partition environment. Considering that both fixed and variable process attributes are specified using APEX services, all the system resources required by a process are statically defined at build time. The implication of this is twofold:

1. It is the application developer's responsibility to define the process attributes that allow the process to fulfill its functional requirements.
2. It is the system integrator's responsibility to define the partition attributes that meet both the partition's process requirements and the system's robust partitioning requirements.

Processes are created and initialized only once during the lifetime of the partition. A partition can, however, re-initialize any of its processes, as well as prevent them from being scheduled.

6.8.3.2.3 Process Scheduling

Process scheduling takes place within the partition activation window. The scheduling model is based on a preemptive model in which the process selected to execute is always the one with the highest priority from the ready queue. This model allows critical sections of the partition code to be executed without the risk of rescheduling. Furthermore, if a process execution is interrupted by the end of a partition activation window, it is guaranteed that this process will be resumed at the next partition activation.

The key features of this model are:

1. The scheduling unit is a process.
2. Each process has a current priority (managed by the partition code).
3. A process can be periodic or aperiodic.
4. All processes share the same resources (i.e., the resources allocated to the partition they are part of).
5. The scheduling algorithm is priority-preemptive. During a rescheduling event, the RTOS selects the process with the highest current priority from the ready queue. If several processes with the same priority are ready, it selects the one waiting for the longest time. That process will control the processor until another rescheduling event occurs.
6. The scheduling of the partition's processes is controlled by the partition via APEX services. The RTOS is only responsible for dispatching and preempting processes based on their priority levels and operating states.

6.8.3.2.4   Deadlines

Each process has an associated time capacity. This attribute represents the response time for the process to satisfy its processing requirements. After a process is started, its deadline is set to a value equal to the current time plus its time capacity. If the process finishes its execution cycle before its time capacity, the deadline is met. Otherwise, the deadline is missed. A deadline can be postponed by a replenish request. Since the time capacity is an absolute time and not an execution period, a deadline can occur outside the partition execution time. In case this happens, an error recovery action will be taken only in the next partition activation window.

6.8.3.3   Interpartition Communication

Interpartition communication is an umbrella term that covers all the mechanisms required to support the exchange of data between two or more partitions.

The services that implement interpartition communication are based on messages. A message is defined as a finite and contiguous block of data that is sent from one source partition to multiple destination partitions.

Partitions exchange messages through well-defined interfaces named ports. A port provides the required resources for communicating messages and defines the message structure and characteristics used during transmission.

The routing of partition ports is realized by channels. A channel is a logical communication path between one source partition port and one or more destination partitions ports.

6.8.3.3.1   Communication Principles

ARINC653 interpartition communication is based on the principle of transport independence. This principle establishes that the transport protocol is responsible for ensuring that messages are transmitted and received in the same order, regardless of the routing performed in the network. In this respect, messages do not have an associated priority level and are treated only based on the order of transmission. Furthermore, this principle ensures that any fragmentation and segmentation required to transport the data from the source to the destination(s) is invisible to the applications. The result is that, at the partition level, messages are atomic entities and are always transmitted and received as a complete unit.

During the system design phase, it is the responsibility of the application developer and the system integrator to ensure that the selected transport protocol meets the latency and reliability requirements for all associated partition messages.

This model provides the ability to upgrade network technologies without application impact and portability of applications across systems that employ different network architectures.

6.8.3.3.2   Communication Levels

The APEX interface provides interpartition communication services that are invariant to system module boundaries. In other words, it supports the transmission and receipt of messages via partition ports, regardless of whether the partitions are allocated to the same core module or to different core modules. Therefore, it is the system integrator's responsibility to configure the channel connections, via the system configuration tables, in a manner that all communication requirements of the individual partitions are met. This mechanism promotes the modularity and portability of partitions across different systems. Messages exchanged across core module boundaries (i.e., between partitions and pseudo-partitions) must be transmitted via a data bus. Similarly, messages exchanged within core module boundaries may be passed via a data bus or directly via RTOS facilities.

6.8.3.3.3   Communication Routing

The configuration of partition ports and the associated channels is entirely defined during the system integration process through the system configuration tables. In this regard, the definition of channels is not restricted to the module being integrated, but also encompasses all system modules. Each module is independently configured, but all must be synchronized to ensure that channels crossing module boundaries are routed correctly and that the associated ports are configured consistently.

6.8.3.3.4 Message Types

Messages are classified according to their length and periodicity.

The message length can be fixed or variable. Fixed-length messages have a constant size for every transmission. This type of message is most suitable for transmitting measurements, commands, and statuses that have a fixed and constant structure. Variable-length messages can have different sizes. This type of message is most suitable for transmitting data whose structure varies with the system operation, such as the list of airframes for the Traffic collision avoidance system (TCAS) function. In this case, the source partition must always specify the size of the valid data payload as part of the variable-length message structure to enable the destinations to interpret it correctly.

In respect to its periodicity, messages can be periodic or aperiodic. Periodic messages are transmitted on a regular, fixed time interval. This type of message is most suitable for transmitting data that continuously varies in time, such as air speed and total pressure. Aperiodic messages are transmitted at random time intervals. This type of message is most suitable for transmitting the occurrence of specific discrete events, such as an aircraft pilot action.

6.8.3.3.5 Transfer Modes

Partition ports can be configured to operate in two distinct operating modes: sampling mode and queuing mode.

In sampling mode, consecutive messages have the same data structure but communicate updated data values. There are no message queues associated with the transmission of sampling messages, and each message remains in the destination port buffer until overwritten by a more recent occurrence. Due to their nature, sampling mode ports can only transmit fixed-length messages.

In queuing mode, consecutive messages have unique data structures; thus, no message can be discarded. In order to handle queuing messages, the associated source and destination ports must implement message buffers according to the First in/first out (FIFO) policy. Queuing mode ports can transmit both fixed- and variable-length messages.

6.8.3.3.6 Port Attributes

ARINC 653 defines the minimum set of attributes required to configure a port. These attributes are fixed and specified via configuration tables.

1. Partition Identifier: the partition identifier attribute defines which partition has access to the port resources.
2. Port Name: the port name attribute defines a unique name to identify the port within the partition that has access to it.

3. Mode of Transfer: the mode of transfer attribute defines the port operating mode (sampling mode or queuing mode).
4. Transfer Direction: the transfer direction attribute defines whether the port allows messages to be transmitted (the partition is the message's source) or received (the partition is the message's destination).
5. Message Segment Length: the message segment length attribute defines the maximum length of the data block that can be transmitted by the port.
6. Message Storage Requirements: the message storage requirements attribute defines how many messages must be stored in the port's buffer. This attribute is only applicable to queuing ports.
7. Required Refresh Rate: the required refresh rate attribute defines the rate at which messages are expected to be received. This attribute is only applicable to sampling ports, and it is used by the RTOS to determine the validity of a message based on its arrival time and the time it was read by the application.
8. Mapping Requirements: the mapping requirements attribute defines the connection between the port and the physical communication medium. This optional attribute can be used to map ports to external physical addresses or procedures (e.g., device drivers) when there are engines for automatically moving data between the communication bus and the port's memory buffer.

6.8.3.3.7 Process Queuing Discipline

Interpartition communication is ultimately implemented by the processes that effectively access the partition ports.

When accessing queuing ports, a process can be blocked on a full message queue (source partition) or on an empty message queue (destination partition). In this case, a process rescheduling event will be triggered to the RTOS. Waiting times can be limited, or even avoided, with the aid of port time-outs.

Processes that are blocked in a queuing port can be queued according to an FIFO or a priority order. In the case of priority ordering, same-priority processes are queued in FIFO order. The port's queuing discipline is defined through APEX services during the port's creation time.

6.8.3.4 Intrapartition Communication

The RTOS integrity requirements that are necessary to ensure robust partitioning demand additional runtime verification that can affect the performance of the communication crossing partition boundaries. To allow processes within a partition to communicate and synchronize without the overhead of a global messaging system, the APEX interface provides a set of intrapartition communication services.

Process communication is based on buffers and blackboards. These services allow multiple source and destination processes to exchange messages in a lightweight manner. In this scheme, a process addresses the buffer or the blackboard, instead of the other process with which it wishes to communicate. This provides an asynchronous and independent communication mechanism.

Process synchronization is based on semaphores and events. Semaphores provide mutually exclusive access to shared resources, while events promote the synchronization of control flows through notification of the occurrence of defined conditions.

6.8.3.4.1   Buffers

In an APEX buffer, each message is considered unique and independent of the others. A message that is sent by one process is stored in a message queue according to an FIFO order. Processes that wait on a buffer are queued in either FIFO or priority order. If a process attempts to read a message from an empty buffer or write a message in a full buffer, the RTOS will trigger a process rescheduling event. If the buffer does not change its state during a specified amount of time, the RTOS puts the process back into the ready queue.

The maximum number of messages that can be stored in the buffer, the process queuing discipline, as well as the maximum process blocking time are runtime attributes defined during the creation of the buffer by the process that owns it.

6.8.3.4.2   Blackboards

In an APEX blackboard, only one message can be displayed at a particular time. Any message written on a blackboard will overwrite the previous one and will be stored until it is overwritten itself. Processes can read, write to, or clear blackboards. If a process tries to read a message from an empty blackboard, the RTOS will trigger a process rescheduling event. If the blackboard does not change its state during a specified amount of time, the RTOS puts the process back into the ready queue.

6.8.3.4.3   Semaphores

The APEX semaphores are based on the counting semaphore model. In this model, a process first waits on the semaphore to get access to the required resource and then signals the semaphore after completing the processing related to it. A semaphore comprises a counter that indicates the number of currently available requests for the resource it is controlling and a queue of waiting processes.

Processes can either wait for or signal semaphores. If the semaphore is not already indicating zero requests, the wait service decrements the semaphore counter by one unit; otherwise, it queues the calling process. A queued process can be blocked until the semaphore counter is incremented or until the expiration of a specified amount of time.

The signal service increments the semaphore by one unit. If there are processes queued on the semaphore, the semaphore queuing discipline is applied, and the RTOS will trigger a process rescheduling event.

Processes that wait on a semaphore can be queued in either FIFO or priority order. The number of requests the semaphore can hold and the process queuing discipline are runtime attributes defined during the creation of the semaphore by the processes that own it.

6.8.3.4.4   Events

APEX events are a communication mechanism that allows a process to notify other processes about the occurrence of a determined condition. An event comprises a state variable (which can be either "up" or "down") and a list of waiting processes. Upon the creation of the event, the initial state of an event is always "down."

Processes can set, reset, and wait on events. The set operation causes the event to transition to the "up" state, while the reset operation causes it to move to the "down" state. If the event is down, the wait service queues the calling process in the waiting list.

When the event is set, the RTOS moves all waiting processes from the waiting list to the ready queue and triggers a process rescheduling event.

6.8.3.5   Health Monitor

The Health monitor (HM) is an RTOS mechanism that provides robust fault isolation and prevents fault propagation across independent partition domains. It is responsible for monitoring and reporting software and hardware errors at different execution levels, providing tiered error handling and recovery actions.

Errors can occur at the module, partition, or process levels. The error level is defined by the state in which the system is operating when the error is detected. Based on the error and the level at which it was detected, an error recovery action is taken. Errors that are detected at one level can optionally be escalated and handled at a higher level. Additionally, errors detected at the partition and module levels can trigger HM callbacks. These callbacks are specific procedures called by the RTOS whenever a partition or module error is reported. HM callbacks can be uniquely and independently defined for each partition in the module and are system-specific. The configuration of all errors, their levels, their associated recovery actions, and the HM callbacks is performed during system integration through the system configuration tables.

6.8.3.5.1   Error Levels

Process-Level Errors

Are related to application execution errors (e.g., buffer overflows, memory violations) and invalid RTOS calls. Other than these, they can be raised via APEX services to indicate application-specific errors. Process-level errors may impact one or more processes inside a partition, but cannot propagate across the partition boundaries.

Partition-Level Errors

Are related to partition configuration and initialization errors or errors in the process-level error handlers. Partition-level errors impact one single partition and cannot violate robust partitioning.

Module-Level Errors

Are related to the configuration and initialization of the core module, partition scheduling, power failures, and other system-specific execution errors. These errors impact all partitions in the system.

6.8.3.5.2   Error Response Mechanisms

Error Handler Process

Process-level errors are handled by a special process called error handler process. This process has the highest priority inside a partition and is automatically scheduled by the RTOS whenever a process-level error is detected.

The error handler process must be developed by the application developers for each partition. The APEX interface provides services to retrieve the error code and the name of the faulty process, so tailored recovery error actions can be taken. If the error handler process is not defined, the RTOS escalates the error to the partition-level HM facility.

In order to standardize application error handling, the APEX defines the following process error codes:

1. DEADLINE_MISSED: The process has violated its deadline.
2. APPLICATION_ERROR: A code for all application-raised errors.
3. NUMERIC_ERROR: All errors associated with numerical processing (e.g., divide by zero, floating point overflows).
4. ILLEGAL_REQUEST: An invalid system call to an RTOS service.
5. STACK_OVERFLOW: The process has tried to allocate more stack memory than its memory requirements.

6. MEMORY_VIOLATION: The process has tried to access memory outside its access rights.
7. HARDWARE_FAULT: All errors associated with hardware faults during process execution (e.g., memory parity errors, I/O errors).
8. POWER_FAIL: A system power failure—notification for the application to save session data.

Health Monitor Tables

Partition- and module-level errors are handled through HM tables specified during the system integration process. For errors detected at these levels, the error response mechanism is a two-step process:

1. The RTOS invokes the associated module/partition HM callback—if defined
2. The RTOS looks up the error code in the associated module/partition HM table and takes the pre-defined error recovery action.

6.8.3.5.3 Error Recovery Actions

Different error recovery actions can be taken, depending on the level at which the error was detected.

Process Recovery Actions

The error handler process can take actions at the process and partition levels. The following is a list of possible recovery actions

1. Ignore the error—possibly log it.
2. Stop the offending process and re-initialize it.
3. Stop the offending process and start another process.
4. Restart the entire partition (set it to either cold or warm start).
5. Stop the entire partition (set it to idle mode).

Partition Recovery Actions

The HM table associated with a partition can define the following error handling actions:

1. Do nothing—the required error handling was performed by the HM callback.
2. Restart the entire partition (set it to either cold or warm start).
3. Stop the entire partition (set it to idle mode).

Module Recovery Actions

The HM table associated with a module can define the following error handling actions:

1. Do nothing—the required error handling was performed by the HM callback.
2. Restart the entire module (all partitions are restarted).
3. Stop the entire module (all partitions are stopped).

6.8.3.6   Time Management

Time management is an important characteristic for an RTOS. Time is an absolute attribute and must be independent of the partitions allocated to the module. All time values used to manage deadlines, activation periods, and delays are based on a unique time base managed by the RTOS kernel. Regardless of this, timestamps employed by the partition to perform function-specific tasks, such as fault recording, might come from other time domains through regular interpartition communication.

6.8.3.7   Memory Management

All the partition resource availability requirements are statically defined in the system configuration tables. Therefore, no services for dynamic memory allocation are defined in the APEX interface.

6.8.4   Service Requirements

The functionality described in Sect. 6.8.3 is provided to the application software through RTOS services. These services constitute the functional requirements of the APEX interface and are grouped into the following categories:

1. Partition Management
2. Process Management
3. Time Management
4. Memory Allocation
5. Interpartition Communication
6. Intrapartition Communication
7. Health Monitor.

The APEX functional requirements are entirely specified in a structured language. This formal language forms a specification grammar based on the syntax of Ada 83 and provides the definition of the service interface and a semantic description of its functionality.

The definition of the service interface includes the name of the service and a list of its formal parameters, including data types, constants, and validity ranges.

The semantic description gives an algorithmic representation of the behavior of the service independent of any implementation considerations and is composed of two parts. The first part specifies the error handling actions that must be performed when invalid input values are detected. The second defines the standard service operation and the expected output when all input values are valid.

Since this work is concerned only with the system configuration requirements (static aspects) defined by the ARINC 653 specification, no further details about the service requirements (dynamic aspects) are presented in this section.

6.8.5 Verification Responsibilities

The ARINC 653 specification defines different responsibilities concerning the verification of individual software applications and their allocation to a particular IMA system.

Verification of the system's availability and integrity requirements—taking into consideration the fulfillment of all applications' functional requirements—is the responsibility of the system integrator.

The verification of functional requirements of an individual application, independent of the system into which it is integrated, is the responsibility of the application supplier.

6.9 Challenges and Ways Forward

The growing customer demands for more connectivity from gate to gate have been driving an increasing concern for digital attacks on board modern civil aircraft. Recently, FAA and EASA proposed cybersecurity amendments to the airworthiness regulation, which effectively impose new requirements on aircraft manufacturers and operators seeking certification of new or modified systems.

The new certification requirements proposed by FAA and EASA require applicants to address threats that can lead to unauthorized access or disruption of aircraft systems, interfaces, or information. These new requirements virtually define a new discipline of airworthiness security, which comprises cybersecurity and information security both at the aircraft level and for the ground support equipment associated with aircraft information systems and data networks.

In this respect, the FAA already recognizes a set of industry guidelines as acceptable means of compliance with this new regulation. The first part of the set comprises DO-326A, entitled "Airworthiness Security Process Specification" [17], and DO-356A, entitled "Airworthiness Security Methods and Considerations" [19]. These documents provide the core guidelines and outline the major steps, activities, and objectives of airworthiness security certification. The second part of the set is defined by DO-355, entitled "Information Security Guidance for Continuing Airworthiness" [18], which contains guidance on continued, in-service airworthiness security.

In contrast to the traditional system safety and system development process guidelines defined by ARP 4761, ARP 4754, and their recommended practices that deal with hazards resulting from "natural" system failures, DO-326A and its companion publications address a new set of risks caused by intentional system tampering.

In summary, airworthiness security is a relatively new concern, but one that will most likely evolve and mature rapidly as new and modern aircraft integrate more systems into the connected environment. Unlike traditional safety, cybersecurity risks are continuously evolving. Thus, avionics systems will require constant assessment as new hostile agents might enter the aircraft environment.

References

1. AC 25.1309-1A, System Design and Analysis. U.S. Federal Aviation Administration (FAA)
2. ARINC Specification 653-2, avionics application software standard interface part 1—required services. Aeronautical Radio, Incorporated
3. ARINC Specification 664, aircraft data network. Aeronautical Radio, Incorporated
4. ARP4754A, guidelines for development of civil aircraft and systems. SAE Aerospace
5. ARP4761, guidelines and methods for conducting the safety assessment process on civil airborne systems and equipment. SAE Aerospace
6. F. Boniol, *New Challenges for Future Avionic Architectures* (Springer, Cham, 2013), pp. 1–1
7. H. Butz, *Open Integrated Modular Avionic (IMA): State of the Art and Future Development Road Map at Airbus Deutschland* (2008)
8. R. Collinson, *Introduction to Avionics Systems*, 3rd edn. (Springer, New York, 2011)
9. K. Driscoll, H., Integrated modular avionics (IMA) requirements and development, in *Proceedings of the ARTIST2 Meeting on Integrated Modular Avionics, November 12–13, 2007, Rome, Italy*. Integrated Modular Avionics Conference For The European Excellence On Embedded Systems (2007)
10. J. Krodel, G. Romanski, Real-time operating systems and component integration considerations in integrated modular avionics systems report, in *Final Report DOT/FAA/AR-07/39, U.S. Department of Transportation Federal Aviation Administration (FAA)* (2007)
11. I. Moir, A. Seabridge, M. Jukes, *Civil Avionics Systems*, 2nd edn. Aerospace Series (Wiley, New York, 2013)
12. P.J. Prisaznuk, Arinc 653 role in integrated modular avionics (IMA), in *IEEE/AIAA 27th Digital Avionics Systems Conference, 2008 (DASC 2008)* (IEEE, New York, 2008)
13. RTCA DO-160/EUROCAE ED-14, environmental conditions and test procedures for airborne equipment. Radio Technical Commission for Aeronautics, and European Organisation for Civil Aviation Equipment
14. RTCA DO-178C/EUROCAE ED-12C, software consideration in airborne systems and equipment certification. Radio Technical Commission for Aeronautics, and European Organisation for Civil Aviation Equipment
15. RTCA DO-254/EUROCAE ED-80, design assurance guidance for airborne electronic hardware. Radio Technical Commission for Aeronautics, and European Organisation for Civil Aviation Equipment

16. RTCA DO-297/EUROCAE ED-124, integrated modular avionics (IMA) development guidance and certification considerations. Radio Technical Commission for Aeronautics, and European Organisation for Civil Aviation Equipment
17. RTCA DO-326/EUROCAE ED-202, airworthiness security process specification. Radio Technical Commission for Aeronautics, and European Organisation for Civil Aviation Equipment
18. RTCA DO-355/EUROCAE ED-204, information security guidance for continuing airworthiness. Radio Technical Commission for Aeronautics, and European Organisation for Civil Aviation Equipment
19. RTCA DO-356/EUROCAE ED-203, airworthiness security methods and considerations. Radio Technical Commission for Aeronautics, and European Organisation for Civil Aviation Equipment
20. J. Rushby, Partitioning in avionics architectures: Requirements, mechanisms, and assurance. Technical report (SRI International, California, 1999)
21. A.S. Subcommittee, Arinc specification 653: Avionics application software standard interface, in *ARINC Project Initiation/Modification (APIM) APIM16-009, Aeronautical Radio, Incorporated* (2016)
22. A.L. Todd Gauer, IV&V on Orion's Arinc 653 flight software architecture, in *Proceedings of NASA's 2010 Annual Workshop on Independent Verification and Validation of Software. National Aeronautics and Space Administration (NASA)* (2010)
23. C.B. Watkins, R. Walter, Transitioning from federated avionics architectures to integrated modular avionics, in *Proceedings of the 2007 IEEE/AIAA 26th Digital Avionics Systems Conference* (2007)

Chapter 7
Reference Architectures for Industry 4.0

Frank Schnicke and Thomas Kuhn

Abstract The adoption of Industry 4.0 requires reconsideration of plant software architecture due to the strict layers of the automation pyramid hindering the implementation of central Industry 4.0 use cases like the changeable plant. Thus, plant software architecture has to change and, for example, adopt concepts such as the digital twin. In this chapter, we provide an overview of current challenges of the status quo of software architecture in Industry 4.0 and describe how they are solved by reference architectures. Furthermore, we provide guidance on how to classify use cases and reference architectures of Industry 4.0 according to various reference architecture models.

7.1 Introduction

Recent events, such as the COVID-19 pandemic, floods, or even the blockade of the Suez Canal, have shown the need for flexible supply chains and productions that can be adapted when necessary, for example, to compensate for important providers dropping out or to react to unforeseen market demands. This requires the digitization of production environments to enable information exchange along the value chains, which is the major mission of the Fourth Industrial Revolution—Industry 4.0 (I4.0). Information exchange will, however, not only improve the efficiency and robustness of production; it will also enable the efficient production of small lot sizes and thus individualized products and new data-driven business models.

Many companies of different sizes have a strong interest in transforming their manufacturing environments into a digitized and interoperable Industry 4.0 environment. Reference architectures are key to realizing an interoperable Industry 4.0. Yet, a prerequisite for choosing the right reference architecture is the existence

F. Schnicke (✉) · T. Kuhn
Fraunhofer Institute for Experimental Software Engineering, Kaiserslautern, Germany
e-mail: frank.schnicke@iese.fraunhofer.de ; thomas.kuhn@iese.fraunhofer.de

© The Author(s), under exclusive license to Springer Nature Switzerland AG 2023
E. Y. Nakagawa, P. Oliveira Antonino (eds.), *Reference Architectures for Critical Domains*, https://doi.org/10.1007/978-3-031-16957-1_7

151

of a common understanding of a company's use cases as well as the use cases addressed by a reference architecture.

To address this issue, this chapter provides an overview of Industry 4.0 reference architectures. First, we will describe current challenges of implementing Industry 4.0 and provide insights into how to classify use cases and reference architectures. Then reference architectures will be described and classified according to the Reference Architecture Model Industrie 4.0.

The outline of this chapter is as follows: Subsections 7.1.1 and 7.1.2 provide the historic context of industrial revolutions and summarize Industry 4.0. In Sect. 7.2, we will outline typical architectural challenges in production systems by describing use cases and architectural drivers and presenting two architecture reference models that can be used for the classification of use cases and architectures. Section 7.3 will introduce the concept of the digital twin and describe its relation to I4.0 system architectures. Next, Sect. 7.4 will introduce the BaSys 4 reference architecture as an example of I4.0 reference architectures and describe its components in detail. In Sect. 7.5, we will describe additional reference architectures and classify them according to RAMI 4.0. Finally, in Sect. 7.6, we will draw conclusions and provide guidance for future work.

7.1.1 A Short History of Industrial Revolutions

As the name Industry 4.0 implies, there have been three industrial revolutions in the past. The First Industrial Revolution was sparked by the usage of waterpower and steam power to ease mechanical tasks, which greatly increased productivity. The next industrial revolution happened with the introduction of assembly lines. This allowed mass production of products with high efficiency.

The introduction of automation by using robots and computers additionally increased production efficiency. This is considered as the Third Industrial Revolution [1]. While productivity greatly increased, flexibility did not increase. Each of these three industrial revolutions introduced an increase in productivity but only when manufacturing the same product with little to no variants. However, changing a manufacturing system that is using a Third Industrial Revolution standard is very expensive due to various factors described in Sect. 7.2.1.

7.1.2 The Fourth Industrial Revolution

In contrast to the previous industrial revolutions, the Fourth Industrial Revolution does not mainly aim to increase the efficiency of producing the same product. Instead, it aims to enable an increase in flexibility to allow, for example, the efficient production of vastly different products on the same production line.

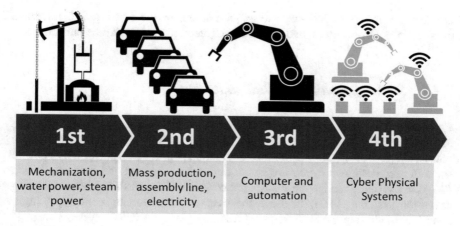

Fig. 7.1 The four industrial revolutions [3]

The authors of [2] name different requirements that the next industrial revolutions have to satisfy. Below, a small excerpt of these requirements is listed:

- Interoperability: Integrating different heterogeneous systems with each other
- Scalability: Integrating new resources into existing systems
- Open and Dynamic Structure: Dynamically integrating new subsystems without having to stop the system
- Agility: Reconfiguring a system quickly to enable adaptation to changing requirements

The Fourth Industrial Revolution aims to address these requirements. Figure 7.1 shows the history of industrial revolutions, including the Fourth Industrial Revolution.

These requirements are motivated by several use cases: (1) changeable plant, (2) process documentation, (3) supply chain integration, and (4) plant data integration. A more in-depth overview of use cases and drivers will be given in Sect. 7.2.

Different names are in use for this Fourth Industrial Revolution. Germany coined the term "Industry 4.0" (*Industrie 4.0* in German), while in the USA, the name "Industrial Internet of Things" or "Smart Manufacturing" is used. In this chapter, Industry 4.0 will be used to refer to the Fourth Industrial Revolution.

7.2   Architecture Challenges in Production Systems

To understand issues addressed by Industry 4.0 reference architectures, it is vital to have an overview of the status quo in manufacturing and its architectural challenges. We will detail these in this section. Additionally, we will describe use cases and architecture drivers of Industry 4.0 as motivation for the existing I4.0 reference architectures. Furthermore, two reference architecture models will be introduced.

7.2.1 Status Quo and Its Challenges

Currently, automation is implemented using the "automation pyramid" reference architecture as defined by IEC 62264 [4] and shown in Fig. 7.2. This architecture consists of separate layers with defined interaction points. PLCs perform the specific steps in predetermined cyclic programs. Supervisory control and data acquisition (SCADA) systems realize the distributed control of several PLCs. Manufacturing execution systems (MES) man-age the overall production by controlling high-level manufacturing steps. Enterprise resource planning (ERP) systems manage resources, for example, the number of items in stock. Cross-layer interaction in the automation pyramid is difficult, as every layer can only access information that is provided by lower layers. Changes therefore require modifications in all layers. In contrast, Industry 4.0 advocates a peer-to-peer communication to enable device-to-device communication. However, this change in architecture only addresses the data acquisition part and does not introduce changeability on its own.

PLCs are programmed using languages defined by IEC 61131 [5]. These languages impose several challenges, e.g., unclear semantics [6]. If a process parameter needs to be changed and the needed variant is not already implemented, the code on

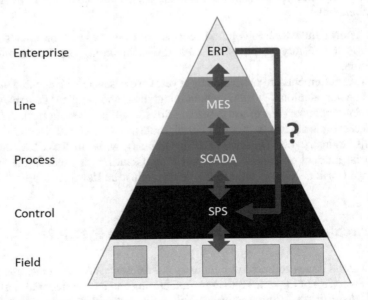

Fig. 7.2 The framework of the automation pyramid and its challenge of layer-spanning access

the PLC needs to change, which may affect PLC cycle times and therefore real-time constraints of the program. Predecessor and successor devices of the changed device depend on this cycle time, and inter-PLC communication through networks must also be considered during reprogramming. As a consequence, a change of a single PLC may produce side effects in other PLCs [7], leading to downtimes and therefore to a loss of time and money.

7.2.2   Use Cases

Industry 4.0 encompasses a plethora of different use cases on different levels of plant automation. The Plattform Industrie 4.0 [1] provides an overview of important use cases in a whitepaper [8], including (1) the changeable plant, (2) smart product design for smart products, and (3) continuous engineering of plants. In the following, a selection of these use cases will be presented in addition to use cases that were tackled in projects by the authors together with industry partners. Section 7.2.3 will then present a selection of architectural drivers derived from those use cases.

- *Changeable Plant*: The use case of a changeable plant focuses on plug-and-playability to enable quick reactions to changes. This changeability includes both the change of a product and the change of manufacturing equipment. In a changeable plant, both can be changed and reconfigured without major manual effort and with setup times reduced to an absolute minimum. However, enabling a changeable plant requires rethinking the plant architecture and transforming it to an I4.0 SOA [9]. This use case is addressed, for example, in the BaSys 4.0 and BaSys 4.2 projects. [2]
- *Process Documentation*: In this use case, production data is acquired during production and can thus be used for detecting quality issues on-the-fly. This data can then be integrated with product lifecycle management (PLM), thus enabling more efficient engineering by learning for future generations of the product. The integration of PLM systems is addressed, for instance, in the BaSysPLM [3] project.
- *Supply Chain Integration*: By creating horizontal integration along the supply chain, data can be passed more efficiently. By using unified data models and interfaces, companies can increase resilience to disturbances in supply chains. The projects BaSys überProd and BaSys4SupplyQ [4] address supply chain issues,

---

[1] A German board consisting of industry and research companies working to define the future concepts of Industry 4.0 (see https://www.plattform-i40.de/IP/Navigation/EN/Home/home.html)

[2] https://www.basys40.de/ (German)

[3] https://www.softwaresysteme.pt-dlr.de/media/content/Projektblatt_BaSys_PLM.pdf (German)

[4] https://www.softwaresysteme.pt-dlr.de/img/content/BaSys4SupplyQ.pdf (German)

e.g., by focusing on passing quality data along the supply chain in a standardized format.

- *Plant Data Integration*: Currently, plant data is typically stored in data silos with little integration. By creating integrated solutions, redundancy can be eliminated. Through unified data formats and presentations, applications can be implemented independent of the specific data silo used. This issue is addressed by the projects DigiPro4BaSys, [5] where plant data is used for visualization, and BaSyPaaS, where data silos are integrated for better cost estimation.

7.2.3 Architecture Drivers

The development of a new architecture has to address numerous stakeholder needs, which have to be formulated and formalized. Architecture drivers support the formalization of stakeholder needs regarding architecture decisions: Architecture drivers are a particular set of requirements classified as new, risky, or expensive to implement or maintain [10] and therefore significantly affect the architecture. The specification of architecture drivers must be precise enough to enable the architecture to properly reason about adequate architecture solutions to address them. In this regard, we adopted the approach proposed by Knodel and Naab [10], who claim that architecture drivers must be specified in terms of (1) the environment or condition in which this driver occurs, (2) the event that stimulates the occurrence of the driver, (3) the expected response of the system to the driver event, and (4) the quantifications associated with the three previous aspects. Each of these measurable effects indicates whether the driver is addressed by the architecture.

The systematic specification of architecture drivers must indicate the quality aspects that characterize the system functions described in each architecture driver specification. For instance, instead of claiming that the light barrier sensors shall transmit signals to the roller conveyor of the production plant, we might characterize the system function by the degree of security of the signal transmission (e.g., the maximum tolerable delay). In this way, the architecture drivers specify not only the what but also the how well (i.e., with what degree of quality), thereby providing proper information for the selection of an adequate architecture solution for each architecture driver. To this end, we adopted the quality characteristics described in ISO/IEC 25010:2011 Systems and software engineering—Systems and software Quality Requirements and Evaluation (SQuaRE)—System and software quality models [11] to characterize the I4.0 architecture drivers described in this chapter. ISO/IEC 25010 comprises the following quality characteristics: functional suitability, performance efficiency, compatibility, usability, reliability, security, maintainability, and portability. Each quality aspect is further refined into

---

[5] https://www.softwaresysteme.pt-dlr.de/media/content/Projektblatt_DigiPro4BaSys.pdf (German)

Table 7.1 Architecture driver describing information exchange between systems of the automation pyramid

Driver	Information exchange between systems of the automation pyramid	Quantifications $\Downarrow$
Quality aspect	• Compatibility (interoperability) • Performance efficiency (time behavior)	
Environment	• Several devices and products exist • Applications exist on a higher layer, e.g., a dashboard • DTs exist for each production entity and for the production management	• Number of devices • Number of products
Stimulus	• A device has information about it being updated, e.g., a change in a critical sensor parameter like energy insufficiency or overheating	• New time stamp Value! = Old time stamp value
Response	• The changed information is propagated to the DT • Another device or application retrieves the information and, for example, sets a control point	• Number of direct communications between physical devices and other applications = zero • Latency requirement violations = zero

sub-aspects. For instance, security is further refined into confidentiality, integrity, non-repudiation, authenticity, and accountability.

In the following, two architectural drivers motivated by the use cases in Sect. 7.2.2 will be described in detail.

7.2.3.1 End-to-End Communication

Enabling end-to-end communication is one of the main goals of I4.0 [12] and provides the foundation for other use cases, such as *changeable plant* or *plant data integration* (cf. Sect. 7.2.2). I4.0 advocates a peer-to-peer architecture that enables cross-layer interaction to allow flexible use of data as the basis for self-adapting processes. Asset Administration Shells (cf. Sect. 7.3.2) provide common data structures and a defined type system and are therefore a valid technical foundation for DTs. AAS submodels enable the definition of tailored data structures and services to describe and represent specific production assets. All assets can access the AAS regardless of their own location within the automation pyramid. This makes the Industrial Internet of Things possible. A common technical requirement in control systems is maximum data latency, which is often constrained to a maximum value. The authors of [13] adapted the end-to-end communication architecture driver initially proposed by Antonino et al. [14] to also reflect access within the same layer of the automation pyramid (cf. Table 7.1), so it also contains quantifications of latency requirements.

7.2.3.2   Plug-and-Produce

Plug-and-play describes the ability of a system to enable automatic discovery and configuration of a newly plugged-in component without the need for human intervention. Plug-and-produce extends this concept to the domain of manufacturing. Thus, Plug-and-produce describes the foundation needed for the use case of a *changeable plant* (cf. Sect. 7.2.2). The common objective is to reduce the effort required to install new or additional devices into a new or existing infrastructure as well as to reduce downtimes. Koziolek et al. [15] identify nine phases for "plug-and-produce," classified into physical device installation in phases 1 to 3 and configuration and system integration in the remaining ones. All 9 phases can be further decomposed into 51 steps in total. The first phase is only necessary when an existing device is replaced. Thus, it is not applicable when a plant is commissioned for the first time. Phases 2–8 focus on the physical integration of the device into the system, while phase 9 focuses on integrating the device into the plant's IT system. In addition to the identification of the nine phases, the authors propose a Plug-and-produce architecture called OpenPnP based on OPC-UA. OPC-UA serves as the basic communication technology from and to field devices and connected components. OpenPnP also uses the built-in mechanisms of OPC-UA for device registration and discovery.

Building on this work, the authors of [13] describe an architecture driver focusing on phase 9 in Table 7.2. The context includes preconditions and assumptions made in order to establish a common understanding of the environment. It is followed by the steps needed to trigger the response of the system.

7.2.4   Classification of Use Cases and Architectures

To improve understanding and to enable a common nomenclature for discussions, reference architecture models can be utilized. These reference architecture models make it possible to classify use cases and architectures in order to identify gaps, for example. In consequence, they allow simultaneously description of the problem space and the solution space. In the following, two reference architecture models will be introduced: RAMI 4.0 and IIRA.

7.2.4.1   Reference Architecture Model Industrie 4.0 (RAMI 4.0)

The Reference Architecture Model Industrie 4.0 (RAMI 4.0) [16] proposes a three-dimensional approach to classifying architectures and use cases. Its three axes are (1) the architectural layers, (2) the life cycle and value stream stages in conformance with IEC 62890, and (3) the hierarchy levels in conformance with IEC 62264 and IEC 61512. Since the model will be used to classify the reference architectures in the following sections, each dimension will be described in detail in the following.

Table 7.2 Architecture driver describing the Plug-and-produce use case

Driver	Plug-and-playability of devices	Quantifications ⇓
Quality aspect	• Compatibility (interoperability) • Maintainability (modifiability)	
Environment	• The production system has been deployed • A DT IT infrastructure is running • The semantics of the new device are already specified and can be interpreted by the enclosing infrastructure	• Number of devices
Stimulus	• An additional device is installed in the described environment • The physical device is set up, including its calibration and configuration of basic communication (i.e., phases 1 to 8)	
Response	• The system discovers the DT infrastructure • It makes its DT available to the system, e.g., by uploading it to a server • The DTs can be found and accessed by other applications or devices	• Integration time of device for phase 9 < 1 minute • Manual interventions = 0

7.2.4.1.1   The Architectural Layers

The *architectural layers* axis of RAMI 4.0 is split into six layers, each describing one structural aspect.

- *Business Layer*: Here, aspects relevant to business goals are described. For instance, organizational issues, business processes, as well as legal constraints are described here.
- *Functional Layer*: This layer describes functionalities in the context of an Industry 4.0 system, such as runtime environments, formal descriptions, and platforms for horizontal integration.
- *Information Layer*: In this layer, data used and/or created is described. This includes, for example, formal descriptions of models and rules, consistent integration of data, runtime environments or data (pre)processing, and the provision of data via APIs.
- *Communication Layer*: Here, Industry-4.0-conformant access to data and functionality is described, which is why today's automation busses are not included in this layer, but rather in the *Integration Layer*. Examples described in this layer include communication using unified I4.0 data formats and the provision of services based on service-oriented architectures.

- *Integration Layer*: The *Integration Layer* builds the bridge between the physical and the digital word. Here, the infrastructures needed for realizing functions of assets are described. Examples include human-machine interfaces and descriptions of assets.
- *Asset Layer*: This layer represents the real world, i.e., the physical assets. For example, the integration between assets and the *Integration Layer* is described here.

7.2.4.1.2   Life Cycle and Value Stream Stages

The different *life cycle and value stream stages* enable the classification of solutions and challenges in terms of the part of the asset's life cycle that is addressed. These stages are divided between the life cycle of an asset type and an asset instance.

The *Asset Type Life Cycle* is subdivided into (1) *type development*, i.e., development of the overall product, and (2) *type maintenance/usage* which includes updating of type definitions with, e.g., lessons learned and design optimizations.

Similarly, the *Asset Instance Life Cycle* is subdivided into (1) *instance production*, i.e., challenges and solutions addressing the creation of the asset, and (2) *instance maintenance/usage*, which addresses, for example, predictive maintenance or human-machine interfaces.

7.2.4.1.3   Hierarchy Levels

The hierarchy levels are defined in conformance with IEC 62264 and IEC 61512, which describe, for example, the reference architecture for factory systems, i.e., the automation pyramid. To reflect the requirements of Industry 4.0, the layers *Connected World*, *Field Device*, and *Product* are added to the layers already described in the IEC standards named above. Thus, the following hierarchy layers are described:

- *Connected World*: This layer describes the relation between assets, which is not necessarily limited to the relations within a single factory or company.
- *Enterprise*: In this layer, enterprise-level aspects like order planning or general production planning are reflected. This is where ERP systems are located.
- *Work Centers*: The *Work Center* layer addresses aspects focusing on single work centers, like production orchestration, execution, and quality management. Typically, MES systems are located here.
- *Station:* Here, aspects of a single station are described. This level focuses, e.g., on monitoring and process management systems like SCADA.
- *Control Device:* The focus of this level is the device controlling a single aspect of the manufacturing process like a robot arm. This control is typically realized via PLCs.

- *Field Device:* Here, the different actors and sensors in a production plant are addressed.
- *Product*: This level addresses aspects related to the product, such as its production plan as well as its status and location within the running production.

7.2.4.2 Industrial Internet Reference Architecture (IIRA)

The Industrial Internet Reference Architecture (IIRA) [17] is specified by the Industry IoT consortium and aims to address the "need for a common architecture framework to develop interoperable IIoT systems for diverse applications across a broad spectrum of industrial verticals in the public and private sectors to achieve the true promise of IIoT" [17]. Similar to RAMI 4.0 described in Sect. 7.2.4.1, it proposes a three-dimensional layout.

However, in contrast to RAMI, it does not focus solely on Industry 4.0 but tries to address various industrial sectors.

To address these industrial sectors, IIRA proposes the following viewpoints:

- *Business Viewpoint*: This viewpoint focuses on identifying stakeholders and their business objects as well as their values and vision. Additionally, it focuses on how a system can achieve these objectives.
- *Usage Viewpoint*: In this viewpoint, the focus lies on the expected system usage. Thus, for example, a sequence of activities delivering the intended functionality is described.
- *Functional Viewpoint*: Here, the functional components of an IIOT system as well as their structure and interrelations are described. Additionally, interfaces and interactions between components are detailed here.
- *Implementation Viewpoint*: The *Implementation Viewpoint* addresses technologies required for realizing the functional components described in the *Functional Viewpoint*.

In addition to the various viewpoints and industrial sectors, IIRA proposes the *Lifecycle Process* axis. However, these lifecycle stages depend on the specific industrial sector. Thus, IIRA does not propose an overall lifecycle model.

7.3 The Digital Twin in the Context of Industry 4.0

Industry 4.0 is typically associated with digital twins (DT). However, there is a plethora of ideas and concepts associated with DTs. In this section, we will therefore establish a common understanding of *what* a DT is in the context of this chapter. Additionally, we will introduce the Asset Administration Shell as specific implementation of the DT.

7.3.1 The Digital Twin

The term digital twin is used in various contexts with different meanings. The range of understanding extends from a simple 3D model of an asset to a complete description of an asset including physical simulation models and access to the real asset. In any case, a digital twin is a digital representation of a real asset.

For the categorization of the terms used for this purpose, the distinction into model, digital shadow, and digital twin as proposed by Kritzinger et al. [18] is suitable. The distinction is derived from the different degrees of integration between the real asset and the virtual representation:

- **Model:** A digital representation, for example, a pure simulation model, without automated exchange between the real and the digital object
- **Digital Shadow:** A model of an asset, including an automated flow of information from reality to the virtual mapping (Fig. 7.3)
- **Digital Twin:** A digital shadow with feedback of any changes from the virtual representation into reality and the ability to influence or control a real system

The digital twin addresses an aspect that is missing in many systems today: Even if entire systems or system components are already digital, there is no uniform digital image of these systems in their entirety. This was precisely the original motivation of Glaessgen et al. [19] for creating the digital twin. They wanted to create a virtual representative that could be tested instead of a real system in order to save costs during development. This virtual representation should behave like its real counterpart in every situation. Even today, the complexity and diversity of current systems lead to challenges that are very difficult to solve without digital system images.

Fig. 7.3 Visualization of a digital shadow of an aluminum cold-rolling mill

If, for example, a new driving function is to be tested today, the test activities must be carried out in real vehicles. Due to the large number of vehicle variants and situations in which a function must be tested, this already leads to great expense. As the complexity of the driving functions increases, more and more tests are required, which can hardly be carried out in a meaningful way in real vehicles. At the latest during the development of autonomous driving functions, a point is reached at which it is no longer possible to test sensibly using traditional means.

In production engineering, too, changes to production often have to be tested on the real system. For this purpose, the running production has to be stopped. If errors occur, they must first be eliminated before production can be restarted with the modified configuration. These downtimes are expensive and significantly reduce the flexibility of a production.

A digital system image would solve both problems. The digital image of a vehicle would enable virtual tests of driving functions. Different situations and the behavior of the new software in different model variants could be tested in parallel in powerful computing clusters. In the production area, changes could be tested on a digital image of the plant before modifications are made to the real plant. A large part of the problems would thus be found in a virtual environment. This would lead to significantly lower downtimes and thus save costs and time.

7.3.2   Digital Twins and the Asset Administration Shell

The Asset Administration Shell (AAS) [20] is a technical realization of the digital twin concept that is currently being defined by the Plattform Industrie 4.0.

The AAS defines a uniform data structure that digitally describes production assets. Specific properties are encapsulated in submodels. The submodels of the AAS are therefore comparable to OPC-UA companion specifications since both encapsulate domain knowledge in models. In consequence, there are activities that want to integrate both approaches with each other. As of now, the AAS is subdivided into (1) AAS Type 1, i.e., the serialized AAS that can be exchanged between entities; (2) AAS Type 2, i.e., the AAS as runtime entity with its own runtime API; and (3) AAS Type 3, i.e., the AAS as an independent agent.

The AAS and its submodels were originally designed for use in the automation domain, but they are largely domain-independent. They can therefore also be used in other domains as a technological basis for digital twins.

Right now, the following technical documents are available:

- *Details of the Asset Administration Shell (Part 1)*: This document [21] describes the overall metamodel of the AAS. In addition to the specification, mappings to specific technologies are provided. These mappings include JSON, XML, AASX (an Open Packaging Conventions-based package format), AutomationML, RDF, and OPC UA NodeSets. This document therefore defines the AAS Type 1.

– *Details of the Asset Administration Shell (Part 2)*: In this document [22], the runtime environment is specified. This includes the HTTP/REST API for infrastructure components such as the AAS Registry, the AAS and Submodel Repository, as well as the HTTP/REST API of the AAS and the submodels itself. Thus, this document defines the runtime API needed to realize AAS Type 2 and therefore provides the foundation for AAS Type 3.

For the AAS as specified in the *Details of the Asset Administration Shell* documents, there exists an open-source reference implementation named *Eclipse BaSyx*. [6] BaSyx provides various SDKs with varying scopes, e.g., Java, C#, and Python as well as C++ and Rust. Additionally, BaSyx provides off-the-shelf components that can be instantiated with little to no programming knowledge.

7.4   BaSys 4

This section provides an overview of the BaSys 4 reference architecture. All software components of this reference implementation are provided as part of the Eclipse BaSyx middleware. [7]

7.4.1   Overview

Many existing Industry 4.0 architectures realize strict layering. This is not so much the result of an explicit decision, but rather a result of the combination of numerous systems that together execute the production process. As described in Sect. 7.2.1, strict layers are defined by the automation pyramid.

A layered architecture has the advantage that interfaces between layers are well defined. The MES system, for example, mediates between ERP and SCADA. However, in a strictly layered architecture, only adjacent layers communicate with each other. Changes that are not part of the layered interface need to be implemented in all layers. Therefore, ERP systems cannot simply access a sensor on the shop floor.

The BaSys 4 architecture realizes decentralized machine-to-machine communication that enables all production assets to communicate with each other. This requires unified interfaces for all assets regardless of the asset type. Products, machines, processes, workers, and all other relevant assets therefore need to provide a unified API to enable decentralized machine-to-machine communication. This change in architecture is illustrated in Fig. 7.4.

---

[6] https://www.eclipse.org/basyx/

[7] https://www.eclipse.org/basyx/

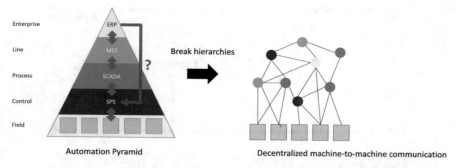

Fig. 7.4 The transition from the automation pyramid to the Industrial Internet of Things

Figure 7.5 illustrates the overall architecture of a BaSys conformant system. We differentiate between the enterprise, field, and digital process levels. The enterprise level consists of enterprise-level applications. These include the aforementioned ERP systems, but also, for example, analysis and optimization applications. Systems on the enterprise level require a holistic view on the production, which includes local production lines and resources, but may also extend to supply chains and remote locations. The field level consists of edge devices, PLC controllers, and devices, which include sensors and actuators. The field level in our architecture model only has a local view on the production and local knowledge. Assets on this level are service providers. Process-level knowledge, e.g., regarding the necessary sequence of process steps to create a specific product, should not be known by assets on this level to maintain flexibility. The digital process between these two layers is the glue that keeps both worlds together. It realizes digital twins for relevant production assets that represent relevant information and services. Digital twins provide unified interfaces that enable accessing and updating all status information. ERP components, for example, update digital twins with information regarding required quality aspects and deadlines, while the process devices provide measured values and live data to the digital twins.

7.4.2 The BaSys 4 Reference Architecture

The BaSys 4 digital process consists of components that communicate through an end-to-end communication medium. Any end-to-end communication is supported. One open-source solution for this end-to-end communication is the virtual automation bus (VAB) [23], which is part of the Eclipse BaSyx distribution. The VAB is a gateway-based system that integrates existing network infrastructures and field buses in a connected network. It adapts to existing network topologies and restrictions. The VAB defines common communication semantics based on a type system and five action primitives: get, set, create, delete, and invoke. Mappings

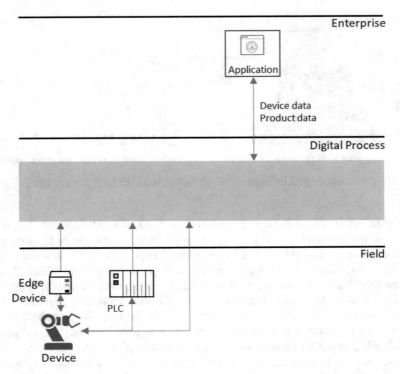

Fig. 7.5 The digital process

define the realization of each of these primitives for a target hardware. VAB gateways translate bus-specific telegrams based on the semantic model and therefore enable end-to-end communication.

Figure 7.6 illustrates the basic architecture pattern of our BaSys 4 architecture. It is a virtual end-to-end communication medium that connects Industry 4.0 components. All of these components speak the same language, use the same type system, and provide the same interface to enable end-to-end communication.

We selected the Asset Administration Shell described in Sect. 7.3.2 of the Plattform Industrie 4.0 as a realization of our Industry 4.0 components. An AAS represents a single, relevant production asset. It defines a unified API that enables access to basic information, which includes the name and the unique ID of an asset. AAS may be defined for any kind of physical or non-physical asset, including products, work pieces, orders, devices, workers, processes, and all other kinds of relevant production assets. As these assets differ greatly with respect to their type, and consequently with respect to the information and services provided and required, all asset-specific data and services are not a direct part of the AAS. Instead, an AAS consists of several submodels providing access to asset-specific data and services as described in Sect. 7.3.2. Every AAS submodel is identified by a unique

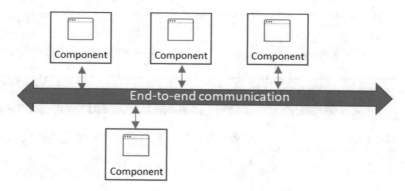

Fig. 7.6 White box view on the digital process

ID that is connected to the ID of its AAS and adds, for example, the submodel type in order to create a distinguishable, unique ID for the submodel.

AAS are defined on the type and instance level. Type AAS define common properties for asset types, i.e., assets that share similar properties. Instance AAS contain data that is specific for a single entity, e.g., a concrete device or a concrete product. Both types of AAS are realized in the same manner in terms of the technology used.

Figure 7.7 illustrates the components of the BaSys 4 architecture and the information flows between them. AAS are hosted by server components that may be deployed to different locations. We differentiate AAS type servers that host type AAS as Type 1 AAS. AAS instance servers host Type 2 and Type 3 AAS that connect to and communicate with process assets. The communication endpoint, which must be used to communicate with an AAS or with an AAS submodel, therefore depends on the server to which the AAS or the submodel is deployed. Therefore, a registry keeps track of the mapping between AAS (or submodel) IDs and communication endpoints. So an AAS and a submodel must first register with the registry to make its communication endpoint available to applications. If the AAS or the submodel is relocated, the registry entry must be updated if the network address changes during the relocation process.

Control components realize a unified interface for controlling a device and for querying the abstract device status. This abstract device status is provided conformant to the PackML standard and specifies an overall device state: whether the device is ready, idle, busy, or in an error state. The control component also defines a unified control interface that enables selection of operation modes and access to services provided by a device. The operation mode conforms to standardized operation modes and includes installation modes with reduced power and speed for safety reasons as well as automatic operation and manual override modes. Device services are device-specific and enable the integration of the device into a dynamic process.

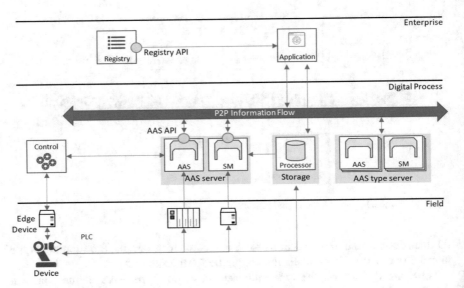

Fig. 7.7 BaSys 4 architecture

Some devices, e.g., high-speed cameras, may provide data at high frequencies. This data is often processed by special hardware and stored in a native storage. A digital process needs to integrate this data through a unified interface in order to enable data access along the value chain. Therefore, for integrating native data, a reference and an access service are relevant. The data reference needs to point to a communication endpoint that enables an application to retrieve data, e.g., via an HTTP call. This data will be provided as a binary blob. If the application cannot process this data, it needs to be converted into a standardized format by a conversation service of an available submodel.

7.4.2.1 C4 Architecture Model

We describe the realization of our BaSys 4 architecture as a C4 architecture diagram and depict it in Fig. 7.8, which shows AAS reference submodels, the AAS registry referencing AAS, and AAS submodels. All data from AAS, submodels, and the registry is stored in the storage backend and is therefore kept separate. This enables the deployment of AAS, registry, and submodels as containers, as well as the dynamic re-deployment of these components. This, in turn, enables load balancing; allows a submodel to follow the work piece, for example; and makes it possible to implement data preprocessing algorithms close to the data source. Only preprocessed data is added to the storage backend. Applications access AAS, AAS submodels, and the registry though a synchronous, HTTP rest-based API. External data sources, e.g., OPC-UA servers or MQTT providers, are shadowed by the AAS

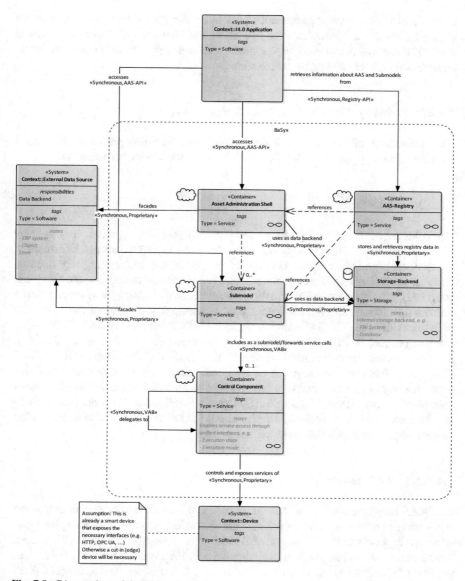

Fig. 7.8 C4 overview of the BaSys 4 architecture

submodels. This means that these provide a unified façade to applications that hide implementation details. Furthermore, the submodels may preprocess data to convert it into a unified format and therefore keep applications independent of characteristic curves of, e.g., sensors. Control components provide a synchronous interface to devices. As many device-specific operations may take considerable time, the control component implements asynchronous semantics. An operation therefore does not wait until the device completes the operation, but changes the control component state. The control component autonomously executes the operation and indicates completion via a change of its device state.

7.4.2.2 Industry 4.0 Infrastructure Components

The realization of the BaSys 4 architecture requires the presence of several infrastructure components. We will detail these components in this section.

7.4.2.2.1 AAS Registry

The AAS registry acts as the central entry point to the AAS system. It is used by I4.0 applications to (1) look up available AAS and (2) retrieve access information, e.g., network endpoints. This concept is similar to the service registry used in classical service-oriented architecture. However, instead of describing only services provided by the different entities in the system, the AAS registry provides additional information about system participants, e.g., semantic descriptions of the asset type or services offered. This information enables I4.0 applications to find entities with specific properties. A service orchestrator, for example, can find all entities that provide specific manufacturing services. The AAS registry maps IDs to AAS descriptors. IDs must be unique in a given context, so they must be either globally unique or, e.g., a combination of a product type and a serial number. The same AAS may be reachable through multiple IDs. Optional additional API functions include an event mechanism to inform listeners about the connection of new assets in the system and about assets that have left the system.

7.4.2.2.2 AAS Server

The AAS servers may be realized on premises or in a private or public cloud. An AAS server hosts AAS and submodels and provides the capability to upload and store AASs persistently at runtime. All AAS data is stored on a storage backend. This guarantees that an AAS is available even in the event of a device failure. To support the realization of an AAS server, an API that enables the handling of AAS on a server, e.g., the upload, deletion, and manipulation of AAS data, has to be provided. In most cases, multiple AAS servers are necessary, e.g., to store product AAS close to manufacturing lines and to reduce network traffic.

7.4.2.2.3   Edge Node

Edge nodes connect devices to the digital process. Edge nodes that provide larger resources may also implement AAS servers and therefore implement AAS and submodels. Smaller edge devices, however, do not need to implement full-featured AAS servers. They may instead natively realize AAS submodels that are created, for example, with one of the Eclipse BaSyx SDKs. This enables smart devices to provide such things as sensor data and digital nameplates.

Edge nodes furthermore enable the retrofitting of existing devices, i.e., the integration of older devices into an I4.0 system. Currently, retrofitting typically focuses on enabling only communication with legacy systems; an example is PLC controllers that use field bus communication [24].

7.4.3   The Service-Based Production Paradigm

Today, the dominant approach for automating a production process is cyclic programs that are executed by PLC controllers. In this approach, every PLC controller executes a cyclic program that implements a part of the manufacturing process. PLC controllers execute the cyclic program that defines input signals, triggers, and output values that control machines to realize a production step. Once the cycle is completed, another product is loaded, and the next cycle starts. MES systems are able to supply parameters, but usually modify the basic cycle execution. Modifying a production process in this case often involves several PLC controllers. As PLC controllers are networked, changes in one controller quickly affect other controllers as well. Complex process changes therefore often yield hard-to-locate side effects that require time for resolving them—time during which the production is halted.

The BaSys digital process (cf. Fig. 7.9) enables a different paradigm, which yields more flexible manufacturing processes. Devices are considered service providers only. They implement callable services that realize individual production steps. Parameters enable the parameterization of these steps. Control components provide a unified interface for selecting and invoking services (the service interface) and for checking whether a service is complete and whether a device is available.

Instead of executing a cyclic production in which every PLC controller executes a cycle and, once this cycle is completed, repeats the cycle, PLC controllers now are service providers. The sequence of services that is executed to create a specific product is controlled by a service orchestrator, which is a specialized control component that controls the invocation and status of dependent control components. Service orchestrators extract the sequence of required services for each manufacturing cell from the product AAS. This way, every product may define an individual recipe—a sequence of process steps—and therefore realize individual production steps that go beyond simple parameter changes. Device AAS specify available services and optional data on cost of operation that may be used to automatically schedule and optimize production steps. Consequently, processes

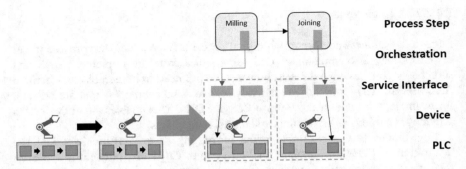

Fig. 7.9 The transition from cycle-based manufacturing to service-based production

are much more flexible with a service-based approach, and small lot sizes can be realized in a better way.

7.4.4 Mapping to RAMI 4.0

In this section, BaSys 4 is characterized according to the three dimensions of RAMI 4.0. For each dimension, a mapping to *no coverage*, *partial coverage*, and *full coverage* is performed. For *partial coverage* and *full coverage*, a reasoning is provided. Additionally, the coverage is visualized based on the RAMI 4.0 visualization.

BaSys 4 covers the following aspects of RAMI 4.0 as visualized in Fig. 7.10:

- Life Cycle and Value Stream:

  – Full coverage through the concept of AAS covering all stages

- Layers:

  – *Functional*: Full coverage through AAS submodels providing formal descriptions
  – *Information*: Full coverage by AAS, submodels, and their API
  – *Communication*: Full coverage by providing I4.0-conformant access to data (i.e., the AAS)
  – *Integration*: Full coverage by providing the VAB for system integration

- Hierarchy Levels:

  – *Connected World*: Partial coverage due to submodels being provided, but lack of integration between factories
  – *Enterprise*: Full coverage by addressing production planning
  – *Field Devices, Control Devices, Stations, and Work Centers*: Full coverage via AAS and their respective submodels as well as through control components

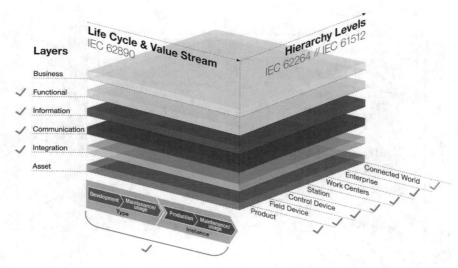

Fig. 7.10 RAMI 4.0 coverage visualization of BaSys 4 (Adapted from [16])

- *Product*: Full coverage through submodels and process BPMN

7.5 Further Reference Architectures

In the following, additional reference architectures will be described. Similar to Sect. 7.4.4, each reference architecture will be classified according to RAMI 4.0.

7.5.1 SITAM

Kassner et al. [25] propose an architecture with a focus on data-driven manufacturing called Stuttgart IT Architecture for Manufacturing (SITAM). The overall setup of the architecture is shown in Fig. 7.11. It covers the complete life cycle of products by addressing processes, physical resources, cyber-physical systems, IT systems, and web data sources. The architecture itself is subdivided into three middlewares: (1) the *integration middleware*, encapsulating resources into services and providing mediation and orchestration capabilities; (2) the *analytics middleware*, providing the means for analyzing (big) data; and (3) the *mobile middleware*, enabling the provision of mobile information.

In the following, each middleware will be described in more detail.

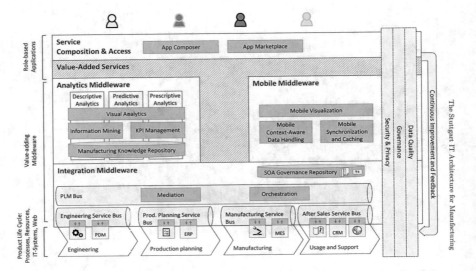

Fig. 7.11 Overview over SITAM [25]

- *Integration Middleware*: The *integration middleware* forms the core layer of SITAM by creating changeable and adaptable integration building on the SOA paradigm. In its core, it leverages hierarchically arranged enterprise service buses (ESB) for specific life cycles. For each phase of the life cycle, there exists an ESB that is responsible for the integration of applications and services within this life cycle. All phase-specific ESBs are integrated using the superordinate product lifecycle management bus. For each phase-specific ESB, SITAM defines a phase-specific data exchange format. Additionally, a dedicated sub-component is provided for real-time capabilities in the manufacturing phase.
- *Analytics Middleware*: This middleware aims to deliver integrative, holistic, and near-real-time analytics. For this purpose, various manufacturing-specific components are provided. For example, it provides (1) the manufacturing knowledge repository used for storing source data and insights; (2) the information mining component providing tooling for data mining and machine learning; as well as (3) support for visual analytics, enabling humans to easily analyze the data.
- *Mobile Middleware*: Here, the provision of mobile information as well as acquisition of mobile data is enabled. Similar to the *analytics middleware*, various components are provided that can be leveraged. It offers (1) the mobile context-aware data handling component, providing manufacturing-specific context models for describing context elements and relations; the (2) mobile synchronization and caching component, supporting offline usage of mobile applications and providing means for determining which data should be cached; and (3) the mobile visualization component, providing tailored visualization schemata.

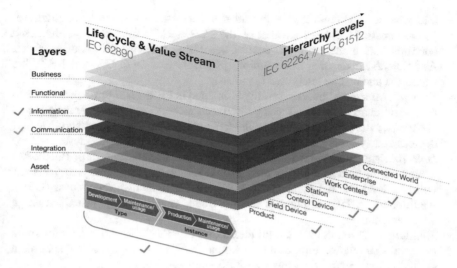

Fig. 7.12 RAMI 4.0 coverage visualization of SITAM (Adapted from [16])

SITAM covers the following aspects of RAMI 4.0 as visualized in Fig. 7.12:

- Life Cycle and Value Stream:
  - Full coverage by providing ESBs for the different life cycle stages
- Layers:
  - *Information:* Full coverage by providing lifecycle-specific data exchange formats
  - *Communication:* Partial coverage by providing unified communication, which is, however, not fully RAMI 4.0 compliant (i.e., does not use AAS)
- Hierarchy Levels:
  - *Enterprise*: Full coverage through integration of ERP via ESB
  - *Work Centers*: Full coverage through integration of MES via ESB
  - *Stations/Control Device*: Full coverage through integration via ESB
  - *Product*: Full coverage through workflow model of product

7.5.2 PERFoRM

The architecture developed in the PERFoRM project aims to enable seamless production system reconfiguration by addressing use cases like plug-and-produce [26]. Its architecture consists of the following components [27]:

- *Middleware*: The middleware provides the necessary core functionalities for communication between entities of the PERFoRM architecture. It defines a common data model with the goal of describing standard data and interfaces. Additionally, it ensures that multiple protocols like OPC UA and REST are supported and can be integrated seamlessly.
- *Standard Interfaces:* Interoperability is enabled in PERFoRM through the utilization of standard interfaces. For the interfaces, a common data model is defined.
- *Technology Adaptors:* The goal of the technology adaptors is to integrate legacy devices and systems like MES or ERP into the PERFoRM architecture.
- *Data Analytics and Visualization:* This component enables users of PERFoRM to analyze the data acquired by means of the middleware to identify, for instance, optimization potential with regard to Overall Equipment Effectiveness (OEE). Additionally, GUI components are provided, enabling easy visualization of acquired data.
- *Simulation:* Through its standard interfaces, PERFoRM enables the integration of various simulation tools and the evaluation of, for example, changes in plant configuration with regard to various KPIs such as OEE.

The PERFoRM architecture is mapped to various use cases [26], e.g., (1) compressor production, (2) micro-electrical vehicle production, (3) microwave oven production, and (4) aerospace component production. Additionally, the architecture was validated in the context of a robot reconfiguration application with a focus on changing robot trajectories [27] as well as in a data mining application with a focus on predicting machine failure [28].

PERFoRM covers the following aspects of RAMI 4.0 as visualized in Fig. 7.13:

- Life Cycle and Value Stream:

  - Partial coverage by providing integration with aspects relevant to the creation of a product instance

- Layers:

  - *Functional*: Full coverage by addressing planning and reconfiguration
  - *Information:* Full coverage by defining data models
  - *Communication:* Partial coverage by providing a unified communication, which is, however, not fully RAMI 4.0 compliant (i.e., does not use AAS)
  - *Integration:* Full coverage by providing data adaptors and interfaces

- Hierarchy Levels:

  - Enterprise: Full coverage through integration of ERP via middleware
  - Work Centers: Full coverage through integration of MES via middleware
  - Stations: Full coverage through integration of SCADA via middleware
  - Control Devices: Full coverage through integration of PLC via middleware
  - Product: Full coverage through workflow model

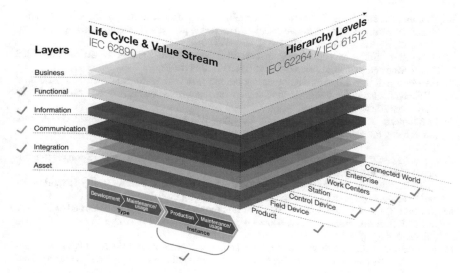

Fig. 7.13 RAMI 4.0 coverage visualization of PERFoRM (Adapted from [16])

7.6 Conclusion

In this chapter, we provided a comprehensive overview of the challenges, concepts, use cases, architecture drivers, and reference architectures of Industry 4.0.

With several use cases as a starting point, we motivated architecture drivers. Next, we introduced RAMI 4.0 and IIRA frameworks for use case and reference architecture classification. Additionally, we described the concept of the digital twin and the Asset Administration Shell as well as the role of the digital twin in Industry 4.0. Finally, we presented several reference architectures for Industry 4.0 and classified them according to RAMI 4.0.

References

1. R. Drath, A. Horch, Industrie 4.0: Hit or hype?[industry forum]. IEEE Ind. Electron. Mag. **8**(2), 56–58 (2014)
2. W. Shen, D.H. Norrie, Agent-based systems for intelligent manufacturing: a state-of-the-art survey. Knowl. Inf. Syst. **1**(2), 129–156 (1999)
3. Roser, Christoph: BWorld Robot Control Software. https://enwikipedia.org/wiki/File:Industry_4.0.png. Last Accessed 13 November 2021
4. International Electrotechnical Commission, *IEC 62264–1 Enterprise-control system integration–Part 1: Models and terminology* (IEC, Genf, 2003)
5. Programmable Controllers—Part 3: Programming Languages, International Electrotechnical Commission, IEC, International Standard IEC61131-3, 2003

6. N. Bauer, R. Huuck, B. Lukoschus, S. Engell, A unifying semantics for sequential function charts, in *Integration of software specification techniques for applications in engineering*, (Springer, Berlin, Heidelberg, 2004), pp. 400–418
7. V. Vyatkin, Software engineering in industrial automation: State-of-the-art review. IEEE Transactions on Industrial Informatics **9**(3), 1234–1249 (2013)
8. Plattform Industrie 4.0, Anwendungsszenarien. https://www.plattform-i40.de/PI40/Redaktion/DE/Downloads/Publikation/fortschreibung-anwendungsszenarien.pdf. Last Accessed 13 November 2021
9. F. Schnicke, T. Kuhn, P.O. Antonino, Enabling industry 4.0 service-oriented architecture through digital twins, in *European Conference on Software Architecture*, (Springer, Cham, 2020)
10. J. Knodel, M. Naab, *Pragmatic evaluation of software architectures*, vol 1 (Springer International Publishing, Cham, 2016)
11. ISO/IEC. Systems and software engineering – Systems and software Quality Requirements and Evaluation (SQuaRE) – System and software quality models. ISO, 2011
12. K. Zhou, T. Liu, L. Zhou, Industry 4.0: Towards future industrial opportunities and challenges, in *2015 12th International conference on fuzzy systems and knowledge discovery (FSKD)*, (IEEE, Zhangjiajie, 2015)
13. F. Schnicke et al., Architecture blueprint enabling distributed digital twins, in *7th Conference on the Engineering of Computer Based Systems*, (Association for Computing Machinery, New York, NY, 2021)
14. P.O. Antonino et al., Blueprints for architecture drivers and architecture solutions for Industry 4.0 shopfloor applications, in *Proceedings of the 13th European Conference on Software Architecture-Volume 2, ECSA '19, 261268*, (Association for Computing Machinery, New York, NY, USA, 2019)
15. H. Koziolek et al., OpenPnP: a plug-and-produce architecture for the industrial internet of things, in *2019 IEEE/ACM 41st International Conference on Software Engineering: Software Engineering in Practice (ICSE-SEIP)*, (IEEE, Montreal, QC, 2019)
16. SPEC, DIN. 91345: 2016-04 Reference Architecture Model Industrie 4.0 (RAMI4. 0). DIN 4 (2016), 2016
17. Industry IoT Consortium, IIRA. https://www.iiconsortium.org/IIRA.htm. Last Accessed 13 November 2021
18. W. Kritzinger et al., Digital Twin in manufacturing: A categorical literature review and classification. IFAC-PapersOnLine **51**(11), 1016–1022 (2018)
19. E. Glaessgen, D. Stargel, The digital twin paradigm for future NASA and U.S. air force vehicles, in Proceedings of the 53rd AIAA/ASME/ASCE/AHS/ASC Structures, Structural Dynamics and Materials Conference (10.2514/6.2012-1818), 2012
20. C. Wagner et al., The role of the Industry 4.0 asset administration shell and the digital twin during the life cycle of a plant, in *2017 22nd IEEE International Conference on Emerging Technologies and Factory Automation (ETFA)*, (IEEE, Cyprus, 2017)
21. Plattform Industrie 4.0, Details of the Asset Administration Shell Part 1. https://www.plattform-i40.de/PI40/Redaktion/EN/Downloads/Publikation/Details-of-the-Asset-Administration-Shell-Part1.html. Last Accessed 13 November 2021
22. Plattform Industrie 4.0, Details of the Asset Administration Shell Part 2. https://www.plattform-i40.de/IP/Redaktion/DE/Downloads/Publikation/Details_of_the_Asset_Administration_Shell_Part_2_V1.html. Last Accessed 13 November 2021
23. T. Kuhn, P.O. Antonino, F. Schnicke, Industrie 4.0 virtual automation bus architecture, in *European Conference on Software Architecture*, (Springer, Cham, 2020)
24. T. Lins et al., Industry 4.0 retrofitting, in *2018 VIII Brazilian Symposium on Computing Systems Engineering (SBESC)*, (IEEE, Salvador, 2018)
25. L. Kassner, C. Gröger, J. Königsberger, E. Hoos, C. Kie-fer, C. Weber, S. Silcher, B. Mitschang, The Stuttgart IT architecture for manufacturing. An architecture for the data-driven factory, in *Enterprise Information Systems (ICEIS) 2016. Revised selected papers*, (Springer, Cham,

2017)
26. P. Leitão et al., Instantiating the PERFORM system architecture for industrial case studies, in *International workshop on service orientation in holonic and multi-agent manufacturing*, (Springer, Cham, 2016)
27. N. Chakravorti et al., Validation of PERFoRM reference architecture demonstrating an automatic robot reconfiguration application, in *2017 IEEE 15th International Conference on Industrial Informatics (INDIN)*, (IEEE, Emden, 2017)
28. N. Chakravorti et al., Validation of PERFoRM reference architecture demonstrating an application of data mining for predicting machine failure. Procedia CIRP **72**, 1339–1344 (2018)

Chapter 8
Domain-Independent Reference Architectures and Standards

Silverio Martínez-Fernández, Xavier Franch, and Claudia Ayala

Abstract To remain competitive, organizations are challenged to make informed design decisions in order to construct software systems with similar architectural needs. They use reference architectures to achieve interoperability of (parts of) their software, standardization of software systems among multiple actors, and faster development with templates and guidelines for designing. In this chapter, we give an overview of domain-independent reference architectures and standards available in the gray literature for practitioners, classified by technology (cloud computing, big data, Internet of Things, and artificial intelligence) and analyzed based on their characteristics (e.g., purpose and contents). The discussed reference architectures are either published by standardization organizations such as ISO/IEC and NIST or fostered by large companies such as Microsoft and IBM.

8.1 Introduction to Reference Architectures and Standards in Industry

Reference architectures (RAs) provide battle-proven (and often generic) design solutions (including generic artifacts, architectural styles, and domain vocabulary) for systems in a particular business domain or technology areas [5]. They include best practices or standards, design guidelines, and sometimes even partial implementations [15]. In this sense, RAs are a blueprint for system development and can act as a foundation for designing a concrete (and more refined and detailed) architecture for a particular system. This allows improvement of the interoperability of the software systems by establishing a standard solution and common mechanisms for information exchange; reduction of the development costs of software projects through the reuse of common assets that worked well in the past; and improvement of the communication inside the organization because

S. Martínez-Fernández (✉) · X. Franch · C. Ayala
Universitat Politècnica de Catalunya—BarcelonaTech, Barcelona, Spain
e-mail: silverio.martinez@upc.edu; xavier.franch@upc.edu; cayala@essi.upc.edu

© The Author(s), under exclusive license to Springer Nature Switzerland AG 2023　　　181
E. Y. Nakagawa, P. Oliveira Antonino (eds.), *Reference Architectures for Critical Domains*, https://doi.org/10.1007/978-3-031-16957-1_8

stakeholders share the same architectural mindset [10]. However, it also influences the learning curve of developers due to the need of learning its features.

In the previous chapters of this book, we have seen RAs for specific critical business domains, like avionics and automotive. Contrasting with the focus of the previous chapters, in this chapter, we present domain-independent RAs and standards that mostly focus on technological areas such as cloud computing, big data, Internet of Things (IoT), and artificial intelligence (AI). These RAs could be a great support to the realization of business domain-dependent RAs by reusing knowledge.

8.1.1   Motivation and Research Goal

RAs from peer-reviewed papers have been already the object of study in existing secondary studies [6]. However, the analysis of gray literature on RAs in industry is scarce [6]. Therefore, this chapter covers this gap by analyzing RAs created and adopted in industry for diverse technological areas. The goal of this chapter is twofold:

- To collect RAs from standardization organizations and large companies for relevant technological areas such as cloud computing, big data, IoT, and AI-based systems.
- To support the construction of business domain architectures by analyzing, customizing, and instantiating the RAs for the aforementioned technological areas.

8.1.2   Research Methodology

To reach our goal, we focused on RAs for key technological areas which have become widely adopted by the software industry in the last years. We searched such RAs in two types of gray literature sources with either high expertise or high outlet control. Expertise is the extent to which the authority and knowledge of the producer of the content can be determined. Outlet control is the extent to which content is produced, moderated, or edited in conformance with explicit and transparent knowledge-creation criteria [7]. Therefore, we targeted RAs published by either (i) standardization organizations (high expertise) or (ii) large companies (high outlet control).

Regarding standardization organizations, we selected five well-known ones:

- The National Institute of Standards and Technology (NIST).[1] It was funded in 1901 as physical sciences laboratory and non-regulatory agency in the US Department of Commerce. Its activities embrace a number of physical and engineering disciplines, information technology among them.
- The International Organization for Standardization (ISO).[2] It is an international standard-setting body composed of representatives from various national standards organizations. Founded on February 23, 1947, the organization promotes worldwide proprietary, industrial, and commercial standards.
- The Object Management Group (OMG).[3] It is a computer industry standards consortium. OMG Task Forces develop enterprise integration standards for a range of technologies.
- The International Telecommunication Union (ITU).[4] It is a specialized agency of the United Nations responsible for all matters related to information and communications technologies. It was established in 1865.
- The European Telecommunications Standards Institute (ETSI).[5] It is an independent, not-for-profit, standardization organization in the field of information and communications. ETSI supports the development and testing of global technical standards for ICT-enabled systems, applications, and services.

Regarding large companies, we considered companies such as Microsoft, IBM, and Oracle, due to their relevant impact on the software practices worldwide. Furthermore, large companies usually share RAs due to their high amount of employees and hence standardization needs within the company, as well as with stakeholders using their software tools.

8.1.3 Structure of the Chapter

The rest of this chapter gives an overview of popular RAs from diverse technological areas might potentially influence and support the realization of domain-dependent RAs (as those related in the previous chapters of this book). The approached areas are cloud computing (see Sect. 8.2), big data (see Sect. 8.3), IoT (see Sect. 8.4), and AI-based systems (see Sect. 8.5). Finally, Sect. 8.6 concludes the chapter.

---

[1] NIST website: https://www.nist.gov/.

[2] ISO website: https://www.iso.org/home.html.

[3] OMG website: https://www.omg.org/.

[4] ITU website: https://www.itu.int.

[5] ETSI website: https://www.etsi.org/.

8.2   Cloud Computing

NIST defines *cloud computing* as "a model for enabling ubiquitous, convenient, on-demand network access to a shared pool of configurable computing resources (e.g., networks, servers, storage, applications, and services) that can be rapidly provisioned and released with minimal management effort or service provider interaction" [12]. This paradigm is mainly characterized by its *service models* and *deployment models*. Traditional service models are software as a service (SaaS), platform as a service (PaaS), and infrastructure as a service (IaaS), but countless new models have emerged and are emerging over time, e.g., blockchain as a service or machine learning as a service (see Sect. 8.5). The main deployment models are private cloud, community cloud, public cloud, and hybrid cloud. Major players in the IT market, such as Microsoft, IBM, Google, and many others, have become *cloud service providers* covering one or more of these service and deployment models. All of these aspects and many others, e.g., on-demand self-service, broad network access, resource pooling, rapid elasticity, and measured service, need to be considered in RAs for cloud computing. In the following, we present two widespread RAs for cloud computing.

8.2.1   NIST Cloud Computing Reference Architecture

In 2011, NIST proposed an RA for cloud computing [9]. Its main planned purpose is to facilitate the understanding of the operational intricacies in cloud computing. Its main characteristics are:

- It separates two delivered assets: the RA itself and a taxonomy that structures and defines the concepts presented in the RA.
- The two assets follow a layered structure, with actors as the main concept, then activities related to actors, and components and sub-components to perform the activities.
- The RA defines five types of actors: consumer, provider, broker, auditor, and carrier. The broker manages the use, performance, and delivery of cloud services, while the carrier is an intermediary that provides connectivity and transport of cloud services from the producer to the consumer.
- Service models (SaaS, PaaS, and IaaS) are contextualized in a generic stack, relying upon a layer of resource abstraction and control, and further onto a physical resource layer.
- Deployment models are basically those mentioned above. Private and community clouds are sub-classified into on-site or outsourced, depending on the organization that hosts the cloud.
- A portfolio of service-related functions conform the cloud service management, which is described from three different perspectives: business support (e.g.,

contract management and pricing), provisioning and configuration (e.g., metering and SLA management), and portability and interoperability.

- Last, security and privacy are identified as crucial cross-cutting aspects and included in the RA explicitly.

8.2.2   ISO/IEC Cloud Computing Reference Architecture

In 2014, ISO/IEC proposed an RA for cloud computing in the form of the standard ISO/IEC 17789:2014 [17]. Its main characteristics are:

- The RA distinguishes four viewpoints for a cloud computing architecture: user view, functional view, implementation view, and deployment view. The first two are covered by the standard, while the latter two are considered vendor-specific and then left out of the proposal.
- The user view includes several inter-related entities already present in the NIST standard, as roles (similar to actors), service models, and deployment models. While the ISO/IEC standard offers less roles than NIST, it decomposes them into up to 15 sub-roles providing a rich role structure. In fact, NIST roles of auditor and broker are sub-roles of cloud service partner in ISO/IEC 17789. Each sub-role has associated a number of activities, up to 41.
- The functional view proposes a functional four-layer structure (user, access, service, and resource) combined with multi-layer functions (development support, integration, security, operational support, and business support). The layers embed RA components, up to 35.
- At a higher level, both views are related with a mapping from the user view to the functional view. Also, they are related to common cross-cutting aspects as governance, auditability, and quality concerns (availability, security, etc.).
- More interestingly, the standard contains a fully detailed mapping reconciling the sub-roles, activities, and components providing a holistic view to the RA.

8.2.3   Analysis for Cloud Computing RAs

Table 8.1 summarizes the main similarities and differences among these two architectures as reported in the two previous subsections.

8.3   Big Data

NIST defines *big data engineering* as "advanced techniques that harness independent resources for building scalable data systems when the characteristics of the datasets require new architectures for efficient storage, manipulation, and analysis"

Table 8.1 Comparison of concepts among NIST and ISO/IEC RAs for cloud computing

Concept	NIST RA for cloud computing	ISO/IEC 17789:2014
Structuring concept	Layered structure	Viewpoints
Roles	Consumer. Provider. Broker. Auditor. Carrier	Customer. Provider. Partner. Two layers of roles
Service models	IaaS. PaaS. SaaS	IaaS. PaaS. SaaS. NaaS
Deployment models	Public. Private (on-site, outsourced). Community (on-site, outsourced). Hybrid	Public. Private. Community. Hybrid
Functional view	Service-related functions over three perspectives	Multi-layer functions over four layers

[2]. There are many RAs for big data, such as Lambda, Kappa, and Bolster [14]. In this subsection, we focus on three RAs for big data, respectively, proposed by NIST, OMG, and ISO/IEC.

8.3.1 NIST Big Data Reference Architecture (NBDRA)

In 2018, NIST proposed an RA for big data (NBDRA). Its main purpose is to develop consensus on fundamental concepts related to big data [2], such as providing a common language for the various stakeholders, encouraging adherence to common standards, and providing a technical reference for US government departments. It comprises three main assets:

- *A conceptual model.* It is a vendor- and technology-agnostic conceptual model for big data systems. In the conceptual model, big data systems are comprised of logical functional components connected by interoperability interfaces (i.e., services). The conceptual model is organized along two axes representing the two big data value chains: Information Value (horizontal axis) and Information Technology (vertical axis). Along the Information Value axis, the value is created by data collection, integration, analysis, and applying the results following the value chain. Along the IT axis, the value is created by providing networking, infrastructure, platforms, application tools, and other IT services for hosting of and operating the big data in support of required data applications.
- *The activities view.* It examines the activities carried out by the NBDRA roles, which are mainly five: system orchestrator, data provider, big data application provider, big data framework provider, and data consumer.
- *The functional component view.* It defines and describes the functional components (e.g., software, hardware, people, organizations) that perform the various activities outlined in the activities view. Two fabrics (management and security and privacy) envelop the components, representing the interwoven nature of management and security and privacy with all the components.

The purpose of the views (activities and functional components) is to provide the system architect with a framework to efficiently categorize the activities that the big data system will perform and the functional components which must be integrated to perform those activities. During the design process, the architect is encouraged to closely collaborate with the system stakeholders to ensure that all required activities for the big data system are captured in the activities view. Then, those activities should be mapped to functional components within such activity view using a traceability matrix.

8.3.2 Cloud Customer Architecture for Big Data and Analytics

In 2017, the Cloud Standards Customer Council by the OMG released a well-tested RA for big data and analytics in a hybrid cloud environment [16]. The goal is to provide guidance to enterprises to understand proven architecture patterns that have been deployed in numerous successful enterprise projects. The RA is described in terms of the components of its three main layers, which are:

- *Public Network Components.* The public network includes cloud users, SaaS applications, data sources, and edge services.
- *Provider Cloud Components.* The provider cloud represents the cloud-based analytics solution. It hosts components to prepare data for analytics, store data, run analytical systems, and process the results of those systems. Provider cloud elements offer API management, streaming computing, cognitive assisted data integration, data repositories, cognitive analytics discovery and exploration, cognitive actionable analytics, SaaS applications, and transformation and connectivity.
- *Enterprise Network.* The enterprise network is where the on-premises systems and users are located: users, applications, data, and user directory.

8.3.3 ISO/IEC 20547-3:2020(E): Big Data Reference Architecture

The ISO/IEC 20547 series are intended to provide users with a standardized approach to develop and implement big data architectures and provide references for systems. In 2020, an overview of the RA and a process for instantiating the RA to design the software architecture of a big data system were released [20]. The key goal of this RA is to facilitate a shared understanding across multiple products, organizations, and disciplines about current architectures and future direction. It has three main elements:

Table 8.2 Analysis of big data RAs

Concept	NIST NBDRA	OMG big data RA	ISO/IEC 20547
Purpose	Standardization (governmental)	Facilitation	Standardization
Context	Single organization (US government departments)	Multiple organizations	Multiple organizations
Roles	Technical: system orchestrator, data provider, big data application provider, big data framework provider, and data consumer. Fabric: management, security, and privacy	Enterprise user, cloud user (knowledge worker and citizen analyst, data scientist, application developer, data engineer, chief data officer)	Technical: big data application provider, big data framework provider, big data service partner, big data provider, big data consumer. Others: general, security and privacy, management, data governance

- Related concepts to the Big Data Reference Architecture (BDRA).
- A *user* view defining roles/sub-roles, their relationships, and types of activities within a big data ecosystem.
- A *functional* view defining the architectural layers and the classes of functional components within those layers that implement the activities of the roles/sub-roles within the user view.

The user and functional views of the RA can be used by software architects to describe big data systems. The RA is vendor agnostic and does not define prescriptive solutions that inhibit innovation.

8.3.4 Analysis of Big Data RAs

Table 8.2 summarizes the main differences of the aforementioned big data RAs. These three RAs are vendor agnostic and do not represent concrete software architectures of big data systems, but tools to describe and design them. It must be noted that all of them support to some extent cloud providers or subsystems.

8.4 Internet of Things (IoT)

An official definition of IoT defines it as "an infrastructure of interconnected entities, people, systems and information resources together with services which process and react to information from the physical world and from the virtual world" [18]. IoT devices and systems have become crucial aspects of modern life in domestic, healthcare, agricultural, and industrial sectors. Actually, any technology prefixed with smart is likely to be part of the rapidly growing IoT family, for example, smart meters, smart cars, smart cards, smart fitness trackers, smart cities, smartphones, smart watches, smart utilities, smart agriculture, smart healthcare, and even smart manufacturing, said to be the next industrial revolution [19].

The benefits of IoT are numerous as to make us more connected, knowledgeable, efficient, effective, and less wasteful. But if handled incorrectly, it can make our computer networks and our data less secure and lacking resilience. Therefore, standards are required to deal with interoperability and security challenges of IoT as well as the usual maintainability and sustainability ones [22].

Academia, industry leaders, and dedicated societies have been active during the last decades to deal with IoT issues and to agree on standards that allow the successful adoption of IoT technologies. Some examples of consolidated efforts from standardization bodies and industrial communities for the development of IoT are detailed below.

8.4.1   ISO/IEC 30141:2018: Internet of Things (IoT)—Reference Architecture

In 2018, ISO, together with the International Electrotechnical Commission (IEC), published ISO/IEC 30141 [18], a standard reference architecture for IoT. The key goal of this reference architecture is to establish common ground regarding IoT in order to make it more effective, safer, resilient, interoperable, and much more secure by facilitating the complex assemblage of billions of smart devices connected through the Internet.

The ISO/IEC 301401 standard is aimed to serve as a base from which to develop (specify) context-specific IoT architectures and hence actual systems. The context can be of different kinds but shall include the business context, the regulatory context, and the technological contexts (e.g., industry verticals, technological requirements, and/or nation-specific requirement sets).

The ISO/IEC 30141 was conceived to provide a foundation and reference framework for the many applicable standards produced by the working group ISO/IEC JTC 1/SC 41 on Internet of Things and related technologies. The ISO/IEC 30141 standard provides the RA for resilience, safety, and security. At the same time, as the Internet of Things continues to evolve and grow, nine further standards for the IoT, to provide for increasing trustworthiness, interoperability, security, and technical specifications, are being developed.

The IoT RA represented in the ISO/IEC 301401 standard describes generic IoT system characteristics and a conceptual model. This allows the definition of a reference model consisting of a number of architectural views aligned with the architecture descriptions defined in ISO/IEC/IEEE 42010.

The main elements of the ISO/IEC 301401 standard are based on a common vocabulary, reusable designs, and industry best practice and define:

- Physical Entities ("things") that need to be connected with IT systems through networks.
- Electronic devices that interact with the physical world such as sensors and actuators. The first ones collect the information about the physical world, while the second ones can act upon Physical Entities. Both sensors and actuators can be in many forms such as thermometers, accelerometers, video cameras, microphones, relays, heaters, or industrial equipment for manufacturing or process controlling.
- Technologies for gathering and processing data such as mobile technologies, cloud computing, big data, and deep analytics used to achieve the final result of controlling Physical Entities by providing contextual, real-time, and predictive information which has an impact on physical and virtual entities [18].

The high-level view of the key IoT concepts contained in the conceptual model of the standard, their relationships, and their interactions can be consulted at [18].

8.4.2   IEEE 2413-2019: IEEE Standard for an Architectural Framework for the Internet of Things

IEEE has also recognized the value of the IoT to industry and the benefits this technology brings to the public. Among the diverse standardization efforts related to diverse IoT aspects (e.g., harmonization and security and sensor performance and quality), they established since 2014 the working group P2413. This group released in 2019 the IEEE 2413-2019—IEEE Standard for an Architectural Framework for the Internet of Things.[6]

An architectural framework is the collection of viewpoints that frame the concerns of an identified group of stakeholders.[7] The standard aims to address the IoT stakeholder concerns to help them build a connected world that can interoperate while meeting both the needs of enterprises and society for the trustworthiness of IoT systems. The adoption of a unified approach to the development of IoT systems will reduce industry fragmentation and create critical mass of multi-stakeholder activities around the world. So, this standard aims to promote cross-domain interaction and aid system interoperability and functional compatibility.

The standard provides a conceptual basis for the notion of things in the IoT, by providing definitions based on IoT domain abstractions from the identification of commonalities from different IoT domains. Six representative domains were

---

[6] https://standards.ieee.org/content/ieee-standards/en/standard/2413-2019.html.

[7] ISO/IEC/IEEE 42010:2011. Systems and software engineering—Architecture description 2011. http://www.iso.org/iso/catalogue_detail.htm?csnumber=50508.

considered: smart manufacturing, smart grid, smart buildings, intelligent transport, smart cities, and healthcare. The six domains were examined with reference to the aspects and concerns of cyber-physical systems identified in,[8] and the outcomes of that process were used to motivate the architecture viewpoints. Thus, the standard presents shared concerns of these IoT domains as a collection of architecture viewpoints. In addition, the standard suggests an architecture development process.

The main motivation of the standard is to provide a framework for:

- Vendors to build conformant, interoperable, secure IoT systems that can span multiple application domains.
- Buyers to make comparisons and assessments of such systems.
- System designers to accelerate design, implementation, and deployment processes for such systems.

This standard is the basis of other IoT-related standards further in specific domains:

- P2413.1—Standard for a Reference Architecture for Smart City (RASC).[9] It provides an architectural blueprint for smart city implementation leveraging cross-domain interaction and semantic interoperability among various domains and components of a smart city.
- P2413.2—Standard for a Reference Architecture for Power Distribution IoT (PDIoT).[10] This standard provides an architectural blueprint for the development of the Power Distribution IoT (PDIoT) engaging various domains and stakeholders, including cloud computing, IoT, and legacy grid systems, and promoting integration and interoperability among various components of electric power grid.

8.4.3 Industrial Internet Reference Architecture: IIRA

The Industrial Internet Reference Architecture (IIRA) for Industrial Internet of Things (IIoT) systems has been designed by the Industrial Internet Consortium (IIC). It was first published in 2015, and its latest release was in 2019.[11]

The IIRA is not a standard, but it is based on the Industrial Internet Architecture Framework (IIAF) that is based on the ISO/IEC/IEEE 42010:2011 standard. The IIAF framework is required to handle the system complexity and helps to identify and classify stakeholder concerns into appropriate categories that allow systematic evaluation of the systems and the necessary resolution to architect

---

[8] NIST SP 1500-201, Framework for Cyber-Physical Systems, Volume 1, Overview, June 2017.

[9] https://standards.ieee.org/project/2413_1.html.

[10] https://standards.ieee.org/project/2413_2.html.

[11] Industrial Internet Consortium. The Industrial Internet of Things Volume G1: Reference Architecture. Version 1.9. June 19, 2019.

and build such systems. The IIAF identifies conventions, principles, and practices for consistent description of IIoT architectures. This standard-based architecture framework facilitates easier evaluation and systematic and effective resolution of stakeholder concerns. It serves as a valuable resource to guide the development documentation and communication of the IIRA.

Thus, the IIRA uses a common vocabulary and a standard-based framework to describe business, usage, functional, and implementation viewpoints. The architecture description and representation are generic and at a high level of abstraction to support the goal of broad industry applicability. Its main goals are:

- To serve as an architectural template and methodology to support system architects to design their own systems based on a common framework and concepts.
- To assist in achieving a common understanding and communication of the overall system among its diverse stakeholders, which will aid in system deployment and significantly enhance system interoperability across industrial sectors.
- To map applicable technologies and to guide technology and standard development driven by broad industry applicability and interoperability.

Furthermore, the conception and evolution of the IIRA are based on distilling and abstracting common characteristics, features, and patterns from use cases defined in the IIC and elsewhere. It is refined and revised continually as feedback is gathered from its application in the testbeds developed in IIC as well as real-world deployment of IIoT systems.

The IIRA first identifies and highlights the most important architectural concerns commonly found in IIoT systems across industrial sectors and classifies them into viewpoints along with their respective stakeholders. It then describes, analyzes, and, where appropriate, provides guidance to resolve these concerns in these viewpoints, resulting in a certain abstract architecture representation. The key constructs of the IIRA, as presented in the official documentation, are stakeholders, concerns, viewpoints, and model kinds.

The IIRA, through its viewpoints, provides guidance to system lifecycle processes from IIoT system conception to design and implementation. Its viewpoints offer a framework to system designers to think iteratively through important common architectural issues in IIoT system creation. It also suggests some common approaches (concepts and models) as views in each of these viewpoints to aid the identification and resolution of important architectural issues. It is not a description of a system lifecycle process, which varies from one industrial sector to another. Rather, the IIRA is an architectural framework and methodology for system conceptualization and architecture highlighting important system concerns that may affect lifecycle process.

8.4.4   Analysis of IoT RAs

We have seen some examples of the diverse efforts to support the conception, design, and evolution of IoT systems: from standardization bodies such as ISO/IEC/IEEE to industry alliances, where the IIC is a very prominent example. In IIC, a large number of actors from different parts of the ecosystem and industry sectors come together to define common best practices on how to build IIoT.

The diversity of approaches to IoT emphasizes the need to correctly position IoT standardization and existing global initiatives such as IIC to promote encouraging results. In the IoT Reference Architectures presented in this book, the use of standards such as ISO/IEC/IEEE 42010:2011 as a reference made the interoperability of the diverse approaches easier.

In addition, the focus on the horizontal systems approach rather than application-specific silos confirms the broad nature of IoT. It is a key approach for IoT solutions to achieve openness, multipurpose, and innovation. It has profound implications on both the technology and business perspectives and offers opportunities and challenges that should be faced by properly evolving the presented IoT Reference Architectures [21].

8.5   Artificial Intelligence- and Machine Learning-Based Systems

AI-based systems are defined by the expert group on AI of the European Commission as either "purely software-based, acting in the virtual world (e.g. voice assistants, image analysis software, search engines, speech and face recognition systems)" or AI that "can be embedded in hardware devices (e.g. advanced robots, autonomous cars, drones or IoT applications)".[12] The emergence of AI-based systems in the last 3 years has triggered the need for software design assets including RAs [11]. In the following subsections, we describe proposals of recommendations for diverse AI technological areas (namely, smart sustainable cities, augmented reality, and packaging and sharing AI and machine learning models as reusable microservices), as well as workflows from large companies, such as Microsoft and IBM.

---

[12] https://ec.europa.eu/digital-single-market/en/news/definition-artificial-intelligence-main-capabilities-and-scientific-disciplines.

8.5.1 ITU-T Y.4470: Reference Architecture of Artificial Intelligence Service Exposure for Smart Sustainable Cities

In 2020, the ITU-T published the recommendation Y.4470 consisting of an RA aiming at establishing AI service exposure for smart sustainable cities [8]. This RA has the following characteristics:

- Usage of capabilities provided by the underlying smart city infrastructures (such as networks, clouds, big data, and security).
- Three groups of logical functional components: (i) AI model training and data management, (ii) supplying AI capabilities (AI model management, AI policy management, AI capability management, AI capability performer, and multiple AI models and AI model agents), and (iii) resource and task management.
- Six reference points to interact with external AI services and smart sustainable cities services.

8.5.2 ETSI GS ARF 003: Augmented Reality Framework Architecture

In 2020, ETSI published an RA supporting augmented reality [4]. The RA structures an augmented reality system in three layers: (i) hardware layer (tracking sensors, processing units, and rendering interfaces); (ii) software layer (vision engine and 3D rendering engine); and (iii) data layer (world knowledge and interactive contents).

Furthermore, the specification of the RA includes details for the functional architecture addressing fully embedded augmented reality systems and implementations over IP networks in a scalable manner. It shows six informative use case implementation samples, by mapping the use cases components to the RA infrastructure and functional architecture. The RA gives support to interoperability requirements for augmented reality components, systems, and services.

8.5.3 Acumos and the AI4EU Platform

In 2018, as part of the European Project AI4EU, the Athena version of the Acumos AI RA was released. It aims at making easy to build, share, and deploy AI-based systems and operates the Acumos portals that enable those capabilities. It standardizes the infrastructure stack and components required to run an out-of-the-box general AI environment. This implies advantages such as allowing data scientists and model trainers to focus on their core competencies: development, training, and deployment of AI models.

The Acumos RA has four main high-level capabilities to build, share, deploy, and operate AI and machine learning models and solutions The Acumos RA has four types of components:

- Core Components: the Portal Frontend, to discover, explore, and use AI models; the model onboarding components, to ingest AI and machine learning models in the Acumos platform; the design studio, to create composite solutions out of basic building blocks (e.g., models); the deployment components, to enable users to launch models and solutions in various run-time environments such as Azure, OpenStack, Kubernetes, and docker; and the catalog and data model and data management.
- Supplemental Components: these components are integrated from upstream projects, in some cases packaged as Acumos images, and provide supplemental/optional support functions for the platform.
- Platform Dependency: upstream components required to support key platform functions such as relational database and docker image creation.
- External Dependency: external systems and services required for the related Acumos functions to be fully usable.

The documentation of the RA is being updated on [1], as the AI4EU project is still under development at the time of writing this chapter.

8.5.4 AI Workflow Proposals from Large Companies

Microsoft's RAs are arranged by scenarios [13]. Each RA includes open-source practices, along with considerations for scalability, availability, manageability, and security. Two examples of RAs showing machine learning scenarios in Azure are batch scoring for deep learning models and real-time scoring of Python models [13].

In 2019, IBM proposed the "Analytics and AI reference architecture." It consists of a flow of activities to develop the model and continuously improve it over time, while the intelligent application is running in production from its collection to its analysis. Indeed, it distinguishes four activities: collect, organize, analyze, and infuse. The two former activities are related to building a predictive model, evaluating data in catalogs and data collections, curating or enhancing the data, and deploying the model. The two latter activities consist of the iterative process of monitoring the deployed model for performance and fairness, interpreting predictions and taking the next best action, and retraining the model in response to skews or bias. Regarding tool support, IBM offers IBM Watson Studio. As noted in the documentation, this RA considers the following key non-functional requirements: performance, stability, maintainability, security, scalability, privacy regulations, and compliance.

8.5.5 Analysis of AI-Based System RAs

AI-based systems have gained an enormous popularity in the last years [11]. As a consequence, several recommendations and platforms including RAs have been published from 2018 onward. Despite being an emerging domain, some of these RAs achieve a high level of maturity, including use case examples in the case of ETSI and tools to support AI model creation and sharing with the Acumos platform. Developers can find useful the aforementioned RAs for creating AI-based systems. While the ITU and ETSI recommendations establish clear building blocks for specific technology areas such as smart sustainable cities and augmented reality, the Acumos platform and RAs from large companies offer support to create diverse types of AI-based systems. All RAs share patterns from service orientation, like the use of reference points, allowing the RAs to aggregate external abilities among functions.

Still, in the upcoming years, there will be more standards for AI-based systems. For instance, ISO/IEC has a few related standards currently under development, such as guidelines for AI-based applications (AWI 5339) and an RA for knowledge engineering (AWI 5392).

Another characteristic is how these RAs aim at being technology agnostic. For instance, ITU claims to be just a recommendation (facilitation rather than standardization), and the Acumos platform offers diverse platforms where to deploy AI-based services.

8.6 Final Remarks

Reference architectures (RAs) are a great asset for knowledge reuse in software systems with a shared domain. In this chapter, we have analyzed existing RAs for relevant technological areas such as cloud computing, big data, IoT, and AI-based systems. They are published by standardization organizations and large companies. In their majority, these RAs follow several many good practices for their sustainability [3]: describing many elements of the ISO/IEC/IEEE 42010 standard (e.g., views and stakeholders), being in repositories with original documents, keeping change history, and being updated with new parts. Being used and published by standardization organizations and large companies, the discussed RAs provide an authoritative source of information about technological areas that could guide and constrain the design and instantiation of multiple architectures and solutions in specific business domains.

Acknowledgments This work has been partially funded by the "Beatriz Galindo" Spanish Program BEAGAL18/00064 and by the DOGO4ML Spanish research project (ref. PID2020-117191RB-I00).

References

1. Acumos: Acumos documentation (2021). https://docs.acumos.org/en/latest/index.html
2. W.L. Chang, D. Boyd, NIST Big Data Interoperability Framework: Volume 6, Big Data Reference Architecture [Version 2]. Special Publication (NIST SP)—1500-6 Version 2 (2018)
3. P.H. Dias Valle, L. Garcés, T. Volpato, S. Martínez-Fernández, E.Y. Nakagawa, Towards suitable description of reference architectures. PeerJ Computer Science **7**, e392 (2021)
4. *ETSI: Augmented Reality Framework (ARF); AR framework architecture* (2020)
5. M. Galster, S. Angelov, S. Martínez-Fernández, D. Tofan, Reference architectures and scrum: friends or foes? in *Proceedings of the 2017 11th Joint Meeting on Foundations of Software Engineering* (2017), pp. 896–901
6. L. Garcés, S. Martínez-Fernández, L. Oliveira, P. Valle, C. Ayala, X. Franch, E.Y. Nakagawa, Three decades of software reference architectures: A systematic mapping study. J. Syst. Softw. **179**, 111004 (2021). https://doi.org/10.1016/j.jss.2021.111004. https://www.sciencedirect.com/science/article/pii/S0164121221001011
7. V. Garousi, M. Felderer, M.V. Mäntylä, A. Rainer, Benefitting from the grey literature in software engineering research, in *Contemporary Empirical Methods in Software Engineering* (Springer, Berlin, 2020), pp. 385–413
8. ITU-T Recommendations: Reference Architecture of Artificial Intelligence Service Exposure for Smart Sustainable Cities (2020)
9. F. Liu, J. Tong, J. Mao, R. Bohn, J. Messina, L. Badger, D. Leaf, NIST Cloud Computing Reference Architecture. Special Publication 500–292 (2011)
10. S. Martinez-Fernandez, P.S.M. Dos Santos, C.P. Ayala, X. Franch, G.H. Travassos, Aggregating empirical evidence about the benefits and drawbacks of software reference architectures, in *2015 ACM/IEEE International Symposium on Empirical Software Engineering and Measurement (ESEM)* (IEEE, New York, 2015), pp. 1–10
11. S. Martínez-Fernández, J. Bogner, X. Franch, M. Oriol, J. Siebert, A. Trendowicz, A.M. Vollmer, S. Wagner, Software Engineering for AI-Based Systems: A Survey. ACM Trans. Softw. Eng. Methodol. **31**(2) (2022). https://doi.org/10.1145/3487043
12. P. Mell, T. Grance, The NIST Definition of Cloud Computing. Special Publication 800–145 (2011)
13. Microsoft: GitHub - microsoft/AI: Microsoft AI. https://github.com/microsoft/AI#ai200---reference-architectures-
14. S. Nadal, V. Herrero, O. Romero, A. Abelló, X. Franch, S. Vansummeren, D. Valerio, A software reference architecture for semantic-aware big data systems. Inf. Softw. Technol. **90**, 75–92 (2017)
15. E.Y. Nakagawa, P.O. Antonino, M. Becker, Reference architecture and product line architecture: A subtle but critical difference, in *European Conference on Software Architecture* (Springer, New York, 2011), pp. 207–211
16. OMG Cloud Working Group: Cloud customer architecture for big data and analytics (2017). https://www.omg.org/cloud/deliverables/cloud-customer-architecture-for-big-data-and-analytics.htm
17. The International Standards Organization: International Standard ISO/IEC 17789. Information Technology—Cloud Computing—Reference Architecture (2014)
18. The International Standards Organization: ISO/IEC 30141:2018(en) internet of things (Iot)—reference architecture (2018)
19. The International Standards Organization. Rick Gould: Architecting a connected future (2019)
20. The International Standards Organization: ISO/IEC 20547-3: Information Technology—Big Data Reference Architecture (2020)
21. V. Tsiatsis, S. Karnouskos, J. Holler, D. Boyle, C. Mulligan, *Internet of Things: Technologies and Applications for a New Age of Intelligence* (Academic Press, New York, 2018)
22. M. Weyrich, C. Ebert, Reference architectures for the internet of things. IEEE Softw. **33**(1), 112–116 (2015)

Chapter 9
Future Advances in Reference Architectures

Elisa Yumi Nakagawa, Pablo Oliveira Antonino, Matthias Galster, and Thomas Kuhn

Abstract The research area of reference architecture will continuously evolve, offering means to increasingly consolidate reference architectures as one of the most relevant reusable artifacts of well-consolidated architectural knowledge and experience. Moreover, existing reference architectures must also continually evolve according to the evolving nature of the different domains where they contribute. New classes of innovative systems with particular characteristics and new technologies (some of which could drastically change the structure of software architectures) will undoubtedly impact the design and evolution of reference architectures. This chapter discusses the main research directions to be taken by reference architectures that will also require a good alignment of efforts from the academic community and industry.

9.1 Perspectives for Future Work

Microservices, cloud computing, IoT, CoT, data science, blockchain, and even mobile apps are mainstream nowadays. Each has its own remarkable benefits and serves as the basis for the development of a considerable number of software-intensive systems. These systems are sometimes *complex* (in terms of complicated business rules and interconnected features), *distributed* (in diverse locations, like clouds, devices, and distributed servers), *large-scale* (involving distributed and large components, such as devices, systems, and equipment), *heterogeneous* (in the sense

E. Y. Nakagawa (✉)
University of São Paulo, São Carlos, Brazil
e-mail: elisa@icmc.usp.br

P. O. Antonino · T. Kuhn
Fraunhofer IESE, Kaiserslautern, Germany
e-mail: pablo.antonino@iese.fraunhofer.de; thomas.kuhn@iese.fraunhofer.de

M. Galster
University of Canterbury, Christchurch, New Zealand
e-mail: matthias.galster@canterbury.ac.nz

© The Author(s), under exclusive license to Springer Nature Switzerland AG 2023
E. Y. Nakagawa, P. Oliveira Antonino (eds.), *Reference Architectures for Critical Domains*, https://doi.org/10.1007/978-3-031-16957-1_9

that different kinds of components take part in), *quality-oriented* (requiring the assurance of different quality attributes), and increasingly *critical* (their failures can cause serious impacts).

These software-intensive systems are also becoming ubiquitous, always-on, and dynamic at runtime and change continuously. Many challenges arise for their development and evolution, and paying attention to the software architecture has proven to be a way to address the design of these systems. In the same direction, the area of reference architectures has advanced in recent decades, thanks to the value that these architectures have provided to industry and academia, while diverse application domains—most of them essential to society, e.g., health, transportation, and manufacturing—have already recognized their value and are benefiting from them. Hence, we have foreseen that reference architectures will constitute the cornerstone of successful application domains and will be essential to the qualities of the software-intensive systems of those domains, mainly regarding interoperability and reusability. But there still remain many issues to be addressed to mature this area, potential needs in such architectures, and research lines for further investigation.

Together with new trends, technologies, and the need for disruptive computational solutions, the **dynamism** in system architectures has become more and more obvious. It is also becoming a challenging issue to be dealt with during the design, operation, and evolution of those systems. In short, dynamic architectures change their structure at runtime in response to changes in the system's environment or operational constraints [1]. Hence, elements (e.g., components, connectors) can be created, added, removed, deleted, reconfigured, or rearranged at runtime, which is also referred to as architectural reconfiguration. For this to be possible, these architectures must contain the specification of all changes that can possibly occur at runtime.

Many application domains require software systems with dynamic architectures, such as robotics, automatic guided vehicles, unmanned vehicles, and intelligent factories. More specifically, matrix production, an upcoming architecture for flexible production systems that dynamically organizes the concurrent manufacturing of products, must include harmonized interfaces to different types of assets from multiple vendors that cover not only functional aspects but also non-functional information, such as offered capabilities, quality, and cost. In this regard, reference architectures also need to encompass dynamism as a core characteristic aligned with existing and future systems; however, most architectures address only the static parts (i.e., those not changed at runtime). Investigating how a given reference architecture could put together all changes of target systems (i.e., instances of such an architecture) is indeed a challenge.

In parallel, classes of systems, including large-scale (or ultra-large-scale) systems, cyber-physical systems, and smart systems, have become necessary and increasingly ubiquitous in our society. These systems arise as a result of the integration of various operationally and managerially independent systems, often developed by different companies with diverse technologies, platforms, and multiple time frames. Sometimes referred to as systems-of-systems (or simply SoS) or smart ecosystems, these systems present operational and managerial independence of their constituent systems, evolutionary development, emergent behavior, and distribution of constituents, as defined in [9, 26, 30].

In this scenario, **integration** (also interoperability or cooperation) of these independent and heterogeneous systems is required to provide more complex functionalities or solutions to broader needs, which could not be provided by any system working separately. Nevertheless, trustworthy and adequate integration is still a big challenge. Future systems-of-systems will not only integrate systems from their domain but must increasingly also interact with other domains. An example is production environments, which often involve just-in-time production in order to reduce the required warehouse space. The current situation, however, shows that supply chains and logistics are tightly coupled and that only the integration of these two systems will yield predictable future stock. In this scenario, reference architectures can serve to promote interoperability among constituent systems by defining the external interfaces of all their components, aiming at facilitating communication and integration with others. However, research on this topic is quite recent, and more investigations must be carried out regarding the design, representation, evaluation, and evolution of such architectures. Additionally, investigations regarding the self-description of systems, including their capabilities, services offered, and quality levels must be also carried out.

Variability has been recognized as an important concept and a response to an even greater necessity of developing a range of similar systems. Current software systems are already built to accommodate variability. This concept appears not only in software product lines (SPL), where variability is well-known, but also in open platforms, self-* systems, service-oriented systems [15], and others. Variability is the ability of software systems or software artifacts (e.g., components) to be tailored to a specific context in a pre-planned manner [38], allowing the adaptation of the software's structure, behavior, or underlying processes and ensuring that the software will successfully adapt to emerging needs [15]. As the main element that could promote variability in software systems is their architecture, variability should be treated as a first-class, crosscutting concern in software architecture design [13]. In SPL, the product line architectures explicitly address variability as features, and variability management is a core activity in SPL engineering, which explicitly represents variations in order to manage dependencies among variants and supports their instantiation throughout the SPL life cycle [5].

However, variability in reference architectures is not clearly understood. There is no real definition of it, and it is unclear how variability should be aggregated or represented in these architectures. Variability can refer to the ability of software systems or artifacts built from such architectures to be easily adapted to a specific context in a pre-planned manner. In another perspective, variability can be the ability of a reference architecture to be more easily instantiated to system architectures by aggregating variation points and variants, where each variant addresses the specificity of a subset of similar systems built from that architecture, as in [16], where a variability viewpoint is introduced to complement the description of reference architectures.

In general, reference architecture engineering has not been concerned with variability from those two perspectives. Most existing reference architectures do not even provide basic variability-related information, e.g., which parts remain variable, and, as a consequence, software systems resulting from them may be difficult to adapt or evolve to new contexts. Architecture instantiation can take more effort and time to find the specificities of each architectural instance, and hence these need to be fully defined during instantiation. There is, therefore, a need to investigate variability in reference architectures, particularly concerning how to identify variability, determine which variability is worth considering in that architecture and reason about them, identify the associated variation points and variants, represent variability, incorporate or remove variations and variants during the evolution of the architecture, manage the dependencies among variations, perform maintenance, and so on. Finally, variability could help manage the differences, while reference architectures have focused on identifying commonalities among systems of a given domain and then framing such commonalities into their design.

Regarding the existing reference architectures themselves, we have looked at many of them **need updating**, mainly those found in the scientific literature. The design of any reference architecture usually consumes considerable time and effort, while any architecture aggregates knowledge and experience that are worth (or should be worth) being reused. Hence, if they intend to be useful, it is undeniable that they need to be updated continuously. Many different aspects lead to the need for an update, including necessary alignments with the domain (e.g., new laws and standards), new technologies (e.g., adoption of blockchain to improve trust, transparency, data security, and traceability), additional features to be covered (e.g., new smart car functions), new ways to organize the systems of the domain (e.g., SOA being replaced by microservices), and so on. In other words, when reference architectures no longer support the development of software systems in their domain or context effectively, it is time for updates.

The possibility of continuous updating of reference architectures is one of the critical factors for the **sustainability** of these architectures. Software sustainability has been previously described in the computing literature as a non-functional, first-class requirement or software quality [33] or as a composite, non-functional requirement that refers to the systems' extensibility, interoperability, maintainability, portability, reusability, scalability, and usability [40, 41]. Concerning software architecture, sustainability refers to the ability of an architecture to tolerate changes resulting from changes in requirements, environment, technologies, business strategies, and goals throughout the life cycle of a software system [3]. Similarly, we can understand sustainability in reference architectures as their ability to tolerate changes needed to remain aligned with a target domain or goal.

Some remarkable examples of sustainable reference architectures are AUTOSAR and ARC-IT. The AUTOSAR project started almost 20 years ago and nowadays presents very extensive documentation organized into four phases and several releases associated with four versions. All updates are documented in detail, with a considerable number of modules updated (refactored, renovated, and re-architected), reallocated, added, or even removed, to accommodate more than

20,000 requirements and 200 specifications. This enables a tight interaction between AUTOSAR components from multiple vendors. ARCT-IT is already 26 years old. During this time, there have been 9 versions with several modules changed, reallocated, added, or removed to cover more than 6000 requirements and around 130 standards. The same is happening in other reference architectures such as AXMEDIS [4], an architecture for automating the production of cross-media content with a life cycle of over 15 years. During its life cycle, AXMEDIS had three big releases with updates in standards to the content management of partners, such as BBC and HP, and refinement of their description with new viewpoints. These architectures are supported by consortia of strategic partners. In the case of AUTOSAR, it is currently maintained by a core of automotive manufacturers, such as BMW Group, PSA Group, Toyota, Ford, and Volkswagen. Looking at these and many other long-lived architectures shows that some of the major critical factors (also discussed in [42]) that could make them sustainable are:

- Existence of a community around the architecture that can sometimes be strengthened via a consortium of partners, including companies, government, standardization organizations, research centers, and universities. For instance, the German government has provided financial support to RAMI (a reference architecture for Industry 4.0), leading to it being one of the most referenced architectures in its domain.
- Reference architectures must be ready to integrate further design decisions that endure over time when the architectures evolve with the addition of new needs, without causing a detrimental effect on existing decisions.
- Alignment to state-of-the-practice scenarios and widely accepted and adopted technologies in the target domains (including architectural patterns and styles, domain standards and legislation, communication protocols, etc.).
- Documentation (i.e., architectural representation) that is suitable for stakeholders of that reference architecture.
- Up-to-date architectures that evolve continuously to absorb new emerging needs throughout their life cycle.

To make reference architectures useful and effective and to assure their long-term existence, sustainability should be considered as a primary, overarching quality attribute in the process of the design and evolution of reference architectures. In other words, we need to address the sustainability *of* reference architectures better. As these architectures are the foundation for the design of sometimes diverse derived system architectures, sustainability of the subsequent systems should also be a concern in a complementary way. In this case, we need to address sustainability *in* reference architectures. Hence, addressing both perspectives—sustainability *of* and *in* reference architectures [43]—is a mid- to long-term investment for both the reference architectures themselves and the sustainability of derived architectures. Thus, it is necessary to open up the research topic of sustainability of/in reference architectures for the next steps.

As discussed in Chap. 2, the systematization of **reference architecture engineering** is necessary, in particular, regarding *how* each main phase of architectural design—namely, analysis, synthesis, and evaluation—is performed. There already exist initiatives to understand these phases better [2, 8, 10, 14, 28, 29]. Regarding **architectural analysis**, there is no formal or practiced way to conduct it. Well-known architectures have somehow proceeded in a particular way that, to some extent, has worked; also, a couple of studies in the literature have addressed the architectural analysis of reference architectures [37], but most of them are domain-specific solutions. Hence, the proposal of methods or guidelines that are generic enough for multiple domains or classes of systems and allow systematically analyzing the requirements of reference architectures could motivate other domains and potential stakeholders to invest effort into conceiving their own architectures.

Concerning what should be done or further researched in terms of the **synthesis of reference architectures**, which are a type of software architecture (but at a higher level of abstraction), their description should also be aligned with ISO/IEC/IEEE 42010, an international standard for architecture descriptions of systems and software [17] that is widely known in academia and industry. This standard establishes definitions and relationships among the main elements that compose architecture descriptions, e.g., stakeholder, concern, architecture decision, architecture view, architecture viewpoint, and architecture model. All these elements are also present in reference architectures; however, we do not see them adequately documented in most existing architectures [37]; an exception is IIRA, whose documentation is based on this standard.

To describe reference architectures, the well-known $4 + 1$ view model (logic view, process view, development view, physical view, scenario view) [23] and Views and Beyond [7], which describes the most relevant architectural views (including modular view, component-and-connector view, and implementation view), can be used or serve as a basis for documenting reference architectures. Additionally, regarding the notation technique used to model these architectures, UML [31], SysML [32], C4 model [6], or other notations are welcome. However, we observe that most architectures, regardless of their scope, are still represented informally and use their formalism and descriptions to express their concepts. This is true not only for architectures with very concrete definitions such as AUTOSAR but also for architectures that classify problem spaces and technical solutions into a taxonomy, such as RAMI 4.0. We have observed that the notation technique adopted does not necessarily imply the success or failure of a given architecture, but a good architectural description is important as it could provide support for wider use and dissemination. A more harmonized formalism for the description of reference architectures would significantly improve the understandability of reference architecture concepts, improve their adoption in different contexts, and, consequently, reduce unnecessary re-work to invent things in one context that have already been solved in other contexts. As observed, the use of reference architectures in industry projects is still costly in terms of the effort and time required, including the task of making several architectural decisions that could already be represented adequately in the architectural documentation. Therefore, special attention must be paid to such documentation.

Initiatives to propose approaches (including processes, methods, viewpoints, architecture description languages (ADL), document templates, and models) aimed at describing reference architectures better mainly emerged in the last decade and are found in little more than two dozen studies in the scientific literature. Most of them address architectures for specific application domains, such as health, automotive, and robotics [37]. Therefore, we foresee that there is still room for investigation as to what might work to adequately document reference architectures. This will certainly depend on the needs of stakeholders or on reference architecture categories (as discussed in Chap. 2).

The investigation of **reference architecture evaluation** is scarce in the scientific literature, while the industry has not been using any formal and systematic way to conduct it. First of all, there is no clear understanding of what qualities in reference architectures exactly refer to, which system aspects they should address, and thus which should be considered in an evaluation. Initial work has suggested the following quality attributes [36]: acceptability, applicability, buildability, completeness, and understandability. Still, we believe this set is larger and also includes, for instance, correctness, consistency, conciseness, currency, conformance to standards, accuracy, structuredness, readability, trust, and other qualities relevant to the evaluation of architectural documentation. In terms of architectural evaluation methods, ATAM (Architecture Trade-off Analysis Method) [20], SAAM (Software Architecture Analysis Method) [19], and their variations, such Decision-Centric Architecture Reviews (DCAR) [39] and Pragmatic Evaluation of Software Architectures [21], could be investigated to find out whether they are suitable (possibly with adaptations) for evaluating reference architectures.

While the three core tasks for designing reference architectures have drawn some attention, two other essential tasks –**evolution** and **instantiation**– have not been studied sufficiently. At the same time, they have already commonly occurred in long-lived architecture projects. In particular, the **evolution** of reference architectures, more specifically their continuous evolution, can assure the value of these architectures throughout their life cycle. Hence, based on the consolidated experience of continuous updates of long-lived architectures, a means to systematically evolve them that can work with multiple architectures could be proposed. This could motivate the update of several outdated architectures, which sometimes have considerable and valuable content but have been left aside, and also facilitate the evolution of those for which continuous updates have been required. At the same time, long-living systems in operation that are bound to reference architectures also require continuous updates to enable migration to newer architecture concepts.

Most reference architectures are informally documented through texts and diagrams; hence, the **instantiation** process is a non-trivial, effort-intensive, and sometimes manual task, performed without any step-to-step guidance being available, for instance. Instantiation refers to an activity that takes part in reference architecture engineering and that is responsible for deriving product architectures (or architectures of given software systems) from reference architectures. In short, the instantiation process (which should be iterative) encompasses (i) reading and understanding of the reference architecture documentation; (ii) selection of the whole architecture or its parts to be reused in the product architectures; (iii) refinement and adaptation of the product architecture and its parts through software system specification, such as requirements, and domain and technology constraints; (iv) documentation (or description) of the product architecture; and (v) evaluation of the product architecture. This process addresses the trade-off analysis of what should be considered, including selecting and detailing elements (e.g., components and connectors), adding new elements, and so on. To facilitate this process, automated tools that can deal with multiple architectures in order to at least partially support this task would be welcome. Each reference architecture should also provide guidance to its instantiation as part of the documentation. Methods for the instantiation process that work with multiple architectures would also be a welcome addition.

Besides instantiation, there are other possible uses of the knowledge encompassed in reference architectures. It could be explored more systematically as a means to standardize the software systems of a given domain. This standardization mainly refers to the interfaces among components (or subsystems) when forming complex and large systems. These architectures can also establish the external interfaces of systems that are built based on these architectures, facilitating the integration of these systems with others. Hence, reference architectures could promote internal and external interoperability in software systems and help guide standard development. Moreover, such architectures could be used to support the evolution of software systems (which present the evolution as a natural process), such as when refactoring, re-architecturing, or simply including new features due to various factors, such as adaptation to new contexts, modification of functionalities, and quality improvement.

In general, designing reference architectures is a time- and effort-consuming task; hence, deriving new reference architectures for the same domain or neighboring ones from existing ones should be considered. A good example is IIRA, which is originally based on IoT and, after evolution and adaptation, has become a reference architecture for industrial Internet (or Industry 4.0). Effort and time reduction could be achieved with this approach, mainly when the previous architectures are more mature and used successfully.

Reuse in the large is a core concern in software product line engineering (SPLE) [34]. In the same direction, reference architectures have indeed presented a valuable body of knowledge that could be reused. The use of existing reference architectures as the basis of SPL and associated product line architectures can be explored. Reusing knowledge contained in these architectures could contribute to reducing the effort required to build SPL artifacts, such as the variability model, implemented components, and the product line architecture, and, therefore, could help to improve productivity during SPLE.

We foresee that there will be concrete evidence of the need to adopt systematized processes for designing reference architectures (from architectural analysis to architectural evolution and uses) in the future. We believe that the community and affected stakeholders will further perceive the relevance of adopting them.

Considering that reference architectures are a particular type of software architecture, we believe that **architectural technical debts** (ATD) are expected to occur during the design and evolution processes of these architectures. ATD refers to immature architecture design artifacts that can compromise the quality attributes of software systems, mainly maintainability and evolvability [25]. Additionally, ATD are the result of sub-optimal upfront solutions or solutions that become sub-optimal when, for instance, technologies and patterns become outdated [35]. The definition of ATD could also be applied to reference architectures, but a deep investigation of the real meaning of ATD is necessary due to the higher abstraction level of reference architectures than product architectures. An examination of technical debt management strategies is also required, including identification, representation (or documentation), monitoring (using specific metrics), prioritization, and mitigation of such debts. We foresee that reference architecture design and evolution processes should incorporate the ATD management process. Not dealing with ATD could directly impact the many benefits of these architectures, such as standardization, quality of the systems instantiated from that architecture, systematic reuse, and interoperability.

As observed in recent years, the software system development has undergone a considerable transformation. The traditional development process has given way to the iterative and continuous development of software, blurring the separation between development time and runtime. This new wave has been referred to as **continuous software engineering** [12], which involves agile methods and is mainstream, also in the context of developing systems that were previously considered critical in terms of being developed iteratively. In this new scenario, it is then necessary to investigate how reference architectures should be incorporated into the software development process when DevOps and BizDev practices, agile methods, or other continuous software engineering activities form the basis of the development. We believe that reference architectures should be a crosscutting artifact in the entire development process, but such inclusion is not a trivial task. It will require software processes to be adequate or remodeled to cover tasks related to reference architecture management. By adopting these new processes, project teams can potentially reduce time, effort, and mistakes and improve productivity.

One class of large-scale software systems composed of other systems and components are **software ecosystems**. They are software platforms and involve communities of external developers that provide functionalities for extending the basic platform [27]. In contrast to other large-scale software systems, such as systems-of-systems, ecosystems usually require a common platform. Ecosystems tend to be "open" in the sense that their architecture enables added-value services by incorporating third-party contributions while retaining essential qualities [22]. These added-value services are typically not known in advance when the platform of the ecosystem is designed. Examples of software ecosystems include Eclipse, Android, Firefox, and Gnome [27]. While these examples are "pure" software ecosystems, in the age of the "Internet of Things," ecosystems can also include hardware components [11].

Jansen et al. argued that software ecosystems usually start with a single provider or a group of providers that open up their business processes to become an open software enterprise [18]. This is similar to reference architectures, which often emerge from community efforts. Let us use the example of a farm software ecosystem to illustrate this. Several agricultural machinery manufacturers have their proprietary platforms (e.g., John Deere's FarmSight or AGCO's Fuse), and there are also multi-vendor platforms (e.g., 365FarmNet, AgroSense). However, it is difficult to establish interoperability with components from different manufacturers. Moreover, existing ecosystems are sometimes too focused on region-specific needs [24]. The agriculture domain could use a reference architecture for ecosystems to map, assess, design, and implement ecosystems that contribute to integrated systems. This architecture could improve communication and collaboration among multiple actors in ecosystems. When defining reference architectures for ecosystems, we need to consider the following drivers:

- Common software: Common software in ecosystems can either appear as a common technological platform or as a software platform. The reference architecture will need to identify common software and software that is specific to a particular ecosystem.
- Business: Business applies to a broader sense than the profit or revenue model, such as the benefits contributors would get from an open platform project (e.g., opportunities for innovation). To build a reference architecture for ecosystems, communities may need to be created around the reference architecture, perhaps within a domain.
- Connecting relationships: Connections can exist in terms of sets of businesses, relationships among businesses, actors in social ecosystems related to the software ecosystem, communities, etc. A reference architecture should, in fact, enable the development of ecosystems collaboratively and in a public manner.

9.2 Final Remarks

Diverse open issues still remain in the area of reference architecture, particularly regarding the various roles that reference architectures could assume, the engineering process involved, and even progress regarding the theoretical foundation.

While the next steps are being taken, the community needs to be aware that outdated reference architectures (unfortunately, many already published) are not helpful, with the effort and time already consumed to design them being wasted in such cases. Strategies for continuously updating these architectures, with a focus on future reference architectures, are fundamental for keeping the community interested alive and successfully taking advantage of the knowledge and well-experienced practices captured by reference architectures.

With continuous software development becoming ever more important, the role of reference architectures in this new scenario needs to be understood better. We also foresee that reference architectures should more explicitly assume other important roles, such as domain systems standardization and interoperability, by capturing and organizing domain-specific interoperability standards and other general standards.

Regarding reference architecture engineering, we can say that it is still relatively immature, with most architectures designed and evolved in an ad hoc way or using specific solutions. Revisiting the need for systematization is therefore fundamental. More importantly, reference architecture engineering should be aligned with the current trend toward continuous software and systems development.

As a result of future research, we also expect that the theoretical knowledge framework in the area will advance further. Also, sustainability of/in reference architectures should be a primary concern of the community and could become the mainstream in this field.

References

1. R. Allen, R. Douence, D. Garlan, Specifying and analyzing dynamic software architectures, in *Conference on Fundamental Approaches to Software Engineering (FASE)* (1998), pp. 21–37
2. S. Angelov, P. Grefen, D. Greefhorst, A framework for analysis and design of software reference architectures. Inf. Softw. Technol. **54**(4), 417–431 (2012)
3. P. Avgeriou, M. Stal, R. Hilliard, Architecture sustainability. IEEE Softw. **30**(6), 40–44 (2013)
4. AXMEDIS, Axmedis (2022). http://www.axmedis.org/com/
5. M. Babar, L. Chen, F. Shull, Managing variability in software product lines. IEEE Softw. **27**(3), 89–91 (2010)
6. S. Brown, C4 Model (2022). https://c4model.com/
7. P. Clements, F. Bachmann, L. Bass, D. Garlan, J. Ivers, R. Little, P. Merson, R. Nord, J. Stafford, *Documenting Software Architecture: Views and Beyond*, 2nd edn. (Addison-Wesley, Boston, 2011)
8. R. Cloutier, G. Muller, D. Verma, R. Nilchiani, E. Hole, M. Bone, The concept of reference architectures. Syst. Eng. **13**(1), 14–27 (2010)
9. P. Dersin, Systems of Systems (2014). IEEE-Reliability Society. Technical Committee on "Systems of Systems". https://rs.ieee.org/technical-activities/technical-committees/systems-of-systems.html
10. L. Dobrica, E. Niemela, An approach to reference architecture design for different domains of embedded systems, in *International Conference on Software Engineering Research and Practice (SERP)* (2008), pp. 287–293
11. T. Eisenmann, G. Parker, M. Alstyne, Opening platforms: how, when and why? in *Platforms, Markets and Innovation* (2009)
12. B. Fitzgerald, K. Stol, Continuous software engineering: a roadmap and agenda. J. Syst. Softw. **123**, 176–189 (2017)
13. M. Galster, P. Avgeriou, Handling variability in software architecture: problems and implications, in *9th Working IEEE/IFIP Conference on Software Architecture (WICSA)* (2011), pp. 171–180
14. M. Galster, P. Avgeriou, D. Weyns, T. Mannisto, Empirically-grounded reference architectures: a proposal, in *7th ACM Sigsoft International Conference on the Quality of Software Architectures (QoSA)* (2011), pp. 153–157
15. M. Galster, D. Weyns, D. Tofan, B. Michalik, P. Avgeriou, Variability in software systems — a systematic literature review. IEEE Trans. Softw. Eng. **40**(3), 282–306 (2014)

16. M. Guessi, F. Oquendo, E. Nakagawa, Variability viewpoint to describe reference architectures, in *11th Working IEEE/IFIP Conference on Software Architecture (WICSA): Companion Volume* (2014), pp. 1–6
17. International Organization for Standardization, ISO/IEC/IEEE 42010:2011 Systems and software engineering – Architecture description (2011). Technical report
18. S. Jansen, S. Brinkkemper, J. Souer, L. Luinenburg, Shades of gray: opening up a software producing organization with the open software enterprise model. J. Syst. Softw. **85**, 1495–1510 (2012)
19. R. Kazman, L. Bass, M. Webb, G. Abowd, SAAM: a method for analyzing the properties of software architectures, in *16th International Conference on Software Engineering (ICSE)* (1994), pp. 81–90
20. R. Kazman, M. Klein, P. Clements, ATAM: method for Architecture Evaluation. Technical report, Carnegie Mellon University (2000)
21. J. Knodel, M. Naab, *Pragmatic Evaluation of Software Architectures* (Springer, Berlin, 2016)
22. J. Knodel, M. Naab, D. Rost, Supporting architects in mastering the complexity of open software ecosystems, in *2nd International Workshop on Software Engineering for Systems-of-Systems (SESoS)* (2014), pp. 1–6
23. P. Kruchten, Architectural blueprints — The "4+1" view model of software architecture. IEEE Softw. **12**(6), 42–50 (1995)
24. J. Kruize, J. Wolfert, H. Scholten, C. Verdouw, A. Kassahun, A. Beulens, A reference architecture for farm ecosystems. Comput. Eletron. Agricult. **125**, 12–28 (2016)
25. Z. Li, P. Liang, P. Avgeriou, Architectural debt management in value-oriented architecting, in *Economics-Driven Software Architecture* ed. by I. Mistrik, R. Bahsoon, R. Kazman, Y. Zhang (Morgan Kaufmann, Burlington, 2014), pp. 183–204
26. M. Maier, Architecting principles for systems-of-systems. Syst. Eng. J. Int. Counc. Syst. Eng. **1**(4), 267–284 (1998)
27. K. Manikas, K.M. Hansen, Software ecosystems – a systematic literature review. J. Syst. Softw. **86**, 1294–1206 (2013)
28. G. Muller, P. Laar, Right sizing reference architectures – how to provide specific guidance with limited information, in *18th Annual International Symposium of the International Council on Systems Engineering (INCOSE)* (2008), pp. 1–8
29. E. Nakagawa, M. Guessi, F. Feitosa, F. Oquendo, J.C. Maldonado, Consolidating a process for the design, representation, and evaluation of reference architectures, in *11th Working IEEE/IFIP Conference on Software Architecture (WICSA)* (2017), pp. 143–152
30. C. Nielsen, P. Larsen, J. Fitzgerald, J. Woodcock, J. Peleska, Systems of systems engineering: basic concepts, model-based techniques, and research directions. ACM Comput. Surv. **48**(2), 1–41 (2015)
31. OMG – Object Management Group, UML – Unified Modeling Language (2017). https://www.omg.org/spec/UML/
32. OMG – Object Management Group. SYSML – OMG System Modeling Language (2019). https://www.omg.org/spec/SysML
33. B. Penzenstadler, A. Raturi, D. Richardson, C. Calero, H. Femmer, X. Franch, Systematic mapping study on software engineering for sustainability (SE4S), in *18th International Conference on Evaluation and Assessment in Software Engineering (EASE)* (2014), pp. 1–14
34. K. Pohl, G. Böckle, F. Linden, *Software Product Line Engineering: Foundations, Principles, and Techniques*, 1st edn. (Springer-Verlag, Berlin, Heidelberg, 2005)
35. E. Tom, A. Aurum, R. Vidgen, An exploration of technical debt. J. Syst. Softw. **86**, 1498–1516 (2013)
36. J. Trienekens, S. Angelov, P. Grefen, R. Kusters, Quality of software reference architectures, in *IADIS International Conference Information Systems* (2011), pp. 145–151
37. P. Valle, L. Garcés, T. Volpato, S. Martínez-Fernández, E. Nakagawa, Towards suitable description of reference architectures. PeerJ Comput. Sci. **7**, e392, 1–36 (2021)
38. J. van Gurp, J. Bosch, M. Svahnberg, On the notion of variability in software product lines, in *2nd Working IEEE/IFIP Conference on Software Architecture (WICSA)* (2001), pp. 45–54

39. U. van Heesch, V. Eloranta, P. Avgeriou, K. Koskimies, N. Harrison, Decision-centric architecture reviews. IEEE Softw. **31**(1), 69–76 (2014)
40. C. Venters, C. Jay, L. Lau, M. Griffiths, V. Holmes, R. Ward, J. Austin, C. Dibsdale, J. Xu, Software sustainability: the modern tower of babel, in *3rd International Workshop on Requirements Engineering for Sustainable Systems (RE4SuSy)* (2014), pp. 1–6
41. C. Venters, L. Lau, M. Griffiths, V. Holmes, R. Ward, C. Jay, C. Dibsdale, J. Xu, The blind men and the elephant: towards an empirical evaluation framework for software sustainability. J. Open Res. Softw. **2**(1), 1–6 (2014)
42. C. Venters, R. Capilla, S. Betz, B. Penzenstadler, T. Crick, S. Crouch, E. Nakagawa, C. Becker, C. Carrillo, Software sustainability: research and practice from a software architecture viewpoint. J. Syst. Softw. **138**, 174–188 (2018)
43. T. Volpato, L. Oliveira, B. Garcés, R. Capilla, E. Nakagawa, Two perspectives on reference architecture sustainability, in *11th European Conference on Software Architecture Workshops (ECSAW)* (2017), pp. 188–194

Chapter 10
Final Remarks

Elisa Yumi Nakagawa and Pablo Oliveira Antonino

Abstract As this is the first book on reference architectures, the plan was to provide an overview of this special type of software architecture and its impact on diverse real-world and use-case scenarios, particularly those addressed in critical domains. This chapter finishes this reference book, highlighting its key messages and presenting issues to consider for further initiatives and improvements.

First Message: The Value of Reference Architectures Has Been Recognized
The value of reference architecture has been increasingly recognized by industry and academia. This is evidenced by the number of reference architectures emerging in several domains, including critical ones, which depend directly on software-intensive systems to realize their processes and where systems development is highly effort-demanding and costly. In particular, we observe that industry has increasingly adopted reference architectures in large, critical, and complex projects as a means to facilitate communication among diverse partners and stakeholders as well as communication among systems produced by them. Reference architectures have been consolidated as one of the most promising artifacts along with other reusable artifacts, like standards, architecture patterns, styles, tactics, and reference models. However, they go beyond this by also aggregating these artifacts together with the body of consolidated and codified knowledge about the structure of domain systems or classes of systems. Hence, reference architectures have reaffirmed their role when we reason about the reuse of consolidated knowledge and experience.

E. Y. Nakagawa (✉)
University of São Paulo, São Carlos, Brazil
e-mail: elisa@icmc.usp.br

P. O. Antonino
Fraunhofer IESE, Kaiserslautern, Germany
e-mail: pablo.antonino@iese.fraunhofer.de

Second Message: Designing and Maintaining Reference Architectures Is Hard
It can be observed that the design and maintenance of reference architectures are
inherently time- and effort-consuming tasks. In most cases, a large amount of
past experience and consolidated knowledge is required to design an architecture;
besides, their continuous update requires trade-off analysis to decide what is worth
being incorporated into, or removed and refined, in the architecture. For that, we
observe that consortia are being formed to support these architectures, also in
financial terms. We also find standardization organizations that are responsible for
supporting the existence of long-lived reference architectures.

Third Message: Reference Architectures Are Built in an Ad Hoc Way Most
reference architectures are built without following a systematic way or process
that organizes all the work. The conception of reference architectures sometimes
emerges from the needs of a group of companies, regulatory bodies, research groups,
or anyone interested in registering a body of knowledge about architecting similar
systems. By examining several architectures over the years, we see that, in general,
the concern has not been the way they are conceived but the presentation of the
resulting architectures themselves.

**Fourth Message: Most Reference Architectures Are Not Yet Sustainable and
Long-Living** The sustainability and longevity of reference architectures should
be a concern, considering that the literature provides evidence that a range of
published reference architectures do not survive. Hence, if the purpose of reference
architectures as well as their design and maintenance are not well-planned and
reasoned, they will probably join others that appear and then disappear because
they not remain effective over time, with the rich knowledge contained in such
architectures becoming outdated or simply being wasted. In this regard, the question
arises of how to assure the sustainability and longevity of reference architectures?

Fifth Message: There Is a Diversity of Reference Architectures Becoming
more popular from the 2000s onward, reference architectures today are very
diverse in terms of shape, description (or documentation), content detailing, size
(or scope), quality attributes, types of stakeholders involved, and so on. On the
one hand, there are successful architectures such as RAMI that are described
as an overall and informal representation with a textual description in a short
documentation. On the other hand, there are big architectures like AUTOSAR and
IIRA that involve several strategic partners with particular interests and a rather
large architectural documentation. There is therefore no widely accepted recipe for
reference architectures to be successful.

Sixth Message: No Consensus of What Reference Architectures Are There is
no consensus about what exactly a reference architecture is nor what it actually
comprises. At the same time, it is observed that different things (such as the
architecture of a given software system at a higher abstraction level) have also been
referred to as reference architectures. We expect this consensus to be hard to achieve

considering the diversity of stakeholders involved, from companies of diverse sectors, like automotive, health, and government, to researchers and practitioners of different areas, such as computing, engineering (electrical, mechanical, and others), and business. However, this reference book intends to draw attention to the need for a widespread definition of the term reference architecture, differentiating it from similar terms –like reference model– in order to mainly facilitate communication among diverse stakeholders.

Seventh Message: Reference Architecture as a Research Area Is Still Maturing
Over the last decade, reference architecture as a research area has advanced, but it is still premature to say that this area is already mature and consolidated. Contributions in diverse research directions are found, but proven theories and well-experimented and widely accepted processes, methods, and techniques for dealing with multiple reference architectures are still needed. In the future, ongoing research needs to drive progress in this area and consolidate the findings.

Printed in the United States
by Baker & Taylor Publisher Services